MW01672807

BEYOND BOOKS

BEYOND BOOKS

HEATHER SHUMAKER

Stories of Traverse Area Libraries

1860–2020

Copyright © 2022 by Heather Shumaker

All rights reserved. No part of this book may be reproduced in any form or by any electronic or mechanical means, including information storage and retrieval systems, without permission in writing from the author, except by reviewers, who may quote brief passages in a review.

ISBN 978-0-578-31508-9
Library of Congress Control Number: 2021921706

Names: Shumaker, Heather, author.
Title: Beyond books : stories of Traverse area libraries, 1860-2020 / Heather Shumaker.
Description: First edition. | Traverse City, Mich. : CRSTAL Publishing, 2022. | Includes bibliographic resources, index.
Identifiers: LCCN 2021921706 | ISBN 9780578315089
Subjects: Traverse Area District Library — History. | Traverse City Carnegie Library (Traverse City, Mich.) — History. | Ladies' Library Association (Traverse City, Mich.) — History. | Libraries — Michigan — History.
Classification: LCC F572 .G5 S58 2022 | DDC 977.4—dc23

Printed in the United States of America

Cover and book design by Saxon Design, Inc., Traverse City, Michigan
Printed by Sheridan Books, Inc.

Published by CRSTAL Publishing, Traverse City, Michigan

Cover map by Herman Brosius: *Bird's Eye View of Traverse City in 1879*

HEATHER SHUMAKER is the author of many life histories as well as fiction and nonfiction books for adults and children. She has been awarded the Michigan Notable Book Award and other honors. She lives in Traverse City, Michigan.

Table of Contents

FOREWORD

CRSTAL, the Committee to Record the Story of Traverse Area Libraries, was established early in 2020. Everyone who was asked to join signed on, probably with no clear idea of what was expected or where it would lead. All had in-depth experience with libraries, mostly local. All have gamely supplied guidance, ideas, recollections, and good humor as the project expanded.

This book began as an effort to tell the story of a group of dedicated citizens in the 1990s who saw a problem and set about to find a solution. Traverse City needed a new library, but attempts to convince the voters had failed. The story is worth telling because it celebrates a community rallying for a common good, regardless of political leaning or personal profit. Before reaching a happy ending, there was drama but, in the end, the focused and committed leadership of local citizens held firm, instilled confidence, and garnered essential support.

That's the story we thought needed telling. When we discovered Heather Shumaker, it was clear that she was just the right person to bring this story to life, to share a shining moment and help remind people how much we can accomplish when we work together.

Then it seemed that this story should be put in context of Traverse City history. That's when our project ballooned into a bigger book of stories about Traverse area libraries going back to the early days of Traverse City. When this little logging community was still very young, a group of dedicated citizens came together and decided that the people needed a library. Their story of how they created a library and managed it for 30 years also deserves telling. And there's more. Fast forward to 2020 when COVID-19 hit, affecting nearly every aspect of life; a new chapter in library history suddenly began.

Heather Shumaker's book is based on interviews and research into many aspects of library and civic history. CRSTAL members helped channel much of the research materials to Heather and provided access to their library-related files. We are grateful for the work of local historians, including many from the early days of Traverse City. For many years, librarian Marie Kulibert maintained detailed records relating to library history and lore. More recently, Amy Barritt, Peg Siciliano, and Richard Fidler have done a great deal of research that helped shape our story. Native American Elder Hank Bailey added depth to this history by sharing information on the Anishinaabek way of holding knowledge and preserving culture.

CRSTAL's project is based on trust and enthusiasm. Publication was made possible by many generous donations from people who love libraries. United Way of Northwest Michigan agreed to hold our funds and oversee disbursement. Leaders of Friends of Traverse Area District Library and Traverse Area Historical Society enthusiastically offered guidance and financial support. Librarians and staff at all the TADL libraries have willingly encouraged and enhanced our process with fact-checking and suggestions. Thanks to all who value community libraries and appreciate their importance.

CRSTAL shepherded the project from start to finish.

Committee to Record the Story of Traverse Area Libraries

Dawn Buchanan
Katheryn Carrier
Jody Clark
Judith Halsted
Donna Hornberger
Anne Magoun (coordinator)
Ann Swaney (coordinator)
Martha Vreeland

This sign hangs above the Nelson Room (Michigan Collection) at the Woodmere Library. Before that, for as many years as people can remember, it hung at the Carnegie Library on Sixth Street. The sign symbolizes what libraries used to mean to people—a building housing reading materials and a place to read them. Today's libraries offer so much more, way beyond books.

Preface

"Write about the library," Anne Magoun told me. "The history of the Traverse Area District Library, and the grassroots effort to build the new library in the 1990s. It's really quite a story."

I started this book thinking I was writing about books in a building. That's what the word "library" conjures up. "Library"—from the Latin liber, meaning "book."

I love libraries. My first step when I moved to Traverse City was to get a library card at the Carnegie library on Sixth Street. Barely a year later, I was delighted with the seemingly miraculous appearance of a brand-new library overlooking the lake on Woodmere Avenue. This library was full of books, but also full of light, lake views, and music. "Come see our library," I prodded out-of-town guests. "It's beautiful."

My earliest memories are of descending to the children's section for Story Time in the old Worthington Public Library in Ohio. Upstairs was all hush: the adult section. A grave place of whispers and intimidating stacks of books. Better to stay below in the children's section, a place of stories, music, and laughter.

Libraries of today are no longer so hushed, but they are no less cherished. Our Traverse Area District Library is more than ever a community center, the heartbeat of the community.

Was it ever just a building with books? Besides housing books, a library is a community's collection of ideas, access, and sharing. Struggles to site and fund library buildings are part of the story. But a library is so much more. It's a collection of humanity's wisdom and knowledge—growing, slipping, expanding, forgetting, remembering—that now includes ukuleles, Wi-Fi hot spots, and baking pans from the Library of Things. It's also the vibrancy of human interaction, from reference questions to children's laughter.

A library is a great gathering of community. It is the best of us: a shared resource, a network of caring. It is the sum of who we are, who we were, and who we strive to be.

The Living Library

What was the earliest library in the region? The Anishinaabe people preserved and shared community knowledge for thousands of years, and their impressive oral tradition, combined with birch bark scrolls and other inscriptions, greatly pre-date the settlers' early bookshelves. What follows is an acknowledgment of this important part of the story of our regional libraries, provided courtesy of Hank Bailey, a tribal member of the Grand Traverse Band of Ottawa & Chippewa Indians.

The Anishinaabe people and their ancestors have lived in the Grand Traverse region for at least 30,000 years. Their cultural and technical knowledge has been passed on verbally from person to person and generation to generation for millennia.

The Anishinaabe created pictorial symbols as memory aids for keeping and sharing their stories and teachings. These simple drawings were scratched on birch bark scrolls or inscribed on rocks and those that remain today are sacred to the People. However, it was the Anishinaabe themselves who served as the knowledge holders – the living library.

The European invaders of what is today Michigan displaced the Anishinaabe people and sought to extinguish their culture. With resilience and wisdom, the Anishinaabe and their leaders adopted and adapted what was useful in the colonial culture.

The Anishinaabe were evicted from their ancestral lands by the 1830 Indian Removal Act which ordered that all tribes east of the Mississippi River be moved to designated land in "Indian Country". In order to protect their people, Michigan's Anishinaabe leaders signed the Treaty of Washington in 1836. In northern lower Michigan the Odawa and Ojibwe avoided removal until the Treaty was signed. Under its terms, the Anishinaabek lost more than 13 million acres of their homeland. However, the leaders secured provisions to protect their rights to traditional natural resources that assured their survival. In addition, Anishinaabe leaders required treaty rights that provided formal education for their people: teachers, school houses, books and technological training. Their initiative has evolved, over time, to support and provide educational opportunities for today's Anishinaabek.

In the Grand Traverse region, these initial services were provided in church-related missions where Anishinaabe children learned to read and write in English and their parents could learn trades such a farming and blacksmithing. Several villages in the Grand Traverse region were founded as missions: Old Mission, Michigan in 1839 (moved to Omena, Michigan in 1852) and Waukauzooville in 1848 (today called Northport, Michigan).

Today the Grand Traverse Band of Ottawa and Chippewa Indians continues to place high value on education for their citizens. In addition to formal education, Tribal members continue to honor, preserve and pass on their traditional knowledge and skills and Anishinaabemowin.

Hank Bailey, Elder of the Grand Traverse Band
of Ottawa and Chippewa Indians

May 12, 2021

Front Street looking east from Union, in 1865. The large two-story building with tower at far left is the Leach Building, located on the corner of Front and Park streets. The next large store is Hulburd's hardware, furniture, and dry goods store (later Hamilton, Milliken & Co.'s first store in 1873); Hubbell Drug Store is the next large building; 2nd small building to its right is the post office; then the farthest right large building is the Kratochvil Saloon at 130 E. Front. There were no buildings on north side of the street at that time.

I shall be miserable if I have not an excellent library.

Jane Austen

CHAPTER 1

Early Libraries

THE LADIES' LIBRARY ASSOCIATION

On a hot Saturday afternoon, eight women gathered in Leach's Hall in Traverse City to discuss a new idea: a Ladies' Library.

The date was July 24, 1869. They were dressed in high-collared blouses, stiff with starch, and full-length skirts that swept the dusty floor. The women filled the front row of wooden benches in the echo-ey hall, vigorously fanning themselves against the stifling July heat, and tried to ignore the droning *buzz* of a blue-bottle fly that batted itself against the hall's dingy windows.

All eyes were on 39-year-old Clymene Bates, also known then as Mrs. Morgan Bates, as she outlined her vision. A library. A *ladies'* library. A sacred space where women could exercise their brains. Where they could read and socialize, discuss literature, access the latest magazines, bring in speakers, and discuss ideas of the day. What Mrs. Bates was proposing was a Ladies' Library Association. Why, they had one in Kalamazoo. An organization, just for women, with a lending library that promoted literacy and equal education for women. The *Grand Traverse Herald* had just reported on similar activity in Flint. The Flint Ladies' Library Association had 3,000 books and a handsome brick building to put them in. It was time for the women of the Traverse area

Ladies' Library Association founder Clymene Cole Bates (1830–1872), native of upstate New York, moved to Traverse City with her husband, Morgan Bates, in about 1858.

to create an educational and cultural center.

Clymene Bates was a natural leader. Vivacious by nature, she had "flashing black eyes," according to her friends, a vigorous will, strong mind, and undaunted courage. She was married to Lieutenant Governor Morgan Bates, former publisher of the *Grand Traverse Herald* newspaper, who was more than twenty years her senior, and staunchly supportive of her efforts. She was the one who'd called the women together at Leach's Hall, which then stood at the southwest corner of Front and Park streets. The little gathering decided unanimously to form a Ladies' Library Association.

In the words of Martha E. Cram Bates: "We merely said: 'Let there be a Ladies' Library Association, and there was.'" Martha Bates was one of the founding members and Clymene Bates's niece by marriage.

Clymene Bates was elected president. Other founding members included: Seraphine (Phenie) Bennett Arnold, Margaret Lackey Ashton, Ella Waterman Fuller, Esther Sprague Day (later Hatch), Mary Knizek (later Buck), and Mina Leach (later Hubbell). They were an impressive bunch: daughters and wives of Congressmen, federal judges, newspaper owners and publishers, lawyers and doctors. Some were immigrants. Some were college graduates, writers, and journalists themselves, such as Martha E. Cram Bates, who was associate editor for the *Grand Traverse Herald*, in charge of the new "Home and Children's" department. They were also young and full of energy, one as young as 17. At founding, their average age was 27 years old.

The accomplishment was noted in the *Grand Traverse Herald*, with a note from the editors: "The Ladies of this village have organized a Library Association…It will prove of great value. Now, in its infancy, let it receive the fostering care of our citizens."

And so the story of a strong library for Traverse City began. A story that again and again invokes the vision of Clymene Bates and a devoted band of determined women.

Mrs. Bates and the Early Ladies

"Books were scarce enough, though we all had a few," recalled Esther Hatch, one of the founding members, in a speech forty years later. "Some had a little more than Dr. Eliot's 'five foot shelf,' but nothing helped out during the long winter evenings like plenty of reading matter." Dr. Charles Eliot compiled the Harvard Universal Classics, known as "Dr. Eliot's Five-Foot Shelf," with works of Plato, Milton, Emerson, and others. Books were expensive and greatly prized, to the extent that people listed volumes of books in their wills among their valuable possessions.

Settler women living in early Traverse Township were isolated and many were desperate for ideas and contact with the outside world. Mail was delivered twice a week. The landscape was either solid forest with few roads and no railroads, or else great swaths of desolate, cut-over landscapes. To get to the railroad in Grand Haven, travelers from Traverse City had to travel overland by stage coach in winter. "The overland route is 175 miles and is performed in four days by daylight," reported the *Detroit Free Press* in 1867.

"For to us, hemmed in by woods and water, the world was literally 'outside,'" remembered Esther Hatch. "Traverse City…at that time had no railroad, no telegraph, no daily paper, no brick blocks, no paved streets, no gas, no telephone, no electric lights, no court house, no business men's association, [but] did have a full-fledged Ladies' Library association, for we not only organized, but we donated from our own scanty store of books a sufficient number to make a beginning."

The Ladies' Library blossomed. Within three short months, they had a collection of 79 volumes housed in the U.S. Land Office located in the Leach Building. It was a friendly arrangement, since Morgan

Built by *Grand Traverse Herald* publisher (1867–1876) D. C. Leach, this unique structure served as home to a number of public and private entities, including the Ladies' Library from 1869 to 1876.

Bates, Clymene's husband, was the land register. Citizens donated the first 54 books, which the Ladies' Library augmented by purchasing books with membership dues and fundraising dollars.

It cost $1 a year to join the Ladies' Library Association. This let members borrow books, have access to the rooms, and have a say in the organization. During their first year, the women decided to allow men to use the collection, but not become full-fledged members. The *GT Herald* reported in 1870: "The Ladies' Library Association has passed a resolution allowing gentlemen to draw books from their library by payment of 50¢ a quarter." This was later reduced to 25¢ a quarter.

The Ladies' group quickly set up a Reading Club, where they took turns hosting literary readings in each other's homes, and put their considerable energy into enhancing the book collection. By the end of their first year they had amassed 829 volumes "most of them valuable and entertaining," as reported by the *Herald*, as well as many national magazines.

Ladies' Libraries were springing up all around the nation. Kalamazoo was an early one, beginning as a book club and sewing circle in 1844 and transforming into a formal association in 1852. It was the first woman's club in Michigan and only the third in the U.S. Flint began its Ladies' Library in 1853. This was a time when women's suffrage was first being publicly explored, starting with the Women's Rights Convention in Seneca Falls, New York in 1848. Founders of Ladies' Libraries were often highly educated transplants from New York and New England who found themselves living in pioneer towns. Some women were activists, eager to secure the vote, but many simply believed an educated woman was better able to fulfill her role as a wife and mother.

"Women desired cultural activities," said local historian Peg Siciliano. "Their political role was limited. All that energy and expertise and talent got channeled into civic activities. [They] knew the benefit of a well-stocked library."

In early Traverse City, the library women threw themselves into an ambitious suite of programs. They started with a free public lecture by Miss Mary Clark of Ann Arbor, an ardent botanist and founder of the Clark Seminary for Young Ladies. The Clark Seminary was a prominent girls' finishing school in Ann Arbor where families from the Midwest and East Coast sent their daughters. "Pleasant as this was," writes Martha Bates, "[it] did not bring any funds into the treasury." So they decided to host an ambitious "fancy fair" and holiday supper. This oyster supper, held at the upscale Gunton House located at the mouth of the Boardman River (southeast corner of Front and Wellington streets), was by all accounts a grand success, bringing in $124 for the new library.

Through ice cream socials, strawberry festivals, dramatic club entertainments, lectures, and donations, the Ladies' Library continued to add to their collection. The local newspaper marked their progress with headlines and news articles like this: "The Ladies…have made an addition of about seventy volumes of valuable books," "Excellent new books," and "The Ladies' Library Association has recently received from friends of Lieutenant Governor Bates…over $60 worth of standard books." The *Herald* noted: "The ladies have been more successful than could reasonably have been expected in accumulating books."

The Ladies' Library hosted boat rides in summer, sleigh rides in winter, fairs, festivals, pumpkin pie socials, and more. "How we worked, and how the men worked, or rather, how we worked the men!" recalled Esther Hatch. "We drew money from husbands, brothers, sweethearts. We fed them and bled them for our pet scheme."

Women around the state were doing the same. Ladies' Library Associations in Michigan staged doll shows, baby judging, flower contests, suppers, needlework contests, and bazaars. The library group in Otsego, Michigan made news by offering "kissing societies" to raise money. The ladies, all "of the highest character, morally, intellectually, and religiously," kissed local men for 5¢ to 50¢. They also did odd jobs, such as blacking boots, washing a milk wagon, and trimming a coffin. Their creative fundraising efforts were picked up by a Chicago newspaper, and soon people from around the country were mailing them gifts of money and books.

Up in Traverse, the dynamic Clymene Bates was behind two more unusual fundraising events, an afghan fair and a squash pie social. The afghan fair was essentially an auction where people bid on items, including a large afghan crocheted by the library women. ("We didn't call it a lottery because that didn't sound well," explained Martha Bates.) The centerpiece was a "brilliant carriage afghan, radiant in hue and fine in texture." Morgan Bates won the afghan, but re-donated it so the Ladies' Library could auction it off again. It was re-sold and re-donated multiple times, before finally ending up in Judge Ramsdell's carriage house. The afghan fair brought in nearly $190.

Then the "big squash" made library history. The big squash took first prize at the fall 1871 Agricultural Fair. It was so mammoth it weighed over one hundred pounds. When someone donated the winning vegetable to the Ladies' Library, Clymene Bates turned it into a profusion of squash pies and sold them at an impromptu squash pie social.

Some years the Ladies raised more than $400. Funds were spent mostly on books. They incurred other expenses like labels for books, and occasionally had to hire a livery team (perhaps to pick up their guest speakers?), from a place such as The European Horse Hotel on State Street.

In July 1871 the Ladies' Library Association formally incorporated, which allowed the group to buy, sell, and own property. That very fall the women bought two lots on State Street with the idea of building a library.

The next fall, however, the library group lost their leader. Clymene Bates traveled east to visit family. She'd not been gone long when news reached Traverse Township: "Mrs. Bates is dead!" She was only 42 when she died of congestive fever (probably malaria). The entire library association attended her funeral in 1872 and wore mourning badges for thirty days.

The Ladies' Library nearly faltered. It had been Clymene Bates's dream from the beginning, and no one wanted to take her place as president. "It was the child of her love and to its advancement she bent every force of her strong mind," said Martha Bates. Some members were all for disbanding. "It is of no use to try to keep up our organization," said Martha Bates. "It is best to give it up now."

LIBRARY HALL

The Ladies' Library Association rallied and continued on for another 70-some successful years. The women proved to be shrewd real estate handlers, and were actively supported by their businessmen husbands who stepped in to help secure loans. In 1874 they swapped the two lots they'd first bought for a well-positioned lot on Front Street owned by Perry Hannah. To make the exchange even, Hannah also gave them $500.

Still, they owned an empty lot in town, not a building. In 1876, the Ladies' Library book collection moved from the Leach Building to the Old Herald building on Cass Street, sharing space with the YMCA. It was housed there for two years. When the YMCA moved out in 1877, talk of creating a brand-new library building accelerated. The Ladies' Library shifted to a better-positioned lot on Front Street, and by December 6, 1878 had finished a handsome building—their own library building—built at what is now 205–207 E. Front Street. It was on the north side of the street, just east of Cass Street in an area known as "the Park."

J.W. Hilton designed the building and must have been a book lover, for he and his wife were given free life-long use of the Ladies' Library. On dedication day in December 1878, the women asked "the gentlemen" for speeches. The men spoke and donated sums of money at the same time, ranging from $1 to $100. The new library building cost $1,940.

Ladies' Library Association built the gabled structure (2nd from left) in 1878 at what is now 205-207 East Front Street, near corner of Cass Street.

"Traverse City is today, well, to put it mildly, not—Chicago," said Martha Bates, in her speech at the dedication of the Ladies' Library building. "Traverse City, that is for its size, is the liveliest, pluckiest, most enterprising and go-ahead little town to be found between Eastport, Maine, and the Golden Gate of San Francisco Bay." The Ladies' Library group was big on pluck, and they intended to make their mark on the town.

Now that they had a building, the Ladies' Library could charge rent for the space. The first floor housed the book collection along with extra rooms for gatherings. The women rented out the front rooms as offices. The original occupants were Seth C. Moffatt, an attorney, and the YMCA, which rented two rooms for reading rooms. Later, different renters used the front offices, such as doctors J. B. Martin and Ziba Evans. The Ladies' Library used the back rooms themselves, regularly renting out the spacious hall above. "They used the building as a meeting room and charged use of the rooms to fund the library," said local historian Peg Siciliano. "That was rather unusual in the early 1870s for women as a group. It was essentially a business."

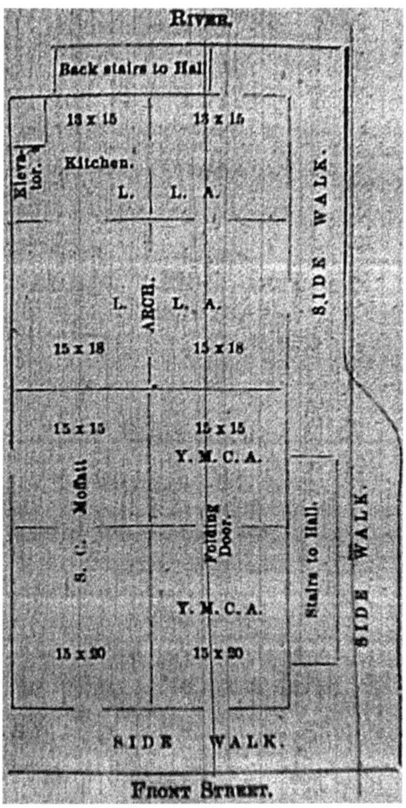

Ladies' Library Building, layout of first floor offices, kitchen, and library, 1878.

The upper floor, called Library Hall, was a large open hall that could seat 300. It was described as "large, light, and pleasant." Library Hall was in great demand for parties, public gatherings, theatrical performances, music, dances, lectures, and any other cultural events since it was the only public hall of its size in Traverse City for many years. Various speakers used the Hall, including James Munson, who gave a talk in 1887 on "The Causes and Prevention of Insanity." He was the first director of the newly opened Northern Michigan Asylum.

We will never know all the events that were staged in Traverse City's first theater, but "Among the Breakers" was one. Produced in the 1880s, the show demanded the sound effects of a storm, so players rigged up a spinning wheel with sand paper to make "waves dash against the shore in fine furry (*sic*)." Library Hall also featured magicians, hypnotists, traveling troupes of players, and hosted masquerades and firemen's balls. "It was probably the worst firetrap anywhere," noted The Observer, a column written by editor Jay P. Smith in the *Traverse City Record-Eagle*, in a retrospective in 1961, "but it escaped any tragedy."

Various speakers used the Hall, including James Munson, who gave a talk in 1887 on "The Causes and Prevention of Insanity."

Plays were audience favorites. "Doubtless more Uncle Tom's Cabin and East Lynne shows played there than anywhere else in the north," shared The Observer. East Lynne shows were wildly popular stage adaptations of the novel *East Lynne* by English novelist Ellen Wood. The story followed Lady Isabel, who scandalously left her husband and ended up returning home disguised as her children's governess, before dying melodramatically and repentantly. Harriet Beecher Stowe, author of the sentimental and influential anti-slavery book *Uncle Tom's Cabin*, never authorized a stage version of her novel, but putting on a "Tom show," was extremely common. It likely helped spread racial stereotypes along with its important abolitionist message. Leon Titus (see page 27) and many others acted in Library Hall shows, which included minstrelsy black-face performances.

The opera houses came later. The City Opera House opened in 1892 and Steinberg's Grand Opera House in 1894, so for fourteen years, Library Hall filled that cultural and community gap. The Ladies did a brisk business and made $500 a year by renting out the hall. One of the groups that used the hall regularly was the Hannah Rifles, who met and drilled in Library Hall. The Hannah Rifles, named after Perry Hannah, was a military group formed in 1895. They sent 110 men to the Spanish-American War to fight in Cuba, and stopped drilling in Library Hall in 1898 when the hall was carpeted.

But besides rifle drills, theater performances, and other activities, the Ladies' Library was primarily about books. Their early collection was impressive. The Ladies' Library had close to 2,000 volumes, mostly fiction. Hot titles on the shelves in 1897 included detective mysteries

The Ladies' Library Hall on Front Street (labeled "2" and circled on page 11) is one of the few structures identified on this *1879 Bird's Eye View of Traverse City* by Herman Brosius.

like *Tracked by a Tattoo* by Fergus Hume or novels such as *Nancy Noon* by Benjamin Swift, *Sir Godfrey's Granddaughters* by Rosa Carey, and *On the Red Staircase* by Mary Imlay Taylor. Also included were nonfiction titles, such as Ralph Waldo Emerson's collection of essays, *Conduct of Life*. As the *Morning Record* observed, they had "the reputation

Other notable buildings include the Park Place Hotel (page 10), and Grace Episcopal Church ("6") on page 11.

among large book houses of being the most up to date of any of their patrons and the latest and best books are always to be obtained at the Ladies' Library as soon as they are published."

Generations of city children grew up making weekly trips to the Ladies' Library. At one time, books for children were rented for 5¢ a week. "Every Saturday afternoon we went to the Ladies' Library with a nickel or a dime and drew books. That's where we got Toby Tyler, Canoemates and Tentmates, Lew and I, and Ben Hur, perfectly wonderful books," recalled The Observer.

The Ladies' Library was a well-beloved part of the community and continued to receive donations, including a sizeable $3,000 bequest from Smith Barnes. Barnes was the former Secretary, Treasurer, and general manager of the Hannah & Lay Mercantile company. He died in 1891 and the estate gift was transferred in 1898. This estate gift gave the Ladies' Library finances a significant boost.

Not even ten years after they moved in, however, the Ladies' Library was beginning to rethink its Front Street location. The large frame building was really bigger than they needed, and now that Traverse City boasted *two* new, flashy opera houses on Front Street, the spaciousness of Library Hall had outlived its purpose. What about something smaller? Something brick and homey? The women toyed with building on a vacant lot on the corner of Boardman Avenue and Washington Street and even bought the land in 1886. In the end, the library re-sold the empty lot to Grace Episcopal Church in 1897. Grace Episcopal had an established building on State Street, but the stench and flies of the new European Horse Hotel that had set up business next door were unpleasant. With Perry Hannah's financial help, they hauled their church building from State Street to a new, quieter location on Boardman Avenue.

The Ladies tried to sell their library building in 1893 and again in 1906, but had no luck. It wasn't until 1909 that the Ladies' Library Association moved from Front Street to a newly built brick building at 216 Cass Street. The original Front Street library was sold for $10,000. The second Ladies' Library building on Cass Street survives intact to this day. It is marked with a state historical plaque and is now home to the State Savings Bank and a law office.

Women's Suffrage and Susan B. Anthony

The women involved in the Ladies' Library Association were passionate about literacy, women's education, and exploring the ideas of the day. Those ideas increasingly included talk of women's public role and voting rights.

On a wintry March evening in 1879, two years after the Ladies' Library got their own building, Library Hall hosted a lecture by noted suffragist Susan B. Anthony. The Ladies' Library and YMCA jointly hosted her, and Anthony held an audience riveted for two and a half hours with her lecture entitled "Woman Wants Bread, not the Ballot," a passionate call for women's suffrage. Although the title of her speech may seem odd, it's based on a story she shared about starving miners and factory workers in England who rioted in protest in the mid-1800s. When Quaker John Bright advised them they needed the vote to ensure cheap bread, the men angrily said: 'It is not the vote we want, it is bread."

Anthony's speech was a popular one she used in cities around the country. She explained how women's well-being depended on having the power to vote, even if people (including women themselves) didn't see the direct connection. "Disfranchisement means inability to make, shape or control one's own circumstances," she said, including the situation of enslaved Blacks, Chinese laborers, women, and others in this definition. "The disfranchised must always do the work, accept the wages, occupy the position the enfranchised assign to them."

She told Traverse City that women, like all disenfranchised people, were like paupers: "You remember the old adage, 'Beggars must not be choosers;' they must take what they can get or nothing! That is exactly the position of women in the world of work today; they cannot choose. If they could, do you for a moment believe they would take the subordinate places and the inferior pay?"

The Ladies' Library turned out in full force, along with much of the town. As Martha Bates' husband, Thomas Bates, wrote in the *Grand Traverse Herald*: "Library Hall was crowded as never before on last Friday evening to hear Miss Susan B. Anthony deliver her noted lecture... [She is] as bright and as sharp as a Damascus Blade."

Anthony also said she appreciated the new boardwalks in downtown Traverse City. Unlike her counterpart Elizabeth Cady Stanton, Susan B. Anthony traveled widely on a speaking circuit and was understandably tired of dragging her long skirts through mud-rutted small town streets.

Times were changing, but slowly. Five years before Anthony's visit, The *Herald* reported results of a survey of 200 homes in Traverse City where only one in six local women favored having voting rights.

Anthony would not have been surprised. It was not "a 'new thing under the sun' for the disfranchised, the inferior classes weighed down with wrongs, to declare they 'do not want to vote,'" she said. "The rank and file are not philosophers, they are not educated to think for themselves, but simply to accept, unquestioned, whatever comes."

That's one reason why the Ladies' Library group worked so hard to create a vibrant library. To create a place where women and men could gather, learn, and expand their thinking.

The Traverse City Ladies' Library Association was among those setting the stage for final passage of the 19th Amendment forty years later.

War, Fire, and Epidemics

War: The Civil War was over by the time the Ladies' Library formed, but it was still recent history. Martha Bates, the new chair, learned that copies of official war records from the "War of the Rebellion" were being distributed to libraries around the country. She immediately wrote to the U.S. Secretary of War, General Alger, and requested a set of documents for the Traverse City Ladies' Library. She was initially denied because all copies had been spoken for. Then six large mail pouches arrived at the Traverse City post office containing 107 clothbound books detailing the "Rebellion Records."

When the Spanish-American War broke out, the Hannah Rifles set off to Cuba in May 1898. The night before they left, Ladies' Library members gathered in Library Hall to prepare a "housewife" kit for each young soldier. These were oilcloth cases lined with silk which contained pins, needles, and thread for mending jobs. According to the *Morning Record*, each case contained a note reading:

> *Our Boys of the Hannah Rifles –*
>
> *With these little home comforts, which you will have no loving hands to use for you but must make serve you yourselves as best you can, go a thousand loving wishes for highest welfare, and earnest prayers will follow you all the way till we welcome you home again. God grant it may be soon. We know it will be triumphantly.*
>
> *Your faithful friends,*
> *The Members of the Traverse City Ladies' Library Association*

When the Hannah Rifles returned from the war at the end of 1898, their health was a concern. "Young men of the High School who went away erect in form and vigorous in health, came back bent from hardships and their systems saturated with malaria," reported the Traverse City High School yearbook in 1900.

Mayor Frank Hamilton urged citizens to add a hospital and also enlarge the public library. A "score or more of the boys were ill" reported the *Morning Record* and stated that these topics were ones "in which the women are vitally interested, and matters which, when energetic women like these take hold of them, are bound to become assured facts and not mere theories." The mayor declared that "a more extensive library with permanent reading rooms would be a boon to young men." Although his idea of a library was primarily aimed at the moral improvement of young men, the *Morning Record* looked to the women of the city to make both the hospital and public library a reality, for "success in promoting them will always follow the efforts of earnest women."

FIRE: In July 1897, the Ladies' Library group was gathered in their library building on Front Street for an afternoon meeting when news reached Traverse City that the nearby village of Lake Ann had been destroyed by a horrendous fire. The fire swept through Lake Ann on July 3, 1897, and rapidly consumed 82 buildings and made 75 families homeless. The Ladies' Library immediately decided to donate $25 to buy clothes and bedding for the fire victims. This was considered a highly generous sum, since many local donations were in the range of 50 cents to five dollars. The Ladies' Library members opened the library rooms to the women of the community and brought in sewing machines. Then they rolled up their sleeves and set to work making bedding and sewing clothes for the Lake Ann families. "It is women's work for women," the *Morning Record* reported. All women were encouraged to bring serviceable cloth, along with pins and needles, towels, handkerchiefs, and dishes.

On a frigid winter day in January 1900, a devastating fire broke out on Front Street, placing the Ladies' Library building and book collection in jeopardy. The horse-drawn fire brigade raced down Cass Street to contain the blaze while the "sharp shriek of the mocking bird whistle sounded the alarm." Mocking bird whistles were a common name for the early steam whistles used as sirens. The fire burned down four buildings: a bakery, a glassware shop, the City Hotel, and the Wood Sisters millinery shop. The fire badly scorched Steinberg's Grand Opera House, and inched closer to the Ladies' Library building.

"It looked at first as though the Ladies Library was doomed," reported the *Morning Record* the next day. Annie Soule, one of the library trustees, rushed into the Ladies' Library to save the records and also hurried out with a portrait of Margaret Ashton, wife of Dr. Benjamin Ashton. Then a team of women and men carried out furniture and books. They saved everything—the entire collection of books—and even the carpets. The Ladies' Library had had a close call, but luckily escaped with only minor smoke damage.

This was the second time the Ladies' Library had been lucky. An even bigger fire had raged through Traverse City on November 11, 1896. That fire burned down fourteen wooden buildings including the Front Street House hotel and several stores and saloons, before being stopped at the brick walls of Steinberg's still-new Opera House.

EPIDEMICS: In the winter of 1901–1902, an outbreak of smallpox hit Traverse City. There was an early hospital in town, but isolation was the best form of containment, so the city designated "pest houses" where people who'd been exposed to smallpox could quarantine. Smallpox was a potentially deadly disease. It began with fever and fatigue, then progressed to vomiting and a disfiguring rash that could lead to blindness and permanent scarring. To stop the spread, people burned all the bedding, clothes, curtains, and furniture in a room used for treating a smallpox patient and even buried the ashes. Michigan had nearly 9,000 smallpox cases in 1901–1902, and another outbreak of smallpox struck Traverse City in 1916. The library trustees' 1916 annual

The November 1896 fire flattened buildings on the south side of Front Street then leaped to attack northside structures.

Leaders of the Ladies' Library Association in the early 1890s (Top row from left): Mary Knizek Buck (charter member); Martha E. Cram Bates (charter member); Mary Ann Stevens Roberts; Margaret Lackey Ashton (charter member); Ada K. Sprague Pratt. Front row: Cornelia Lathrop; Estella I. Udall Kneeland; Adelaide Hoxie Haviland; Janet Bates Boyd; Callie Lackey Thacker.

report notes a decrease in circulation: "This fact is due almost entirely by the smallpox epidemic which existed in the city during the early part of the school year." (See page 63 for effects of 1918 influenza).

An Early Nonprofit

The Ladies' Library Association ran a private library that was open to the public. Today they would likely be termed a nonprofit organization: a group with a vision and a mission, privately managed, but with public service as its goal.

For their first 35 years, the Ladies' Library focused on founding and managing a library and community hall for the public. This was a labor of love and a public service. Although it was privately organized, the Ladies' Library was the go to library for the region, not an exclusive club like a private country club. The library was prominently located, and for many years served as a welcoming downtown fixture for the public's benefit.

Once the Traverse City Public Library was well established and settled comfortably in the Carnegie building in 1905, the Ladies' Library group shifted their focus. They were able to shed some of their larger responsibilities—running the region's main library, managing office rentals, and Library Hall—and enjoy their own company with social and educational programs. The new Ladies' Library on Cass Street represented this second era of the Ladies' Library Association (1909 to 1944).

By creating a well-run, beloved library for the community, the Ladies' Library set a standard for excellence and service and can be considered the main predecessor of the Traverse Area District Library.

By creating a well-run, beloved library for the community, the Ladies' Library set a standard for excellence and service and can be considered the main predecessor of the Traverse Area District Library.

The Township Library

Although many library enthusiasts proudly point to the Ladies' Library as the first local library, Traverse City already had a library, a small public library funded by the fledging Traverse Township government. It began with a modest collection of two rows of books on a bookshelf in the 1850s.

Dr. David Goodale hosted the first library, according to Ada Sprague Pratt, sister to Esther Sprague Hatch and Elvin L. Sprague. Dr. Goodale was also the local postmaster. He arrived in 1853, and his house served as home, library, and post office. Traverse City was still a small lumber town, not yet incorporated as a village. No roads or train lines connected the Grand Traverse region to the outer world, and travel was by schooner, sloop, canoe, or multi-day treks by foot on trails. It wasn't until 1881 that the settlement became an official village, and then a city in 1895.

The Township Library, or later, The City Library, was a somewhat haphazard affair. It enjoyed some built-in funds from the Township budget (for example, $77.80 in the Library Fund in 1861), but the library kept limited hours and had no stable home. Books were borrowed, but not always returned. Notices in the *Grand Traverse Herald* exhorted citizens to bring back their library books.

Dr. Albert Holliday described it like this: "township property... housed in an old wooden building at 115 Park Street." The library landed on Park Street around 1865 and was run by township clerk Jesse Cram (father of Martha E. Cram Bates). At that time, the entire library consisted of two rows of books set on a dark-stained wooden piece of furniture—a combination table, desk, and bookcase.

The Township Library changed locations regularly, depending on who was the current township clerk. For some time it shared space with a drug store run by Lucius Hubbell, then moved on to another drug store, this time run by Eddie Miller. Myron Haskell, who owned a bookstore, was clerk next. For a time, the Township Library was located on the second story of the Hamilton & Milliken store, then it was back to Haskell's when he was re-elected.

Local newspapers noted upgrades to the library. "An addition of $70 worth of new and valuable books has been made to our Town Library" said the *Herald* in 1870, and "Two Hundred Books—New Volumes Added to City Library" said the *Morning Record* in 1897.

Despite its new title as a "City" library in 1895, the public library limped along. According to Mabel Bates Williams (daughter of Thomas and Martha E. C. Bates), the collection was old and dusty and sat in a forgotten corner of the drug store. Years later in 1946, she reminisced over the city's early attempts at a library:

> *I can go back to the time when the so-called City library was a 2 by 3 foot book case, which was housed in the back room of Eddie Miller's drug store when it was located somewhere in the middle of the block east of Hamilton & Milliken's. I don't know how I discovered it, for nobody had taken a book from it for many years. You went through the store, back of the mysterious prescription desk and into a storeroom way in behind. It smelled of dried senna leaves, patent medicine, and dust.*
>
> *You opened the book case and found a whole set of The Rollo Books. Rollo belonged to the era of my mother's childhood circa 1840–1850. He was always the Perfect Gentleman, a Paragon, aged somewhere around seven. He never did anything wrong, and Virtue floated around his brow like an aura.*

The City Library floundered along, floating from space to space. Sometimes the volumes were read, sometimes they weren't, but the

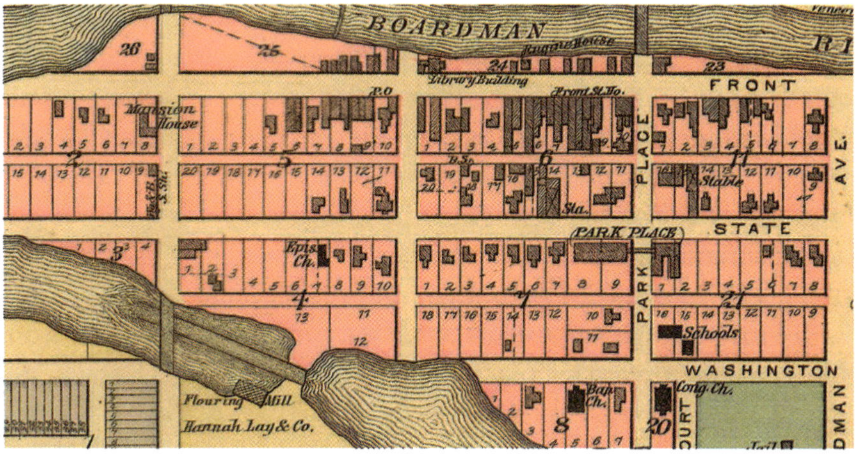

1881 Atlas of Grand Traverse County. Note Ladies' Library Building on Front Street, one of few identified buildings.

city kept accumulating books as the budget permitted. By 1899, they had amassed more than 2,000 books. It was getting harder and harder to move those volumes.

"The room now used for the public library is entirely inadequate…[It] is inconvenient of access, poorly lighted, and entirely too small," stated Thomas Bates and other library trustees in early 1901. Traverse City's population was growing fast, and access was a problem. By 1899 the public library was open only one day a week. As a temporary solution, the men proposed renting space from the Ladies' Library, arguing that Library Hall would provide a pleasant environment with reasonable rent. The Ladies were happy to oblige.

Now two libraries were housed under one roof, the City Library and the Ladies' Library. After they settled into their accommodations at Library Hall, the City expanded hours and installed Lucille Dusenbery as their part-time librarian, at a salary of $30 a month. In 1901, a committee of aldermen reported to the city council: "We believe no better investment can be made…[than] in affording our citizens, and especially our boys and girls, a well lighted, ventilated, comfortable and pleasant room for a library, and a quiet, cheerful reading room." The City Library rented from the Ladies' Library from 1901 until the Carnegie library opened in 1905.

The room now used for the public library is entirely inadequate… [It] is inconvenient of access, poorly lighted, and entirely too small.

Perhaps it was appropriate that the Ladies' Library and the City Library shared space under one roof, for together they formed the core of today's Grand Traverse regional public library system. In 1884, a third local library had also formed, a school library housed at Traverse City High School. Now with three separate libraries all growing, the *Grand Traverse Herald* suggested combining forces to create one good, public library for all local residents.

Traverse City Public Library benefactor Andrew Carnegie (1835–1919)

There is not such a cradle of democracy...as the Free Public Library, this republic of letters, where neither rank, office, nor wealth receives the slightest consideration.

Andrew Carnegie

CHAPTER 2

Carnegie Libraries

THE LEGACY OF CARNEGIE LIBRARIES

About this time, steel tycoon Andrew Carnegie was beginning a new type of philanthropy and ushering in what's been called the Golden Age of public libraries in America.

Over the course of thirty years, Carnegie provided funding to build 2,500 library buildings, 1,689 of them in the United States. The first Carnegie library commissioned in the U.S. was in 1886, in Allegheny, Pennsylvania. Carnegie's last library grant was in 1919, the year he died.

Andrew Carnegie was born in Dunfermline, Scotland. His father was a handloom weaver at a time when the Industrial Revolution was in full swing. Steam-powered looms pushed him and other linen weavers out of work. His mother took to mending shoes and selling groceries, but the family fell into poverty. In 1848 they auctioned off their possessions, borrowed money for passage on the sailing ship *Wiscasset*, and immigrated to the United States. Young Andrew was 12 years old.

The family settled in Allegheny, near Pittsburgh. Andrew worked as a bobbin boy in a textile mill, making $1.20 a week to help support the family. His quest to learn was unstoppable. He attended night school and read voraciously. He also borrowed books from a man

Andrew Carnegie, circa 1861, aged 26 or 27.

named Colonel James Anderson. There was no public library in Allegheny at the time, but Colonel Anderson opened his home library to working boys. Andrew credited Colonel Anderson with opening "the intellectual wealth of the world" to him.

In his teens, Carnegie became a telegraph messenger, joined debating societies, studied bookkeeping and investing. He caught the attention of Thomas Scott of the Pennsylvania Railroad, who made him his right-hand man. Scott became president of the railroad in 1874, and Carnegie rose up the ranks in the railroad, then moved into iron, and finally steel. Already rich, he made an additional fortune with his Carnegie Steel Corporation based in Pittsburgh. In 1901, he retired and sold his steel company to John P. Morgan for $480 million.

This left Carnegie with a lot of money. Carnegie had always grappled with wealth and the responsibility of wealth. Although his relations with steel workers were a mixed bag (he asked the Pinkerton detective agency to hire 300 thugs to break up a strike in Homestead, Pennsylvania. This left twelve dead as the two sides fought with guns, bricks, and dynamite), he always remembered his father's quest to work and his family's poverty.

He coined the term "excess wealth" in his two-part essay entitled "Wealth" published in the *North American Review* in June and December 1889. It opens like this: "The problem of our age, is the proper administration of wealth, so that the ties of brotherhood may still bind together the rich and poor in harmonious relationship." Perhaps the violent Homestead Strike still haunted him.

The essay, commonly known now as "The Gospel of Wealth," is considered a guiding document in American philanthropy. Carnegie argued that the rich have "a moral obligation to distribute [their money] in ways that promote the welfare and happiness of the common man." People should give away any extra money which wasn't needed to take care of their own family. What's more, he said, people should give away their wealth *during* their lifetime, not perpetuate social imbalance with vast inheritances. "The man who dies rich, dies disgraced," he famously said.

When thinking of how to give away his fortune, Carnegie's eye fell primarily on libraries. Carnegie Hall, the world-class concert hall in New York City, was one of his gifts, as well as Carnegie Mellon University, and other concert halls, art galleries, science institutes, and organizations for world peace. He also supported churches, giving away 7,600 church organs. But libraries became his special passion.

Founding libraries was not so much an act of charity, as an act of access.

Libraries supported the self-educated and the self-motivated. Perhaps he was thinking of himself as a young boy, or the generous colonel who opened his private library to boys with the penchant to study. "In bestowing charity, the main consideration should be to help those who will help themselves," he wrote. Founding libraries was not so much an act of charity, as an act of access.

To begin with, Carnegie established libraries in places where he had a personal connection. His first library, donated in 1881, was to his boyhood town of Dunfermline, Scotland. Next he set up libraries in Pittsburgh, center of his steel empire. His library gifts might have ended there, if an earnest senator from Iowa hadn't taken a train to

New York City to ask Andrew Carnegie to fund a library building in Fairfield, Iowa.

Senator James Wilson's surprising request was immediately granted. Carnegie promised Fairfield, Iowa $40,000 for their new library building.

Soon word got out, and people from across the country began writing heartfelt letters to the new patron saint of public libraries.

Like Traverse City's early Township Library, small-town libraries in the 1800s often started out homeless. A library was no more than a collection of books housed somewhere—anywhere. Libraries were located in bowling alleys and private homes. Some citizens borrowed books from millinery shops, grocery stores, or drug stores. Sometimes libraries shared space with noisy places like the town jail or local fire department. One small-town library in Minnesota was actually housed inside a public restroom, and the restroom attendant also served as quasi-librarian.

Letters poured in from eager citizens in Indiana, Ohio, Nebraska, California, Oregon and more, sometimes merely addressed: "Andrew Carnegie, New York." A library. A permanent building, please. Somewhere to put our precious books and create true community space. Anyone could make the request. Sometimes it was the train station manager who wrote, or the newspaper editor. Other times it was a local school superintendent. But it wasn't just men in public positions who wrote to Andrew Carnegie. Women often took the lead in requesting funds for a library, many times women from Ladies' Library Associations. Carnegie's office was soon deluged with 500 to 3,000 letters a day.

With so many requests, Carnegie and his personal secretary, James Bertram, developed a system. They created a simple questionnaire, leaving most details up to the local community. One question was population. How much money a town or city got depended on its size. Big cities like Detroit received $750,000 to fund the main library plus eight branches. Small towns, like Redfield, South Dakota, population 1,015, received only $10,000. Some towns tried to fudge their numbers, claiming more inhabitants, but Bertram referred to official census data.

Carnegie's library grant program was simple: Carnegie provided money for construction, but the local community had to offer a site plus commit to funding the library's operation and maintenance.

To receive a library grant, all communities needed to do was declare their need, provide land for the building site, and promise to support the new library with public tax funds. This was an important point. Carnegie wanted the community to care about its library. At that time, local governments typically limited tax collection for traditional public services like fire and police departments, water works or schools. Libraries? Hardly ever. The standard formula was that local governments were asked to pay 10% of the grant amount Carnegie offered. Suddenly Carnegie's terms made officials consider libraries in a different light. Maybe libraries *were* an essential public service, a public institution deserving of tax money.

Carnegie also deferred to local laws. Although he strongly believed in educational access for everybody, many Carnegie public libraries were "whites only" in the Jim Crow South until the 1960s. When a Carnegie library was built in Atlanta in 1902, W.E.B. DuBois and others spoke out against the injustice of a public library that collected taxes from everyone, but refused to serve a third of Atlanta's population. They insisted on integration. Carnegie continued to work with segregationist cities and towns, but he funded twelve public libraries specifically for African-Americans, such as the Carnegie Negro Library in Greensboro, North Carolina. He also funded fourteen libraries at Black colleges.

Carnegie wanted the community to care about its library.

In the last 18 years of his life, Andrew Carnegie gave away $350 million, a sum equal to about $5.5 billion in today's dollars. That amounted to about 90% of his total fortune.

A CARNEGIE LIBRARY FOR TRAVERSE CITY

In the last few months of 1901, 29-year-old Leon Titus, an assistant bank cashier in Traverse City, wrote a letter to Andrew Carnegie at the behest of the library board. "Mr. Andrew Carnegie, New York City. Dear Sir," he wrote.

Perhaps he'd seen *Harper's Weekly Magazine* that spring. The *Harper's* cover from March 30, 1901 featured Carnegie and his extraordinary grant program to fund libraries. Why, he was even funding libraries in tiny prairie towns, towns like Hawarden, Iowa and Valley City, North Dakota. Traverse City's population was rapidly growing. True, it was still officially under 10,000 according to census data, but if

March 30, 1901 cover of *Harper's Weekly* acknowledges both sides of Carnegie's public persona.

other towns could do it, why not Traverse City?

Although the city was pleased with its temporary location in the Ladies' Library, it was adding books each year, and would soon be outgrowing its space. Also, $300 spent on yearly rent was money they'd rather use for library books and services. In early 1901, there was already murmuring about looking for an outside library benefactor.

"Neither a Carnegie or a Reyerson [*sic*] has struck Traverse City yet, but we live in hope," read a statement in the *Traverse Bay Eagle*. They were referring to Martin Ryerson (great-nephew of Grand Rapids founder Louis Campau), who donated $150,000 to build a library in Grand Rapids.

Would Traverse City attract the interest of a Ryerson or a Carnegie?

Carnegie did not reply. Maybe Traverse City was too small. Maybe he was done giving away his money for libraries. But Titus did not give up. He sent a second letter written

Leon Fayette Titus (1872–1946) intiated correspondence with Andrew Carnegie that led to the building on Sixth Street.

in his elegant, slanted handwriting, using First National Bank letterhead. The second letter is dated January 3, 1902 and he repeats his request, noting that he'd heard nothing from Carnegie in two to three months, so perhaps his first letter had "miscarried." Perhaps it was due to Titus' persistence that Traverse City received a Carnegie library. Columbia University maintains an extensive microfilm database of all the correspondence between local communities and Carnegie. Titus's first "lost letter" is not among them.

> *We read very often of your most generous gifts to other cities, and thinking that you must be continuing your good work, I thought if we presented our conditions to you and they met with your ideas, we might learn what action we could take to secure your aid for a library building for Traverse City.*
>
> Leon Titus to Andrew Carnegie in January 1902

Library trustee Elvin Sprague echoed his initial request with another plea:

> *Andrew Carnegie,*
> *Dear Sir—I write you in the interest of Traverse City, Michigan Public Library. We have a library containing about 4,000 volumes of carefully selected books…We have no building in which to keep it except by renting one. This we do, and are expending nearly $1,000 a year…*
>
> *Our city is comparatively young and with its rapid growth in population a large amount of money has necessarily to be expended for building School houses and street improvements and renders it impossible for us to erect a Public Library…*
>
> *If we can secure the means to build we can get a splendid site in one of the very best and most central parts of town.*
>
> *Respectfully yours,*
> *E.L. Sprague*
> *Member Board of Library Trustees*

Titus' second letter did the trick. Soon Titus was corresponding with Carnegie's personal secretary, James Bertram. He submitted the standard Carnegie questionnaire and other data. Satisfied, Bertram passed Traverse City's application on to Carnegie for his approval.

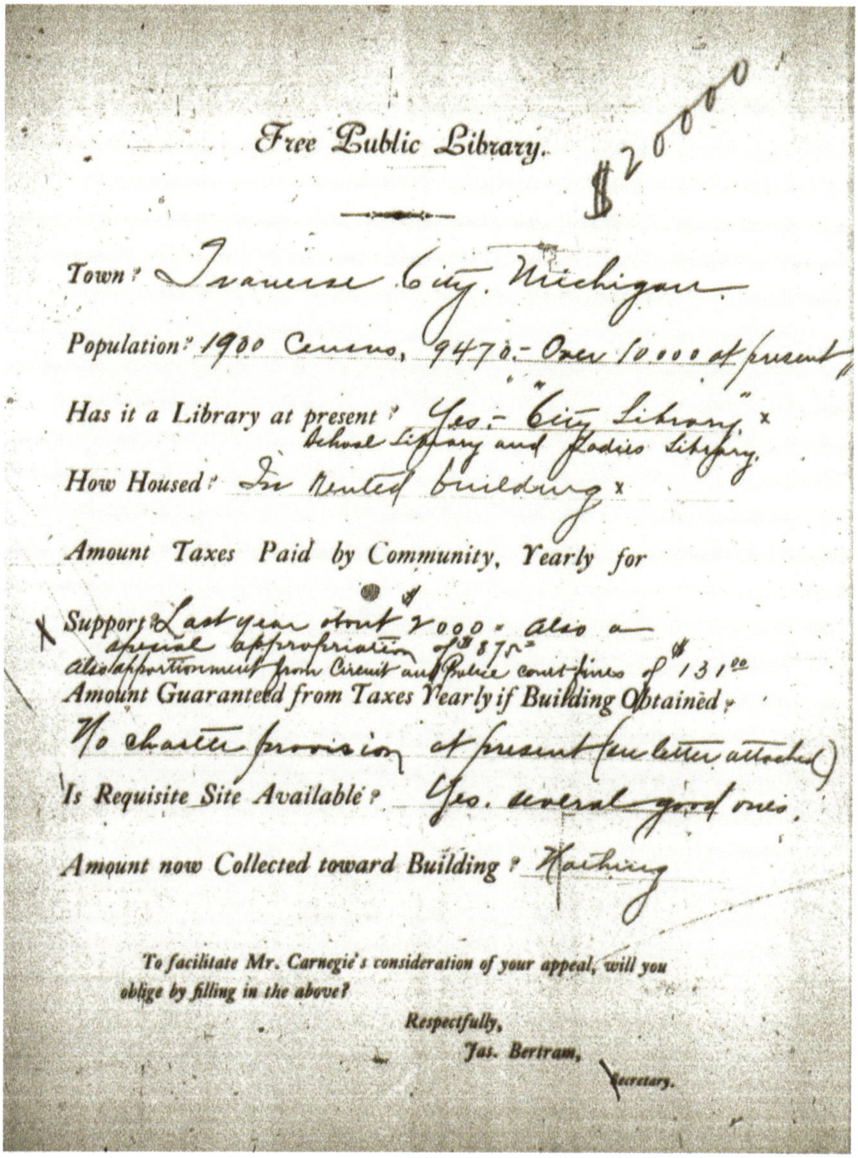

Free Public Library. $20000

Town? Traverse City. Michigan

Population? 1900 Census, 9470.- Over 10000 at present

Has it a Library at present? Yes - "City Library" School Library and Ladies Library.

How Housed? In rented building

Amount Taxes Paid by Community, Yearly for Support? Last year about $2000. also a special appropriation of $875 also apportionment from Circuit and Police court fines of $131.00

Amount Guaranteed from Taxes Yearly if Building Obtained? No charter provision at present (see letter attached)

Is Requisite Site Available? Yes. several good ones.

Amount now Collected toward Building? Nothing

To facilitate Mr. Carnegie's consideration of your appeal, will you oblige by filling in the above?

Respectfully,
Jas. Bertram,
Secretary.

Application to Carnegie for library funds, as submitted by Leon Titus in 1902.

The whole process was quick and easy. A few short months later, the *Evening Record* joyfully reported the news: "Leon F. Titus Has Been in Correspondence with Noted Philanthropist for Months—Favorable Reply Has Just Been Received." The terms: $20,000 for a Carnegie library. All the city had to do was commit to $2,000 per year to run it and provide a site.

> *New York, April 8, 1902*
> *Mr. Leon F. Titus*
> *Traverse City, Mich.*
> *Dear Sir—Responding to your communications:*
>
> *If Traverse City pledges itself by resolution of council to support a free public library at cost of not less than two thousand ($2,000) dollars a year, and provides a suitable site, Mr. Carnegie will be glad to furnish twenty thousand dollars ($20,000) for the erection of a free public library building.*
>
> *Very respectfully yours,*
> *Jas. Bertram*
> *Private Secretary*

The newspapers gave in to much rejoicing. They called the yet-to-be-built building an "ornament to the city" and declared the public library was worthy of tax dollars, just like schools. After all, the city was already spending nearly $2,000 a year in library expenses, such as rent, books, and librarian salary, so the commitment to give $2,000 a year would not be a great hardship. Patronage was skyrocketing. Just last year, in 1901, book circulation had been 37,576, a 70% increase from the year before. This was indeed a golden opportunity. The *Evening Record* proudly said: "There is no city in the state of this size whose public library is better patronized than that here, the number of people taking books from the library is an illustration of the intellectual tendency of our people." In short, Traverse City was the perfect place to welcome a new Carnegie library.

"Traverse City comes in for an improvement through the munificence of Andrew Carnegie," the *Evening Record* wrote. "Traverse City should not let this offer go by. It should be accepted and at once."

It turned out not to be that easy. The trouble was the "suitable site."

Map of downtown Traverse City (2021) adapted to depict layout of 1902

Key

- Hannah and Hull sites that were sources of great controversy 1902–1904
  - **A** Sixth Street Site
  - **B** Ashton-Hobbs Site
- Sites for Carnegie library that were not seriously considered
- Other buildings mentioned in the text
  - **1** Perry Hannah Home
  - **2** Ladies' Library 1878
  - **3** Leach Building
  - **4** Lardie Potato Warehouse
  - **5** Gunton House
  - **6** Henry Hull Home
  - **7** Oval Wood Dish Company

The only thing that you absolutely need to know is the location of the library.

Albert Einstein

Chapter 3

The Great Site Fight 1902–1904

Siting the Carnegie Library

Perry Hannah was the city's most famous Founding Father and indisputably its wealthiest man for many years. As Traverse City's one and only millionaire, he wielded considerable influence and power. But there was another millionaire coming up.

Hannah arrived by schooner to Grand Traverse Bay in 1851. He bought up Harry Boardman's land holdings and lumber mill, and established a Hannah, Lay & Company presence in what would become Traverse City. There he made a vast fortune cutting northern Michigan's timber and selling it to Chicago and elsewhere. Later Hannah, Lay & Co. expanded into milling, banking, real estate, and other businesses. Hannah set up Traverse City State Bank, the region's first bank, and its first store, the Hannah Lay store, which at first stocked "a few pieces of calico, and just dry goods enough to supply the little community."

Hannah had always been a lumberman. He started rafting logs down the St. Clair River from Port Huron to Detroit as a teenager, and later worked in a lumberyard in Chicago, where he met Albert Tracy Lay. In the Traverse area, some people placed Hannah on near-hero status. He was addressed as "the Honorable" and acted as village president, and later became Traverse City's first mayor. Hannah platted

Perry Hannah (1824–1904)

Henry S. Hull (1845–1923)

out Old Town, Oak Park, Boardman, and Slabtown neighborhoods, represented Traverse City in Lansing as a member of the young state legislature, made donations to several churches and to the local synagogue (although he didn't belong to any of them), and donated land for Oakwood Cemetery.

Timber barons like Hannah also left an enormous mark on the natural landscape. Before long, Michigan's unbroken forests had vanished. What was left was a barren landscape, denuded of trees and wildlife habitat. Stumps dotted thousands of acres of razed timber. "Slash fires" broke out, fueled by piles of logging debris. The Traverse City region was no different. After the lumber boom peaked, the area around the new city was a ghost land: a cutover landscape, with eroded river banks, and industrial pollution in the bay.

Whatever his full role, Perry Hannah was a very rich man. For many years he lived in Hannah Cottage at what would be 233 Bay Street, just west of his sawmill, but in 1893 he moved into a new 40-room mansion on Sixth Street.

Meanwhile, a newcomer had come to town: Henry Hull, owner of the prosperous Oval Wood Dish Company. He'd been in business more than ten years when he moved his company to Traverse City at the north end of Boardman Lake. Soon Hull's company had 500 men and women working for him, exceeding Hannah's company as the largest employer in town.

The Oval Wood Dish Company used wood, too. Their signature product was the oval wood dish itself, a thin, disposable plate meant for wrapping butcher meat. By 1899, Hull was making many thousands of them and his bowls were in "every grocery store in the nation." Oval Wood Dish also manufactured other practical wooden items like clothespins, toothpicks, rolling pins, and wooden spoons, using sawmill waste for the smaller items.

Now there were suddenly two millionaires in town. Henry Hull was ready to flex his muscles and show Hannah that he was not the only successful Traverse City businessman.

THE START OF IT

Gratified by Carnegie's generosity, the city immediately appointed a library committee to find a good site. They asked the three library trustees: Thomas Bates, Elvin Sprague, and Ella Perry, to work with three members of the city council: Aldermen Frank Hamilton, George W. Lardie Jr., and Harris Cunningham. The committee was appointed on May 19, 1902, and, because of his involvement with Carnegie, Leon Titus was requested to join them. Titus became Secretary of the new library committee, and Thomas Bates was made chairman.

Full of high hopes, the library committee asked for proposals. Who had property that would be suitable for a public library? Who was willing to sell it to the city? They published ads in both the *Record* and the *Grand Traverse Herald* asking for proposals by August 5, 1902.

When the proposals came in, the library committee did what all diligent committees do. They met. They investigated. They discussed. And they came up with a recommendation: of all the possible sites offered in Traverse City, the very best one was located on Cass Street. Two adjacent lots, one owned by Dr. Edwin Ashton and the other by his brother-in-law, William Hobbs. Both owners were willing sellers. The Ashton-Hobbs Cass Street spot was beautifully located in the central business district, just east of the Boardman River, near the corner of Cass and Washington streets (where Central United Methodist Church stands today). The two Cass Street lots together would cost about $6,000.

Of course, the Ashton-Hobbs spot on Cass Street wasn't the only option. The Grand Traverse Grange offered property (also on Cass Street), as did Samuel Brown. Founding father Perry Hannah had an offer, too. In fact, his offer was a gift. He offered 100 feet on W. Front Street next to Straub Bros. & Amiotte candy factory (near the present-day Record-Eagle offices). Or, if the city preferred, Hannah offered to give $1,000 to improve the grounds of an alternate site between Pine and Union streets. This site was located on the north side of the Boardman River, and was land Hannah had sold to the city earlier for use as a market.

It was hard to say no to a gift of free land, but as the site committee deliberated, they decided that a good location was more important than saving money. After all, the building itself would be constructed for free. Why not choose the best location? Not only did Hannah's Union Street site need fill dirt, it would have too much "noise, confusion, constant passing to and fro of teams and animals [that] would be annoying and strongly objectionable." Hannah's Front Street offer was an odd-shaped, smallish lot on the main business corridor, full of "noise and confusion" and "unpleasant close surroundings." Its near neighbors were the candy factory, the gas works, and the increasingly busy freight and passenger train depot. There would be no room to appreciate the beautiful architecture of the new library. Besides, new factories might easily be built nearby, since the waterfront was industrial. Trains belched coal smoke, as did the nearby water works and Michigan Starch Company factory. Smoke would stain the library building and hurt the books. A library should enjoy a little breathing space, they argued. Somewhere still central, but with a lot large enough to allow green lawns and pleasant shade. The Ashton-Hobbs Cass Street site offered all that.

> *The lot is a most beautiful one, perfectly level, high above the river, overlooking that and up the stream to Boardman Lake and away off to the highlands beyond the Boardman river valley. No possible obstruction can ever shut off this view.*

In fact, the site committee declared, this Cass Street site was as near to ideal as a site could be.

"This work is not for a month or a year but for many years to come," the library committee wrote in its report. "The site that is now selected should be considered in the light of the future as much as the present." A few thousand dollars for the site should not stand in the way. Andrew Carnegie was footing the main bill; their job was to provide the city with the absolute best site.

City Tussles with Library Trustees

Things got tricky when the library committee presented their report. The city council didn't like it. They buried the site committee's report, refused to print it, and instead shared Cunningham's minority report that suggested that the city ought to take Hannah's free gift of land on Front Street.

It was free, and "a kind and generous offer from the founder of our present city." What could be more central than a choice spot on Front Street, the local main street? Besides, the money could be better spent on new bridges or pumps for the water works.

The *Evening Record* took the city council to task. How can you ignore your own committee? the paper demanded. You asked for this report. You appointed this library committee. Let them do their job.

Perhaps they saw reason. Two weeks later the city rejected Hannah's Front Street gift.

With his Front Street property off the table, Hannah moved in quickly with a substitute offer. If Front Street wouldn't do, how about a gift of land along the Boardman River on Sixth Street? He wouldn't just bestow a building site for the library, but also sweeten the pot with a gift of parkland right next door to the library site. How could the city resist?

The *Evening Record* raved over the benefits of the new site. It "will make a magnificent park," they wrote. "On one side one of the city's handsomest residence streets, and on the other the Boardman river." Hannah himself lived on Sixth Street. The new library would be placed a little to the west of the Hannah house "so as not to obstruct the view from his residence." Though it might "seem somewhat out of the way for the east side of the city," they wrote, it wasn't just a library site, the city would gain a park.

It appeared the Carnegie library had a site. On September 16, 1902 the city council voted unanimously to accept Hannah's gift of land on Sixth Street.

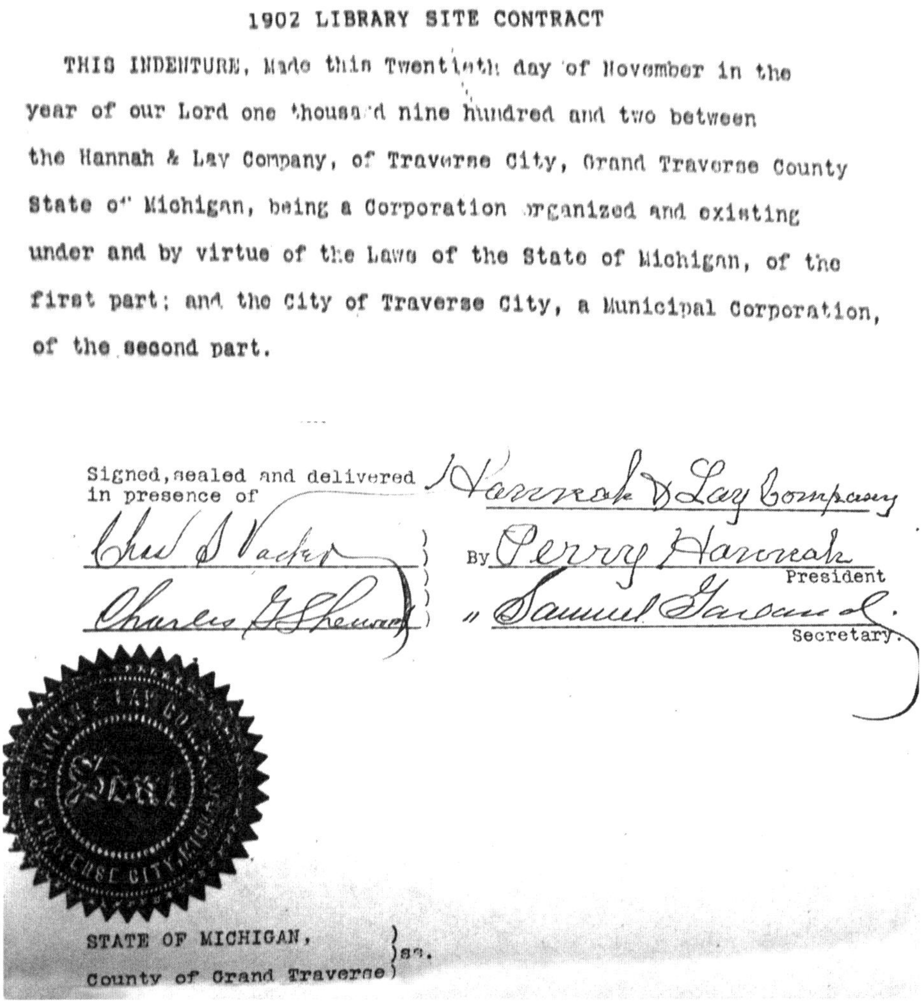

1902 LIBRARY SITE CONTRACT

THIS INDENTURE, Made this Twentieth day of November in the year of our Lord one thousand nine hundred and two between the Hannah & Lay Company, of Traverse City, Grand Traverse County State of Michigan, being a Corporation organized and existing under and by virtue of the Laws of the State of Michigan, of the first part; and the City of Traverse City, a Municipal Corporation, of the second part.

Signed, sealed and delivered in presence of

Hannah & Lay Company

By Perry Hannah
President

" Samuel Garland
Secretary

STATE OF MICHIGAN,) ss.
County of Grand Traverse)

Signed deed from Perry Hannah for proposed library site on Sixth Street, 1902.

EAST VS. WEST: BATTLE OF THE MILLIONAIRES

That might have been the end. As we all know, the Carnegie library was eventually built on Sixth Street, just across from Perry Hannah's house. But that was without reckoning with Henry Hull.

"Some people wanted it on the east side of town or west side of town," said local historian Peg Siciliano. "Perry Hannah was leading the west side. As we know today, he won, because it sits across from his house.

Hull, owner of the prosperous Oval Wood Dish company and president of the First National Bank, was frustrated that the citizens' choice for the library was rejected in favor of Hannah's free gift. He'd do one better. He'd buy the "ideal" Cass Street site and give it to the city.

Hull made his offer public on October 28, 1902. The next day, Perry Hannah delivered the deed to his Sixth Street land to the city.

Now the city was in a quandary. The Cass Street site had seemed pricey at $6,000, but now it was free. Cass Street was a perfect location—central to everyone, level for building, a beautiful view looking over the river—besides, it was the one the library committee recommended. Most of the city's residents favored it, too. But could they go against Hannah? They'd already said yes. The city clerk held the deed, though he'd been instructed not to file it yet.

Traverse City divided in two. One side shouted about moral issues. The city had already accepted Hannah's gift! There was no turning back. A gentleman's word was a gentleman's word, and this was the word of the city.

The other side extolled the benefits of the Cass Street site, particularly its more central location. Hull said the library needed a central spot since it was meant to be a "monument for all time." The library board argued that Cass Street had been their number one choice in the first place. Others said: "young men coming down town evenings will drop in and spend an hour or more, if centrally located." Also, as Hull pointed out, the new federal building for Traverse City's brand-new Post Office had just been chosen to sit on Cass Street. This changed things entirely. Having the post office next door to the library would be perfect. With these new circumstances, the city should reconsider.

Neighbors held huge meetings. On one Saturday evening in November, neighbors crowded into the State Street schoolhouse to protest Hannah's gift and vouch for Cass Street. They thronged to city council meetings, where the reporters described the atmosphere as if there were "a volcano in the room."

"Does this council want to go back in its acceptance of the site offered by Mr. Hannah and insult him?" demanded Alderman Wilhelm, springing to his feet. "Don't let's be cowards."

The fate of the library became a battle of the east side versus the west side of town. Mr. Hull lived on the east side, at 229 Wellington Street. Mr. Hannah lived at 305 Sixth Street on the west side. The river was the divider. The Cass Street site lay east of the Boardman River, the Sixth Street site lay west.

East vs. West. It seems a laughable difference now, when both sites were centrally located by today's standards. However, the sense of a city center was different then. Neighborhoods tended to have distinct divides, often ethnic or occupational. Slabtown was home to lumber families. Catholic parishes drew in different nationalities. Immaculate Conception Church, west of Union Street, mostly served Czech and Polish families. St. Francis, just a mile to the east, had more French, English, and Italian families living around it. So a mile, or even half a mile, could make a difference.

Since people got around mostly by foot, distance also mattered more. The Sixth Street site was "quite distant from the center of the city," complained Leon Titus, an east-sider. Even so, the two sites were less than half a mile apart, an easy ten-minute walk. The controversy seemed much more personal: who was going to boss around Traverse City? Should we be beholden to Perry Hannah forever? What about other people's opinions, or space for newcomers to make their mark? Was there room for everybody? What about what the citizens want? Should we honor our promises?

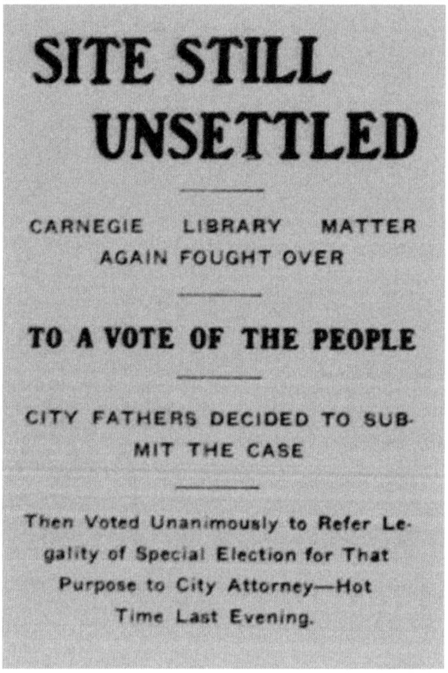
SITE STILL UNSETTLED

CARNEGIE LIBRARY MATTER AGAIN FOUGHT OVER

TO A VOTE OF THE PEOPLE

CITY FATHERS DECIDED TO SUBMIT THE CASE

Then Voted Unanimously to Refer Legality of Special Election for That Purpose to City Attorney—Hot Time Last Evening.

Heated arguments over the location of the new library dragged on from August 1902 to March 1904. This headline is from the *Evening Record,* January 6, 1903.

The majority of the library trustees sided with Hull. They voted to accept Hull's Cass Street site in November 1902. "SETTLED," blared the *Evening Record* headline. "Carnegie Library will go on Cass Street...Offer of Oval Wood Dish Co. Accepted and Deed of Sixth Street Site Will Be Returned to Mr. Hannah."

There were only three library trustees, however, and one of them was a woman. What right did they have to decide such things of importance to the whole community? Women didn't even have the right to vote yet in the U.S. The vote was 2 to 1. Thomas Bates voted for Sixth Street and Elvin Sprague was a staunch advocate for Cass Street. That effectively gave Ella Perry the deciding vote.

Some people called for a city-wide vote, which would allow the matter to be settled by male citizens. Lawyers were called in. Tempers rose. Prominent citizens on both sides feuded with each other. People complained of all the "wranglings, feuds and dissentions." The battle between Hull and Hannah dragged on for a year and a half, leading to fights, possibly fist fights, and lawsuits. "Hot Time Last Evening," announced the *Traverse City Evening Record* in spring 1903, reporting on a city council meeting. After the meeting, two aldermen had "a little tilt."

Richard Rastall, an optician and jewelry store owner in Traverse City, poked fun of the rift with editorial cartoons posted in his shop windows on Front Street. The first one appeared in late October 1902. The *Evening Record* described his cartoons in detail for those who could not get into town to see them:

> *The drawing shows a caricature of Hon. Perry Hannah and H.S. Hull, each grasping an end of a library building and each trying to pull it from the other. Mr. Hannah is made to say: "Hands off. you needn't think you're the 'Hull' thing. I had it first."*
>
> *Mr. Hull says: "Not muchy; this ain't going to be another Perry's victory."*
>
> *Mayor Carver is shown at one side and is represented as saying: "Quit your monkeying, boys. I guess the people will settle this."*

Rastall, seemingly a bit of a rascal, delighted in lampooning both sides. He posted a new cartoon about once a week in November 1902. The next one, entitled "Latest Move," showed the city councilmen creeping out at night to leave a foundling infant in a basket on the doorstep of a library trustee's house. The infant is labeled "Library Site." Perry Hannah is lurking around the corner, while the moon looks down in disgust and says "I have nothing to say." This is just after the city council punted the controversy back to the library trustees.

His last cartoon was sure to get a chuckle: "It's Broke Out Again:"

> *The cartoon shows a nest marked "Library Site," upon which is sitting a hen, whose features show an unmistakable resemblance to Hon. W. H. Foster.* The hen is marked "The Law," and is represented as saying, "If I can only scratch out these 'Oval Dish' eggs, everything will be hunky-dory."*

> *Near at hand is a man with long whiskers who, as Alderman C___, [Cunningham] is saying to a spectacled companion, "By George, Will, there's a hen on!" The companion, who is labeled "Un-d-rt-k-r,. says, "Yes, sir. A Foster mother, though. Hope she'll hatch soon."*
>
> **William H. Foster was the attorney for the Sixth Street side.*

The winter and spring of 1903 were spent in court battles. The library site fight went first to the circuit court and then on to the Michigan Supreme Court in April. At issue was who had decision-making control: the city council? Or the library trustees? The courts sided with the city council.

The Ladies' Library Association entered the fray with an offer of their own. Would the city accept a donation of land from the ladies, if the Ladies' Library was allowed to meet in one of the library rooms? Carnegie said no. It wasn't anything against the Ladies' Library group, but all Carnegie libraries had to be strictly public buildings with no special concession to private groups.

Disgruntled citizens decided to appeal even more directly to Carnegie. It was reported in The Observer and elsewhere that several Traverse City men even traveled to Pittsburgh, home of Carnegie's steel empire to make their case. Was Carnegie there to receive them? After all, by 1902, Carnegie mostly split his time between his New York mansion and a castle in Scotland. Whether Traverse City delegations actually traveled to Pittsburgh is unclear. Carnegie himself preferred the Cass Street site but, as was his way, left the decision to locals.

Grand Rapids Weighs In

Fresh off their own library benefactor battle, Grand Rapids poked fun at Traverse City's dispute. Martin Ryerson and Andrew Carnegie had both offered funds to build a Grand Rapids library. Ryerson won. The *Grand Rapids Herald* ran a tongue-in-cheek story called "Traverse City's Luck" on February 12, 1903.

> *Traverse City is one town in Michigan that is in luck. It has two citizens so public spirited that a law suit is necessary to determine which shall have the privilege of donating a site for the public library which Andrew Carnegie will build... Traverse City is to be congratulated not only upon having two public spirited citizens, but also upon being able to furnish so unique a spectacle.*

The wranglings went on. Strategies ranged from the legal to the definitely illegal. At one point, several city councilors tried to buy Councilman Lardie's vote. George Lardie was the owner of nearby property at the corner of Eighth Street and Lake Avenue (this triangular lot is now Thirlby Automotive). He had plans to build a potato warehouse there, and had been pushing to get a railroad side track to go right up to his business. The city council repeatedly turned him down, William Loudon stating at one point: "If the potato warehouse is located as proposed, property in that section will not be worth 50 cents on the dollar...The smell from the warehouse is enough to knock a man down." Then in April 1903, at the height of the library lawsuits, four fellow city councilmen promised to vote for his side track if Lardie would change sides and vote for the Sixth Street location. He refused indignantly.

OTHER CARNEGIE LIBRARY SITE FIGHTS

To be fair, Traverse City wasn't the only town to have trouble locating its library.

Site fights broke out around Michigan and across the U.S. The honor of placing the public library was often hotly contested. Citizens in Waterloo, Iowa fought over which side of the river to place their public library. When they finally decided to locate the library *in the middle of the river,* Carnegie benevolently stepped in, and gave the warring town money enough for two libraries, one on each side of the river.

Lansing was not so lucky. Carnegie awarded them $32,000, but they couldn't agree on a site. Lansing turned down the money in 1902, making do with keeping their books in city hall.

It looked like Traverse City was headed that way, too. Make up your mind, the Carnegie Foundation said. But Traverse City was still roiled in controversy and couldn't decide. Would they have to give up the promised Carnegie grant and their dream of a new public library?

1903: A NEW MAYOR

A full year had passed since Carnegie's offer of $20,000 for a library, and Traverse City was no closer to resolution. Thomas Bates resigned from the library board. Henry Hull demanded a vote of the people. Perry Hannah waited.

In April 1903, the city voted in a new mayor, John Santo, who brought matters to a head. In his inaugural address on May 4, 1903, Mayor Santo suggested rejecting Carnegie's offer. "We are a city of promise," he declared. It would be better "a thousand times" to return the gift of $20,000 than to continue all the bitterness and indulging in a "spiteful controversy." He deplored all the fighting and questioned why people should fight over "a building we could well dispense with. Why should we presume to ask Mr. Carnegie or anyone else for a gift?" he asked the city council. "Where is the parent who would not speedily reprimand his child for asking a neighbor, let alone a stranger, for a present?"

Either give back the money, or just settle on Sixth Street, he said. We are getting nothing done with all this squabbling. We can't pass the water works bond. We can't pass the bridge bond. Everything is at a standstill because of the library site.

"Never was there a time in the history of our city when it was so important that we should be governed by a unity of purpose," Mayor Santo declared, "and walk shoulder to shoulder as at the present time."

Not only was there a new mayor, but also a new face on the library board. Dr. Albert Holliday had replaced Thomas Bates. By this point it was clear to many that some people were more worried about offending Perry Hannah than coming up with a good library site.

Never was there a time in the history of our city when it was so important that we should be governed by a unity of purpose and walk shoulder to shoulder as at the present time.

By mid-May 1903, there was a breakthrough. The courts decided that the true authority lay with the board of public works. This meant, in effect, that the city council won since the board of public works served under the city. Now, which site would it be? Cass or Sixth Street? Again, the city council split down the middle. They voted 5 to 5. Mayor Santo, who lived equidistant from the two sites on Eighth Street, cast the tie-breaking vote for Sixth Street.

The city authorized the public works department to use $250 to begin planning the building design. In the same city meeting, Lardie got approval for his potato warehouse side track.

Perry Hannah and the Sixth Street site had won.

Still, Leon Titus was not done. He'd been the one to first contact Carnegie, and he fervently believed the Cass Street site was superior.

Kendallville (Indiana) *Daily*, March 23, 1908

Carnegie stands ready with library offers

Perhaps he was prodded to take action by his boss. After all, Henry Hull was president of First National Bank, where young Titus worked (now promoted from assistant cashier to cashier). A month after the mayor's tie-breaking vote, Titus wrote a lengthy letter to Carnegie's office detailing a litany of "illegal and inequitable acts" made by the city council and begging Andrew Carnegie to intervene. Couldn't Carnegie himself decide? Or force a vote in Traverse City, by making a special election a condition of his gift?

Titus's last ditch "Hail Mary" did not work. It's believed he did not even receive a response. When it came to siting the library buildings, Carnegie firmly believed in local home rule.

However, locals were *still* divided. Even after the legal ruling and decisive vote, Cass Street proponents weren't ready to give up. When the board of public works tried to move forward by presenting a contractor, the city council dragged their feet and tabled the library construction vote indefinitely. "Library Blocked," reported the *Evening Record* as late as March 8, 1904. "Councilmen Opposed to Sixth Street Site Cause Delay." The excuse was that one city council member was absent. Given that he was ill, out-of-state in Kentucky, it could be a long time before he returned. Why all the needless delay?

"It is Wrong," screamed an editorial headline from the *Evening Record*. The article urged a stop to all opposition and delays, calling the decision to table things an "unjust slap at the board of public works and contrary to the best interests of the city." A citizen's letter to the editor agreed, saying: "Let us have no more sulking in the harness."

Finally, the warring city council members agreed. At a special meeting on March 17, 1904, Lardie and Hamilton yielded. "I do not want this fight to keep up," said Lardie. He made the case one last time that the Cass Street site was better, then conceded for the sake of peace. After that, the city voted unanimously on plans for the Carnegie library building.

Still, in a plot twist, it could be said that Hull emerged the final victor. A library was never built on the Cass Street spot—that location became home to Central United Methodist Church in 1913—but today a new modern library sits next to Hull Park at the north end of Boardman Lake. Who could have known that nearly a hundred years later, Hannah's Sixth Street Carnegie library site would be abandoned, and the new district library would be associated with Hull Park instead?

A Branch for East Traverse City

Even after the Carnegie library was built on Sixth Street, concerns lingered about improving library access for eastside neighbors. In October 1906, library trustees opened a branch library on the east side, close to Hull's neighborhood. The branch was set up in Oak Park School's basement and filled with duplicate books from the Sixth Street stacks.

"Appreciating the great inconvenience to which the residents of the eastern part of the city were put in order to receive any benefit of the Public Library, the Board of Trustees thought best to establish a branch in that part of the city," states the 1907 annual library report. By then Leon Titus had become one of the three library board trustees, along with Elvin Sprague and Minnie Minor. At that time, Oak Park School was located at the southwest corner of Rose and Webster streets.

The Oak Park branch was open for 54 years, and as long as he lived, this is the library Henry Hull reportedly used. He walked to the Oak Park branch from his house on Wellington Street. Although the Oval Wood Dish Company relocated to Tupper Lake, New York in the Adirondacks in 1917, Henry Hull and his wife remained in Traverse City.

The original eastside branch of the Traverse City Public Library was in the basement of the Oak Park School at the corner of Rose and Webster streets from 1906–1917. From 1900 Traverse City High School yearbook *The Traversensian*.

There were drawbacks. The school basement was not heated after school hours. Did the city want to pay to heat the building so patrons could be comfortable in the reading room, or just let them quickly check out books in the cold? Also, wiring needed to be done, so there were no lights at first. The library was supposed to be open from noon until 8 pm, but was limited to daylight hours for a while. Ten years later, the east branch had definitely outgrown its humble school housing. Conditions were deteriorating. Ventilation was poor, lighting was still bad, and, according to Dr. G. Arthur Holliday (brother of Dr. Albert Holliday), the worst part was that the "stone walls sweat continually." The library space was condemned.

In January 1917, library trustees wrote a letter to the city: "Gentlemen: The room used by the Oak Park library has been condemned by the City Health Officer on account of its unsanitary condition. Therefore, we respectfully petition your honorable body to grant the use of the Fifth Ward hall for library purposes until other arrangements can be made." The nearby Fifth Ward Hall was not used much, except for voting. It functioned as a temporary solution, but the Fifth Ward Hall was still an "old frame building which...[became] a detriment rather than a credit to the library institution."

Still, there was strong city support for an eastside branch library. Partly this was a question of morality. "Every child that the Oak Park library or the main library keeps off the street is worth more than the annual amount expended," opined editors at the *Evening Record.* The editors worried about girls of 14 or 15 walking at night with older men. Keeping the library open at night would help keep the children off the streets and give them a place full of morality. The Oak Park branch was good at drawing in neighborhood children, at least the younger ones, and school children at Oak Park School used the library. Story hours at the main library attracted 2,590 children in six months, according to the library board report of 1907, but the branch drew even more at 3,682. In terms of circulation, however, the main library had a far more robust collection. Patrons checked out more than 15,000 novels from the main library compared to only 1,000 at the branch.

In 1926, twenty-five years after his initial request, Leon Titus boldly wrote to the Carnegie Foundation once more, this time asking

After the health officer condemned the space in the old Oak Park School in 1917, the eastside branch moved into the little-used Fifth Ward Hall at the northwest corner of Washington and Rose streets.

The city tore down Fifth Ward Hall in 1928 and built the Oak Park branch at Washington and Rose streets with the proviso that the lower level would still serve as a voting precinct for the city. It is now a private residence.

for construction funds for a branch. Carnegie had funded branch libraries for larger cities, like Detroit, in the past.

Unfortunately, his was one of hundreds of letters that arrived too late. The Carnegie Corporation had formally ended the program and given out its last library grants in 1919. That was also the year Andrew Carnegie died. The era of building Carnegie libraries was over.

The city forged ahead independently, however, and built a permanent home for their branch library. It replaced the deteriorating Fifth Ward Hall on the corner of Rose and Washington streets. The sturdy, brick building blended beautifully with the surrounding residential neighborhood, and was a favorite for many people. It opened its doors in 1928.

The branch stayed open through the 1950s. In 1961 the Oak Park branch building was sold to the Traverse City Woman's Club, and today is a private home. When the eastside Oak Park branch closed, a new library was opening on the east side: the Mark Osterlin Library, part of the brand-new Northwestern Michigan College.

Carnegie Library as it looked in 1908. Note the fences along the walk and the decorative urns at the entrance.

From this time on, we hope and expect that every man, woman, and child will have at his tongue's end the history of the Traverse City public library at any moment and for all time to come.

Albert. H. Holliday

Chapter 4

Carnegie Library on Sixth Street

Building the Carnegie Library

With the controversy finally settled, the actual building of the Carnegie library moved quickly. Carnegie's first installment of $5,000 arrived in January 1904. Fred Moore was approved as the architect, and George Lather as the construction contractor.

The city was agog with excitement over their new landmark building. "Plans call for a classic Greek structure, repressed brick, Berea sandstone facings," reported the *Evening Record* in July 1903. "The building is to be exceptionally well lighted."

The donated money covered not only the library's construction, but also "complete furnishings." This included seventy two oak chairs for the reading rooms, a swivel chair and a rocking chair for the librarians, and six heavy oak armchairs for library trustee meetings. The furnishings cost $2,500, and also included tables, a marble reception desk, dictionary stands, magazine racks and bulletin boards.

Some people hoped there'd be a gymnasium in the new Carnegie building. This was not uncommon. Communities around the country begged for swimming pools and gyms as part of their Carnegie library design. In December 1904, the *Evening Record* reported that the

Despite delays caused by materials shortages, the Sixth Street Library was built in 10 months.

basement was high and well ventilated and "contains a perfect room for gymnasium purposes."

The chosen library site on Sixth Street had once been the location of Traverse City's first cemetery. Construction did not disturb the resting place, however. All the bodies (about twenty) had been moved to Oakwood Cemetery back in 1861 when the new cemetery opened.

Perry Hannah would have seen the construction going on across the street from his house, but he never lived to see it finished. Hannah died on August 14, 1904 at the age of 79 and was buried in Oakwood Cemetery, property his company had donated to the city.

HORSES, LAMP SHADES, AND *THE SATURDAY EVENING POST*

The city library now had 7,000 volumes. They enlisted a one-horse dray to shift their books from the Ladies' Library building to the brand-new Carnegie building. A dray is a strong cart without sides used to haul heavy loads. The dray must have made several trips, and the library was closed for about a week during the move.

Then on February 28, 1905, the public library opened for business at 9 am. "Everything very conveniently arranged" the *Evening Record's* headline read. "It is roomy, light and airy...The reading rooms are light by day and the system of shaded electrics makes them very comfortable in the evening." That first day, 390 books were checked out, mostly fiction and children's books.

Much was made of the library's design, from its imposing classical design to its cork carpeting, Italian and Grecian marble reception desk and its green-shaded electric lights. The circulation area was tiled with terrazzo tiles, and the *Daily Eagle* positively gushed when describing the reading rooms. "The building is lighted by handsome electroliers," it reported. Reading tables were "all supplied with electric lights shaded with green shades. The lights are operated singly by switches placed

Just before opening of the Sixth Street library. The big marble desk is in front of empty shelving in the half-rotunda. Shelves behind the desk will be filled with fiction books, which librarians will retrieve for patrons.

under the librarian's delivery desk so that any of the lamps when not in use may be turned off by her." Electric lighting was still new in 1905 and many people still lit their homes with gas lights.

After nearly 50 years, the city library finally had a home for its collection. Gone were the days of moving the library from drug store

One of the two reading rooms, looking toward the delivery desk and half-rotunda; nonfiction books will be on the shelves lining the reading room walls. Note the latest in electroliers (reading lamps) on tables.

to drug store. Not only did the new library building have room for books, but also separate children's and adult reading rooms, designated space for book repairs, a librarians' room, library trustees' room, plus extra space in the basement.

Many public libraries across the country were beginning to allow patrons to browse the shelves themselves, no longer requiring them to submit book requests to librarians. In Traverse City however, the fiction collection was "placed in the shelves back of the librarian's desk" and had "to be called for to be obtained," explained the *Evening Record.*

The library also carried "all of the leading periodicals of the day," which meant the magazine racks in the adult reading room were undoubtedly stacked with *Saturday Evening Post, Harper's, McCall's, Ladies' Home Journal, Collier's, the Atlantic Monthly, American Magazine,* and others. Readers were increasingly gobbling up magazines, and there were at least 50 national magazines being published by 1900. The children's room also had popular magazines such as: *Youth's Companion, Jack and Jill, American Boy, Harper's Young People, St. Nicholas (Scribner's Illustrated Magazine for Girls and Boys),* and *McClure's Children's Annual* for 1905.

The new Carnegie library building said in block capitals: "CITY LIBRARY" in stone above the front door.

Sixth Street Library as seen from Wadsworth Street. Perry Hannah house is to the left of the library.

Grand Opening on Sixth Street

On Friday night, March 10, 1905, library lovers in Traverse City flocked to Sixth Street for a gala affair to formally dedicate their "magnificent new Carnegie library." The Steward & Steffens orchestra sat in the balcony and played from 8 to 10 pm. Another new mayor, Mayor Elisha Fulghum, spoke. So did the two male library trustees, Elvin Sprague and Dr. Albert Holliday. Also Cassius Prall, head of the public works board, who said he was not a speech maker, but would do his best.

"The Traverse City public library now has a home equal to that of any city of its size in the state and far superior to many," boasted the *Daily Eagle* the next day.

Helen Stout served as Traverse City's head librarian from 1903–1911.

Alice Wait started working at the Traverse City library in 1903. She continued as a library volunteer after her retirement in 1949.

Helen Stout, the librarian, and her assistant, Alice Wait, gave tours. "Miss Helen Stout, the efficient librarian, is a graduate of the Traverse City High School...Miss Stout is a very popular member of society and has a wide circle of friends which is of great benefit to her in her official capacity." Stout was 18 when she began her library job in July 1903. For a few weeks she worked as assistant librarian to the main librarian, Lucille Dusenbery (now married and named Lucille Keith). When Keith resigned, Stout took her place as head librarian. The library at that time was still housed in the Ladies' Library. Alice Wait, apparently, did not enjoy such an elevated social circle as her counterpart. As assistant librarian, she "fills her place with a dignity and promptness which assures her success in her chosen work," wrote the *Daily Eagle*. The third employee was Freeborn Gardner, who worked as library janitor. The library would soon be open every day from 9 am to 9 pm, and 2 to 5 pm on Sundays.

Trustee Sprague acknowledged the foundational work of the Ladies' Library at the dedication. He thanked them for "the good seed sown in the early days by that most prosperous and character-building organization, the Ladies' Library Association. May it long continue to prosper and work hand in hand with the city public library for the moral upbuilding and intellectual growth of our people."

Everyone knew Miss Wait, who was active in civic affairs and an avid traveler throughout the 46 years she worked at the Traverse City Public Library.

When I got [my] library card, that was when my life began.

Rita Mae Brown

CHAPTER 5

Library Days 1905–1940s

CARNEGIE LIBRARY EARLY DAYS

After the festivities were over, it was time to get down to work. The library bought more books, including many encyclopedias and dictionaries, and greatly augmented their reference section. They made sure to stock the shelves with the latest *Century Atlas* and *Century Biography* as well the *Encyclopedia Americana*. This was partly financed by a gift of $875 from the West Side Chapel Society. The interdenominational group agreed to sell their chapel and give the proceeds to the library.

It was also time to professionalize. The librarians bought a typewriter for $30 and started the grand task of cataloging the books.

"Now we had our new library the Board were most anxious the books be cataloged and a card catalog started," recalled Alice Wait in written memoirs. "So they wrote to the University of Illinois Library School to send some[one]." They brought in a Miss Pugsley to start the process. She likely arrived by train from Chicago, and was soon giving Helen Stout and Alice Wait lessons on cataloging for an hour a day in addition to their other library duties. Miss Pugsley departed suddenly when her mother became ill. "From then on the cataloging was up to Helen and myself, but she left us in good shape, all the books were cataloged except for a few gov't Documents."

Meanwhile, down in the basement, the trustees found themselves with extra rooms that they didn't need for library use. The idea of a gymnasium had floundered. Instead, they reached out to the Traverse City Woman's Club, and offered to let them use the rooms rent-free if they would clean and lay the old library's carpet and furnish the rooms with chairs and a piano. So for $17.50, the Woman's Club arranged to clean and install the carpet, bought chairs, and rented a piano. The new setup gave the library room to seat 150 to 175 people for gatherings of "educational character only."

Owing to a lack of funds we have been unable to add nearly as many books to the library as we should have liked to, or as was actually needed.

Budget woes seemed to plague the early library. Despite Andrew Carnegie's stipulation that the city pay $2,000 a year for operating costs, the library trustees continually asked for even more money. They went back to the city council again and again requesting a larger budget to work with.

"Owing to a lack of funds we have been unable to add nearly as many books to the library as we should have liked to, or as was actually needed," wrote the trustees in a representational sample from their 1907 board report. "We have added only 276 volumes...Very few books of fiction have been bought during the year, although the demand for them has been great."

The Quiet Library and Shh! Librarians

Alice Wait was still at the library, retired but volunteering, when young Fred Nelson (later Traverse City mayor in 1984) got his first library card at the Sixth Street library. "Miss Wait had glasses perched on her nose," he said. "Mrs. Brown—she was a little, tiny, woman who was just a dear. She worked there probably for half a century."

For years, the library staff was the domain of women.

"All librarians were women, like all teachers were women," Nelson recalled. Although both men and women sat on the library board, the job of being a librarian was considered to be women's work.

Traverse City's first librarians were "Miss Ruth" and "Miss Tina," Ruth Barlow and Tina Holdsworth, unmarried women who served the library when it was located up a steep stairway above Milliken's store downtown. Next was Lucille Dusenbery Keith, who managed to keep her paid job after she married, but had to resign when she had a baby two years later.

"When Aunt Tina recommended a book, you could gamble that it was worth reading," remarked Jay Smith in The Observer. "Favorites for the boys, of course, were the Horatio Alger books…The girls had the Elsie books…Bertha M. Clay and Mary Jane Holmes were top authors for the women and the men didn't read much."

The library was certainly popular with children, but perhaps the men read at different hours. Men used the reading room 2,907 times in 1907.

By the time the Carnegie library was built, Helen Stout and Alice Wait were in charge. They worked for a year when the city library was still housed in the Ladies' Library building. Stout's librarian salary was $30 per month, while Wait made $20 a month as assistant librarian. Wait's position was added to help expand hours and services.

As described by the local papers, Stout was a socialite. Her every move was written up in the *Evening Record* and *Daily Eagle,* including which trips she took, which train she rode, and who she visited. She was the daughter of the Reverend Charles Stout, who was the minister at Grace church (Grace Episcopal Church) from 1897 to 1906. Helen Stout was born in 1884 in Kansas, graduated from Traverse City High School, and began working as the city's head librarian while still a teenager. She worked as librarian for eight years, though likely viewed her library job as a temporary position until she got married.

Neither librarian had much training at first. Miss Pugsley's visit from Chicago to show the local librarians how to set up a card catalog was their first serious library training. Later, Stout was sent to Cleveland for four months to study "advanced library methods." There she took courses "under the best instruction" on how to lead children's story times, and began "Story Hour" in Traverse City in 1906. She read four stories a week to local children, two programs at Sixth Street and two at the Oak Park branch.

This trip to Cleveland came about after the State Library Institute held one of its statewide meetings in Traverse City in January 1906. Caroline Burnite, head of the children's department at the Cleveland public library, spoke at the conference. She had many ideas about how to welcome children into libraries. "Miss Burnite stated that the problem of fines was a delicate one, and that it was not advisable to force a boy to pay money for damage to a book if his spending money was limited," reported the *Evening Record.* Burnite advised giving the boy a dust rag and letting him work off his fine by dusting books.

Helen Stout traveled extensively while she was head librarian, often taking a few months off. She visited her parents in Florida by train to enjoy the "flowers and ocean bathing," planned trips to Europe, and toured "the orient." In 1909, Stout's parents asked her to take a leave of absence from her job so she could join her aunt and uncle in the Philippines, where her uncle had a new military assignment. The library board readily granted her a one-year leave, and the *Evening Record* reported: "As her uncle is one of the higher officers, her opportunity for meeting the best of people in Manila is good."

Indeed, Stout soon married Lieutenant James Rivet, a military man she'd met on her travels. The 1911 wedding was considered to be one of the most lavish and notable weddings Traverse City had seen. White cosmos, marigolds, and woodland ferns decorated Grace church, the chandeliers were draped with clematis, and the bride's veil festooned with orange blossoms. The marriage abruptly ended her librarian career. Stout resigned, and the new couple moved to California.

This made room for assistant librarian Alice Wait to step up as head librarian. Unlike Stout, Wait made a long career of 46 years at the Traverse City public library. The daughter of pioneers, she graduated from Traverse City High School at age 20, and was hired by the library two years later in 1903.

Alice Wait, always known as "Miss Wait," at her retirement in 1949

Wait was soon in charge of both the main Sixth Street library and the branch library, making a salary of $480 a year. At $40 per month, this pay was double her starting salary, though the library janitor made considerably more ($564 per year).

The library board also supported Wait's training. She was sent to study in Lansing at a summer library school, and also to Columbia University in New York for a six-week course in library economy. This was an unusual opportunity for women at the time, and although she did not receive a formal degree, Columbia University was proudly mentioned in her obituary. Alice Wait did not marry. Her brother Roy Wait was her main companion. She traveled with him and lived with him in Traverse City during her last years.

This was the era of the Quiet Library. Children and adults were expected to be silent in the reading rooms, and even the Carnegie library's cork carpet was installed specially to make footfalls noiseless.

When Wait started as librarian, the most popular children's books were the rags-to-riches stories about saintly young orphan boys by novelist Horatio Alger. He painted a picture of the American Dream with titles like *Mark the Match Boy*, *Luck and Pluck*, and *Ragged Dick*. The main characters were usually bootblacks, newsboys, street musicians, and peddlers, who all gained great fortunes and rose up the ranks of society (often impressing kindly rich gentlemen with their impeccable character and marrying the boss's daughter). Young readers at that time also read Oliver Optic battle stories or historical adventure stories by G.A. Henty. Optic was the pen name of William Adams, an American who loved boats and wrote about sailor boys, as well as tales of the Civil War with titles like *Cringle and Cross-tree or, The Sea Swashes of a Sailor* and *Now or Never, the Adventures of Bobby Bright*. Henty, a Victorian British author, touted the glory and power of the British empire in glorified tales taking Britain's side in colonial fights against Africa, America, and India.

While Optic favored the North in his Civil War stories, children's book author Martha Finley set her Elsie series in the American South. The character Elsie Dinsmore was an exceptionally devout Christian girl who defied her father's authority, preferring to follow God instead. The series continued into the aftermath of the Civil War when Elsie, then grown, tried to restore the family plantations.

Meanwhile, the adults were reading Richard Harding David romances, like *Vera the Medium* and *The Princess Aline,* or other best sellers from Anthony Hope and George Bair MacCutcheon. Mary Jane Holmes was popular among women for her novels set in the South dealing with gender, race, class, and slavery.

Not all adults were fluent readers, however. As Wait remembered:

> *In the long ago an old gentleman said to me when he returned his book he [had] trouble with this book. "It has so many big words, I cannot pronounce them but I call them 'horse blanket' and go on."*

Another long-serving librarian was Evelyn Hammond, who was known to Traverse City library patrons for many decades as Mrs. Brown. Right after graduating from Traverse City High School in 1906, she began working at the city library as a substitute. In 1920, she accompanied Alice Wait to Columbia for library training. Hammond was well established in her library career when she eventually married Claude Brown. He died of tuberculosis just twelve years later. Evelyn Brown continued at the library, raising their son on her own. Brown worked a total of fifty years at the city library, and then volunteered for another fifteen years part-time.

More Wars and Pandemics

Fifteen years after he first wrote to Andrew Carnegie, Leon Titus was still involved with the library. By 1916 he served as library board chair. Little did he know that the next few years would prove extremely challenging for the library.

War was already besieging Europe. In 1917, the U.S. joined the fray. Titus and the other library trustees had been continually asking the city to properly fund the library. Now budgets were extremely tight. The cost of coal shot up to exorbitant prices. The library was forced to cut back its hours to save the cost of heating the building, reducing its hours to 2 pm to 8 pm.

Librarian Alice Wait organized book drives to send to soldiers. She asked for historical fiction and modern scientific books (published no earlier than 1916), as well as biography, history, and current fiction. Two titles that were particularly popular among the soldiers were *Over the Top* and *Private Peat*, books set in the current war. "Books on electricity, aviation and such things are 'eaten up' as the boys put it," reported the *Record-Eagle,* and "A special 'S.O.S.' call has gone out for German dictionaries." The German dictionaries were particularly needed for officers' training.

In a letter to Alice Wait, Glenn Griffin urged even more book donations. Griffin was a Traverse City local serving as camp librarian at Camp Shelby, Mississippi. "The soldiers are eager readers," he wrote. "The Camp Library is the most popular institution in the camp. We are counting on the home folks to send the books."

Traverse City wasn't the only town donating books. Altogether, Americans donated 10 million volumes during World War I to camp libraries. The American Library Association set up nearly fifty camp libraries between 1917 and 1920 as part of its Library War Service, which included major support from Carnegie.

On top of the war, the 1918 influenza pandemic hit northern Michigan and affected library service. The 1918 flu pandemic killed a tremendous number of people worldwide. It's estimated that between 25 million and 100 million people died in total, (between 2.5 and 5 percent of the global population). The first person to die in the Traverse City area was a 14-year-old boy named Smith Bright. The state health director put Traverse City under strict quarantine orders and closed theaters, churches, and other non-essential public gatherings.

Still, deaths kept coming. By the end of December 1918, flu had killed 34 locals, and the virus was spreading to Cedar, Fife Lake, Maple City, and other outlying communities. The library board shuttered the library for three weeks in January 1919 to help contain the virus. However, many Traverse area residents resented shut-down restrictions and continued to go to dance halls and billiard parlors, and visit quarantined households. The U.S. suffered 675,000 flu deaths from 1918 to 1920, and worldwide it infected one billion people.

The Library in the 1940s

The City Library organized more book drives for soldiers during World War II. These were called "Victory Book Drives," and were part of the nation's larger Victory Book Campaign, which eventually secured 17 million donated books. People were asked to donate books on "mechanics, aviation, and all branches of engineering" as well as fiction, biography, and history.

During the 1940s, the new best sellers were *Forever Amber* and the Jalna books. *Forever Amber* followed the fortunes of the orphan Amber as she married increasingly rich men, all set against the backdrop of 1600s

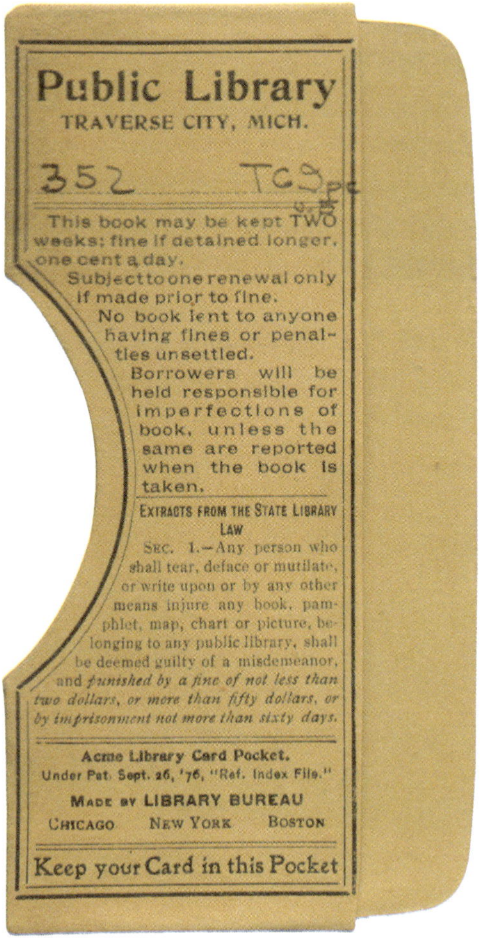

Book cardholder from 1917. Each book held a book card until a patron checked out the book, when it would be clipped with the patron's library card until the book was returned.

A WWII veteran, Karl Burg attended college after the war. He was Traverse City's librarian 1949–1951.

England, complete with the Great Fire of London and the plague. It was so popular locally that the Traverse City library had to buy an extra copy since thirty-eight people were on the waiting list to read it. The Jalna series, written by Canadian author Mazo de la Roche, followed adventures of the Whiteoak family at their manor house called Jalna.

Early library cards were small cardboard ones with metal tabs. To check out a book, the librarian took out the card inserted into the book and put it together with the patron's library card. Then they were stamped together in a machine that stamped the date. Children's cards had a "Y" marked on them for Youth. "I remember wearing them out," said Fred Nelson. Nelson checked out so many books as a child that he wore out several library cards.

Alice Wait and Evelyn Brown presided over the Carnegie library in its early era. Wait retired in 1949, and died in 1965. Evelyn Brown died in 1982 at age 97. A male librarian, Karl Burg, followed Miss Wait, but did not stay long. Burg directed the city library from 1949 to 1951.

The Ladies' Library Once Again

Despite having a fine new public Carnegie library, plus an active east side branch, the Ladies' Library remained strong. As the Carnegie library settled into its new home on Sixth Street, the Ladies' Library continued to buy books. In 1905 the women bought additional property on Cass Street and constructed a grand new Ladies' Library building there in 1909.

This new Ladies' Library also marked a new era for the group of dedicated women who had served the city for four decades as unpaid library volunteers. They were done with rentals. Finished with managing Library Hall and larger public responsibilities. It was time to focus on their own needs. As the *Evening Record* wrote in early 1909:

> *This structure will be a very handsome ornament. It is not designed by the ladies to devote it to rental purposes but to use it exclusively for the association and have it provided with every appointment for convenience and comfort. The idea of renting a home is not at all attractive to the members of the association. They have worked many years for the home they now have and now desire to take a rest.*

It may seem odd that a city the size of Traverse City felt the need to maintain three robust libraries, but the need for a separate Ladies' Library may never have felt more vital. It was the lead up to the 19th Amendment, which passed in 1920 and legally acknowledged women's right to vote. Focusing on their own needs may have meant education and social advancement.

Women's suffrage battles were ongoing. Despite progress over the past sixty years, no one knew how many more generations it would take before women everywhere could legally vote. The second decade of the 1900s was near the height of the women's suffrage battles. During this period, Ida B. Wells was organizing the Alpha Suffrage Club in Chicago, and Alice Paul was locked in solitary confinement in a prison's mental ward. Women with banners were picketing the White House, and thousands of pro-suffrage women were wearing white dresses and marching down city streets.

Although Traverse City was remote from that big city energy, members of the Ladies' Library were well-read and sure to be up to date on the latest developments. It could be a long haul, and the women

The stately Ladies' Library on State Street has more recently served as police headquarters, law office, and bank.

of the city were determined to have more than a room of one's own. They determined to have an entire building of their own. A new one. A grand one. Located in the absolute best position in town: a library on Cass Street.

It is unclear how many Ladies' Library members were active in the pro-suffrage movement, but on the whole, they were more involved than their sister organization, the more conservative-leaning Traverse City Woman's Club. Two of the Ladies' Library founders, Clymene Bates and Martha Bates, were married to men who held strong progressive views. Morgan Bates, early publisher of the *Grand Traverse Herald*, wrote in the 1850s: "We hate slavery in all its forms and conditions, and can have no fellowship or compromise with it." His nephew Thomas T. Bates continued that tradition as editor of the *Herald*. He was openly pro-suffrage and applauded Susan B. Anthony's arrival in Traverse City. The Ladies' Library was founded on ideas. And the idea of the day was voting rights for women.

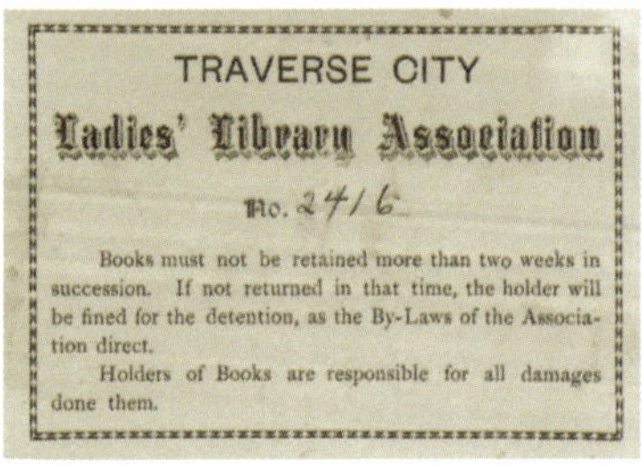
TRAVERSE CITY

Ladies' Library Association

No. 2416

Books must not be retained more than two weeks in succession. If not returned in that time, the holder will be fined for the detention, as the By-Laws of the Association direct.

Holders of Books are responsible for all damages done them.

Bookplates pasted inside books were used to indicate ownership of the book and library lending rules. This particular plate was found inside a 1916 book, *The Girl at Big Loon Post*.

Whatever its political role, the Ladies' Library continued to stock up on popular fiction. Popular new fiction titles in 1907 were *The Midnight Guest*, *The Princess and the Ploughman*, and *The Crimson Conquest.*

The Ladies' group now had 128 members, each still paying $1 dues to join, and 25¢ each quarter to check out books. The group had amassed considerable business savvy. They accounted for every penny, from selling an old stove pipe for 65¢ to renting out Library Hall and enacting real estate sales.

The new property the Ladies' Library bought on Cass Street was a prime lot. The women bought it for $1,800 and refused an offer to resell it for $2,200, recognizing its choice position. It was located right between the original Federal Building (Post Office), later city hall (now old city hall), and the Ashton-Hobbs lots (now Central United Methodist Church). Almost the exact spot where library advocates had wished to place the city library a few years before. Was this the Revenge of the Ladies? If the men couldn't put a library on Cass Street, the women could.

The Ladies' Library designed their new library out of red paving brick, a "harmonious color" and "roomy enough for decades to come." The building was designed by Fred Moore, the same man who had designed the Carnegie library on Sixth Street. The *Evening Record* called it "one of the most convenient and perfect library buildings of its class in the state" and suggested that Traverse City businessmen should follow the Ladies' example in keeping such a united front with practical success.

> *Yesterday was a red letter day in the history of the Ladies' Library association...The splendid building...is a monument to the energy, persistence and culture of a band of Traverse City's most estimable women.*
>
> *Since 1869, they have worked and exercised their business ability and intellectual effort with commendable devotion in securing one of the most conspicuous monuments to woman's work in all of Northern Michigan.*

The brand new Ladies' Library building was celebrated with great fanfare. The day the cornerstone was laid, Campbell's concert band played while the Ladies marched en masse from their temporary library headquarters on State Street to the Cass Street site. There they placed a time capsule in the cornerstone and participated in an elaborate Masonic ritual. "Most worshipful sir," began the Ladies' Library

President Estella Kneeland, as she addressed the Grand Master Mason. The entire Masonic Lodge 222 was there, and the event was important enough that Grand Deacons, Grand Wardens, Grand Tylers, and other Masonic officers arrived by train on the Pere Marquette and GR & I (Grand Rapids & Indiana) lines from Bay City, East Tawas, and Detroit.

Estella Udall Kneeland (1846–1915), president of Ladies' Library Association for many years.

The Cass Street library was the Ladies' Library Association's last permanent home. Early in 1909, they sold their Front Street property for $10,253.75, more than doubling what they'd paid for the lot and building, and moved to temporary quarters until their new building was ready.

Despite their business savvy, in the middle of building the Cass Street library, the Ladies suddenly discovered that they might not be able to legally own the land or the building. Had they accidentally let their corporate status expire? It seemed so. The *Evening Record* reported that the Ladies' Library Association, which incorporated in 1871, only had a legal charter for thirty years. It looked as if they'd been operating without a license for the past eight years. The women quickly filed new paperwork with Lansing to get back on their legal feet. However, this scare might have been just a mix-up about paperwork. An earlier news article from the *Traverse Bay Eagle* in 1901 explained that at the end of the original thirty-year charter, the Ladies' Library Association of Traverse City decided to change its name to the Traverse City Ladies' Library Association, and filed the new charter paperwork on time.

The lavish new Ladies' Library building opened in September 1909. It featured oak staircases, two levels of reading rooms, and plenty of room for their book collection. This second Ladies' Library building cost $8,000 to build, and was generally admired as one of the most attractive buildings in Traverse City. Four years later, the Central United Methodist Church moved next door as its neighbor.

In 1910, the Ladies' Library Association voted to become part of the greater Traverse City Woman's Club federation. They made this decision at the same time librarian Helen Stout presented a talk about her recent experiences in Japan, and "Mrs. Leon Titus [Alice Titus] and Miss Blossom Garland each favored with songs."

The Ladies continued to use their new Cass Street building as a library and meeting space for more than 35 years. Over time, the need for a Ladies' Library gradually lessened, and the group functioned more and more as a social club. By the 1940s, the library building was being used for bandage rolling during World War II as women threw themselves into the war effort. It was referred to as the "Red Cross Building" in 1945 since the Red Cross was located in the basement.

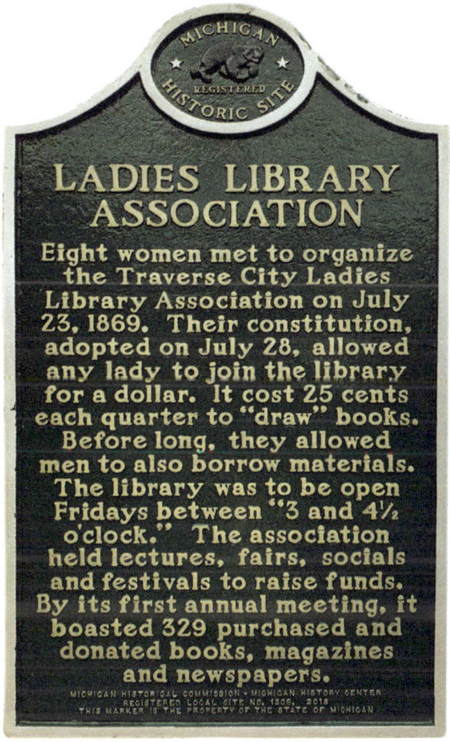

Historical marker recognizing the Ladies' Library Building at 216 Cass Street in Traverse City.

The final meeting of the Ladies' Library Association was held on April 25, 1945. The group effectively disbanded, though it took another ten years or more before they disbursed their assets. The Ladies donated the building to the city, with the provision that women's groups could continue to use the space to meet until 1959. The primary group that took advantage of that provision was the Traverse City Woman's Club, which met there for several years. In the end, the city turned the Ladies' Library into a police station, which served the city from approximately 1958 to 1971.

The Ladies' Library came to an official end in 1958 when they drained their bank account. After 89 years they were ready to move on. The Ladies' gave their remaining assets, $1,461.37, to the much anticipated Northwestern Michigan College library, which was then in the works. Their gift was matched by state funds.

Sixth Street Library with Cornwell addition. Limited parking; old railroad track running near the "bump" of the original Carnegie building.

A trained librarian is a powerful search engine with a heart.

Sarah McIntyre

Chapter 6

Library Days 1950s–1970s

The Post-War Library and McCarthyism

The next city librarian to make her mark was Terese O'Connor Flaherty. Flaherty arrived from Detroit, where she'd worked as chief of book selection and initiated a successful bookmobile program, but she was also a hometown girl. Terese O'Connor had been born in Ontario in 1901 or 1902, and arrived in Traverse City as a young girl to live with her uncle and aunt, William and Maria Heydon. She even worked in the early city library, as an assistant librarian under Alice Wait in 1920.

"We are rather proud of our Traverse City libraries. Traverse City people are great readers and they read good books, but we want them to read even more," said Flaherty when she assumed the director position in 1951. "Our libraries belong to the people. Their money supports them and they are entitled to the best service our staff can give."

Flaherty served as Traverse City library director from 1951 to 1966, and brought the Carnegie library into the modern era. During this time, she also had to navigate a difficult era of censorship that affected libraries all over the country: McCarthyism.

Libraries increasingly came under attack in the 1950s during widespread fear of communism. Senator Joseph McCarthy led a crusade of political repression against many citizens for "un-American activities." Thousands were blacklisted and lost their jobs, hundreds were imprisoned, and public institutions around the country began to demand employees swear loyalty oaths.

This put public libraries in a bind. Librarians either had to remove targeted books and magazines like the *Nation* or *New Republic* under local pressure, or fight back and risk losing their jobs.

The issue was not new. Issues of censorship continually loomed, from what to put in school history textbooks, to whether or not to allow books with swear words or sexual content. In the 1950s, book banning intensified. Groups such as veterans' organizations and churches targeted libraries and demanded that books by communist authors—or even by people perceived as communist—be withdrawn from the collection.

What was being banned? Poems by Langston Hughes, *The Grapes of Wrath* by John Steinbeck, *Civil Disobedience* by Henry David Thoreau, and even stories about Robin Hood. After all, Robin Hood stole from the rich to give to the poor. Books that suggested challenging authority and redistributing wealth struck many people as suspiciously communist.

Locally, a Traverse City minister did manage to get *The Grapes of Wrath* removed from the library. The story follows the Joad family from Depression-era dustbowl poverty in Oklahoma to new jobs as farm laborers in California. It was branded as "communist" and despised for its positive portrayal of labor unions, plus sexual scenes and bad language. The fight against *The Grapes of Wrath* began as soon as the novel was published in 1939. Kent County, California banned the book from its schools and libraries, and people posed for photographs burning it.

The American Library Association passed the Library Bill of Rights based on troubling trends librarians saw, from reactions to *The Grapes of Wrath* to growing intolerance of dissenting views during Hitler's rise to power. The first version came out in 1939 and was revised many times. One significant set of revisions was added in 1948 during the McCarthy era. The first three right*s* state:

> I. Books and other library resources should be provided for the interest, information, and enlightenment of all people of the community the library serves. Materials should not be excluded because of the origin, background, or views of those contributing to their creation.

II. Libraries should provide materials and information presenting all points of view on current and historical issues. Materials should not be proscribed or removed because of partisan or doctrinal disapproval.

III. Libraries should challenge censorship in the fulfillment of their responsibility to provide information and enlightenment.

In 1952, the American Library Association passed a Freedom to Read statement. "The freedom to read is essential to our democracy," it said. "It is in the public interest for publishers and librarians to make available the widest diversity of views and expressions, including those that are unorthodox, unpopular, or considered dangerous by the majority." This was in response to an Eisenhower-administration policy to remove books "by Communists, fellow travelers, et cetera" from the approximately 230 American libraries abroad.

The freedom to read is essential to our democracy.

It is unknown exactly how much pressure local librarians faced in Traverse City during this time. No one kept lists of challenged books. The only notice that remains is from the library notes about removal of *The Grapes of Wrath,* but Traverse City was not immune to cultural pressures.

The question of "appropriate" books had been debated for years. Back in 1906, when the State Library Institute came to Traverse City for its conference, the director of Western Reserve University Library School cautioned against stocking many current fiction titles. "Fiction is good for the library if well used, as it is good bait," she said. "But care should be exercised." The *Evening Record* reported how she selected good books: "She would not put in a library book [that] she would not let a younger sister read and believes the public should be treated with the same consideration."

In 1957, Michigan's supreme court also took a stand and struck down a state law that had been in place for 118 years aimed at "obscene books." In a unanimous ruling, the supreme court decided that the law's aim would "reduce the adult population of Michigan to reading only what is fit for children." Michigan readers should be able to decide for themselves what they want to read.

The issue of banned books did not disappear, but it died down when the McCarthy era ended.

Rise of Community Libraries

As in Traverse City, smaller libraries in the surrounding townships also got started early, many in the 1800s, and grew and blossomed during this time.

Peninsula Community Library was the first local library to spring up in the outlying area. Located on the Old Mission peninsula, it was run by the local township, and its growth follows a similar pattern to Traverse City's main library.

As early as 1859, Peninsula Township voted to form a public library, and at first it was housed in a private home. In 1910, it was considered more practical to spread the books around the peninsula, so the books were dispersed among the township's one-room schoolhouses. Old Mission's one-room schoolhouses were still functioning in 1955, though only seven of them were left. Shortly after the last of the one-room schools closed and consolidated to become Old Mission Peninsula School on Island View Road, the township library moved into the new school building. As the library's history reads: "The Peninsula Community Library, one of Peninsula Township's most beloved institutions, opened on a summer's day in 1957."

Peninsula Community Library started with 700 books, mostly borrowed, displayed on the school stage. They soon settled into more permanent quarters as a library room attached to the elementary school.

Fife Lake Public Library was housed in an old schoolhouse from the early 1950s to 2000.

The community of Fife Lake was also early in starting a small library. In 1887, the county gave Fife Lake Township $17 to start a library. That small seed grant turned into the Fife Lake Public Library. Located east and south of Traverse City, Fife Lake also served many residents in nearby Kalkaska and surrounding areas. They formed an independent board, not governed by the township. In 1939, they moved into in a historic, little white one-room schoolhouse in downtown Fife Lake at 137 West State Street.

In other parts of Grand Traverse County, other communities did the same. Like the Ladies' Library Association in Traverse City, the effort was often driven by women. The Kingsley Woman's Civic Club's first project in 1914 was to create a library. It was an all volunteer-run library, initially stocked with fifty books. Eunice Stinson acted as head librarian for more than twenty years, and she initially opened the library two days a week, four hours each on Fridays and Saturdays.

The Kingsley library was first called the Kingsley Woman's Civic Club Library. Later it became known as the Kingsley Library when it moved into a former bank building in downtown Kingsley in 1939. The Woman's Civic Club purchased the bank building to use for their club and the library. Kingsley residents loved their library, and when it moved, volunteers carried books across the street. After Eunice Stinson stepped down, her daughter-in-law Nell Stinson became the new head librarian and continued that post into the 1960s.

Much later, a community library in Interlochen formed. A small band of women, led by Green Lake Township Supervisor Judith Lindenau, set up a makeshift library with donated books in a corner of the township hall in 1976. With no real space of their own, the library had to move all the books, shelves, and furniture every time the room was needed for something else. After retired schoolteacher Marge Dilley moved to Interlochen, she revitalized the struggling library. By 1981 the Interlochen library was hosting Story Hour for children and cataloging books. The Interlochen library was still a private, volunteer-led library that charged $1 annual dues and had no real building. They no longer had to shift the books and furniture to make room for other events, but the budget was minimal, and their dream of becoming a public library was still off in the future.

Even Long Lake Township had a rudimentary library by the 1980s.

"Long Lake had a closet in the township hall," said Jody Clark. "That's what it was. A few people wanted more books than they could afford to buy."

The Long Lake Reading Center had 2,500 books and operated two days a week. During limited hours (Tuesdays 9 am to 1 pm and Wednesdays 2 to 8 pm), people could check out books, and the "Reading Room" even hosted children's Story Time.

Library Director Terese Flaherty (shown here with Helen Langworthy in December, 1964) spearheaded regional cooperation and book services to outlying areas.

TRAINS & BOOKMOBILES

Back in Traverse City, for many years an active train line ran right below the city library along the Boardman River. The train didn't seem to bother library patrons with its noise. Indeed, a friendship struck up between the railroad workers and the librarians.

Library staff would wave and put up friendly messages in the windows overlooking the tracks, "for the railroad men who wheel by several times a day with a friendly toot for staff members and single workers." This was especially true at holidays. Library employees would paste foot-high letters up on the north window with messages like "Happy Thanksgiving R.R. Men."

Today, the former rail bed can easily be seen. It's that wide, flat part of Hannah Park that runs in a straight line and parallels the Boardman River.

In the 1950s, the Traverse City library began reaching out to surrounding rural areas with a bookmobile. Terese Flaherty knew the advantages of bringing books to patrons. She'd headed up a successful bookmobile project in Detroit, and was eager to launch something similar up north to reach rural residents, to supplement service by community libraries.

Easy access for people living out on farms and in rural areas had always been a challenge. Back in 1873, the Ladies' Library posted a notice in the *Grand Traverse Herald* welcoming women from the region: "Ladies in the country need not necessarily come in person for their books, but may send by others who may be coming to town. We hope many ladies in the surrounding country will become members of the Association. It would be well for them, and help the Association in the noble work it has taken in hand."

The Bookmobile project launched in the mid-1950s, but lapsed when the Grand Traverse County board of supervisors balked at asking taxpayers to fund it. Flaherty persisted, and the Bookmobile returned in the 1960s for a time.

By bringing books out of the city, the Traverse City library was beginning to embark on a new mission: connecting the city and surrounding villages. As the Bookmobiles showed, the library could promote regional cooperation with improved access and literacy for all.

RENOVATIONS: OUT WITH THE MARBLE, IN WITH THE VINYL

Librarians Theresa Schaub (left) and Terese Flaherty with December 1904 *Daily Eagle* article that shows a drawing of the original library building, as they plan for major remodel in 1963.

This was also a great period of modernization. What had seemed up-to-date and exciting in 1905—including the green lamp shades and high ceilings—was no longer desirable. In 1963, Flaherty oversaw major renovations to the Carnegie building. A mezzanine was built over the main stacks, which doubled the bookshelf area. They lowered the 18-foot-high ceilings in both reading rooms, installing white ceiling panels that covered up decorative plaster rosettes and lowered the ceiling height by 10 feet. This move was designed to improve lighting and save heating costs for the massive building. The library installed fluorescent tube lighting. The old much-extolled cork

Space for book shelving nearly doubled after the 1963 interior remodel of the Sixth Street library. (Compare with photo of half-rotunda on page 53)

carpeting was ripped out and replaced with "modern floor coverings," and all the old tables and chairs were replaced or refinished. The children's chairs were pint-sized wooden ones, and chairs in the adult reading room were wooden chairs cushioned with olive green vinyl.

They added a microfilm center and "duplicating machine," doctored up the front entrance with glass and metal, and triumphantly removed the "huge obsolete circulation desk," which had been much applauded by library patrons as the "Italian and Grecian marble" centerpiece of the library at the 1905 dedication ceremonies. Circulation was also modernized, doing away with the old cardboard-card stamping machines. The new system didn't even require patrons to carry a library card. "No library card or registration is required," reported the *Record-Eagle* in 1962. Instead, patrons had to write their name and the book's title on a charge slip. "The library, too, is discarding old, mechanical methods for clean-cut, modern routines," Flaherty said proudly. Two small wooden desks were installed on either side of the entrance for check-out and returns.

Down in the basement, the library fixed up rooms for the Grand Traverse Area Library Federation to meet. This was a new cooperative effort involving 22 libraries in an eight-county region. Flaherty was a main driver and huge proponent of this regional cooperation. The Federation met in Traverse City and included libraries as far away as Cadillac. The Federation shared knowledge and services, plus was able to obtain bulk discounts by doing central ordering. One of its main functions was to create an inter-library loan system, particularly benefiting small, rural libraries.

Upstairs, Flaherty was able to establish the Michigan and Local History Room in April 1962. This was a long-held dream she'd had since first arriving as librarian: a room devoted to Michigan books. The Michigan Room held a collection of local and state-wide historical books, documents, and photographs, many from the Grand Traverse Historical Society. The *Record-Eagle* heralded it as: "An ambitious dream come true with its arresting décor and impressive collection... a memorable achievement which will always be associated with Mrs. Flaherty's ability to attain the impossible."

The "Michigan Room," as it was lovingly called, was built by renovating the building's original balcony. The Carnegie library had a balcony over the entrance, and this was where the Steward & Steffens orchestra performed at the 1905 grand opening. This balcony was enclosed and paneled to create the Michigan and Local History Room.

The new history room housed rare manuscripts such as Civil War muster lists from northern Michigan, and archives of local government

1965 photo of Phyllis Babel in the new Michigan Room (later Nelson Room), designed to feel like a cozy living room. She worked at the library from 1963–1999.

records. It included regional stories like *A Child of the Sea*, a story of Beaver Island by Elizabeth Whitney Williams, and Harold Titus's novel *Timber!* as well as books from early Traverse City settlers. These included Martha E. C. Bates who wrote *Along Grand Traverse Shores*, and Dr. Morgan Leach's *A History of the Grand Traverse Region* from 1883. The cozy, wooden-paneled room was furnished with coffee tables, desks, and armchairs to make it feel like a home sitting room or study. Later the Michigan Room was re-named the Nelson Room, after Jack Nelson, longtime library board trustee (1957–1991) who served as board president for many years.

Evelyn Hammond Brown, known as Mrs. Brown to patrons, on bottom left, surrounded by the all-women library staff in 1965.

The general collection shifted, too. In the earliest years, fiction was in greatest demand, but over time patrons clamored for more nonfiction and reference materials. High school students crowded into the library on weekday evenings to research class assignments. The library added a modest record and film collection as well. Circulation numbers reached 100,000 in 1962. The library staff grew to six full-time staff, including its first designated children's librarian, Theresa Schaub, who'd previously worked at the Carnegie library in Pittsburgh. A photograph from 1965 shows all fourteen staff (full and part-time) were female. Working in the library was still firmly the domain of women.

NORTHWESTERN MICHIGAN COLLEGE FOUNDING

As the library grew, so did Traverse City. Northwestern Michigan College (NMC), a two-year community college, opened in 1951.

It was recognized that a college needed its own library, and Les Biederman put out a call on his radio station for people to "search their attics" and bring books to the brand-new college. People responded with an outpouring of generosity. They donated hundreds of books, which launched the college library collection.

Not many libraries begin life at an airport, but that's exactly where the NMC library began. The college opened before it had its own buildings or campus, so early classes were held in a former Coast Guard barracks at the airport. After four years of airport life, NMC got its own campus in 1955.

When Bernard Rink arrived to take over the reins of the college library in 1957, it still didn't have its own building. That was rectified in 1961 with construction of the new library, which was named for college trustee Dr. Mark Osterlin. "The community kept donating books," said Ann Swaney, NMC archivist. "Bernie Rink kept everything."

Besides meeting student needs, the Osterlin Library collection was designed for the "continuing self-education of intelligent and interested adults in northwestern Michigan." Rink welcomed non-college residents who came to check out books from NMC and said: "Paperbacks, too, are potent tools of culture. They have put more ideas in the pockets of Americans than any other cultural device in the last twenty-five years." Mass-market paperbacks appeared for the first time in the U.S. in 1939, originally called "Pocket Books."

For many years, the NMC library acted as a branch library for residents on the east side of the city.

THE CORNWELL ADDITION

Sixty years after the Carnegie library was first designed, it was clear the city's book collection was outgrowing the building. Ivy covered the outside walls. Books were crowded and the stylish turn-of-the-century furniture was getting old. Despite adding a mezzanine level for more book space, there still wasn't enough room to meet the needs of a growing city population. The Oak Park branch library had closed. The Ladies' Library had closed. Although the newly founded Northwestern Michigan College allowed public use of its library, it was more focused on academic material. The city library now had 30,000 items in its collection and was straining to keep up with demand.

Patronage was also booming. At one point, the children's room was so busy that children's librarian Theresa Schaub declared that "every book in the children's room had been checked out."

It was the 1960s. Manual typewriters were still king and horn-rimmed glasses were fashionable, but tastes were shifting, and change was afoot throughout the city. In 1956, Grandview Parkway was constructed, a major artery running east-west along the Grand Traverse Bay. Young men who'd been overseas in World War II and seen the

Theresa Schaub, assistant library director and children's librarian, was a popular storyteller.

world, such as Julius Sleder and Jack Nelson, had returned to Traverse City. Sleder and Nelson, among others, ran for city council, and "dragged Traverse City into the 20th century," said Fred Nelson, Jack's son. "They paved thirty-five miles of streets...[and] built the parkway." Fred Nelson served as city commissioner, mayor and library board member, like his father before him.

It was decided to keep the library in its home in the Carnegie building for the time being, but add on to the original building with a modern structure. The architect was Gordon Cornwell, so the addition soon became known as the Cornwell extension. The new addition cost $156,000—most of which was paid for by a federal library grant. The federal government paid two-thirds, and the city paid the rest. The addition added 7,900 square feet of space on two floors.

Gordon Cornwell was a well-known local architect. He'd already designed several notable public buildings around town, including Traverse City Central High School, West Junior High (now West Middle

School), St. Francis High School, and Oak Park School. He also designed churches like All Faiths Chapel, Bethlehem Lutheran Church, and several additions to the First Congregational Church. Later, in 1978–79, Cornwell helped design the Governmental Center.

The Cornwell extension was a modern and flat-roofed structure, typical of 1960s square-angled design. It was constructed of concrete and brick, quite different from the original classical stone of the Carnegie building. Some people were delighted with the modern look, others called it "that ugly addition," but people generally agreed that the extra square footage was most welcome. Inside, the spacious addition fit a new children's room, audio-visual space, staff work room, staff lounge, plus meeting rooms. It also boasted large, attractive windows that looked out on Hannah Park and the Boardman River.

The addition was dedicated on September 29, 1966. The mayor, Carter Strong, said: "A library is a symbol of the community and the volume of usage demonstrates the quality of that community." He praised the building for the combination of old and new "with no loss of harmony." Everyone gave a cheer for long-time librarian "Mrs. Brown," who still worked part-time. Library Director Flaherty, wearing a corsage, was singled out as a pioneering library director by Michigan's State Librarian, Genevieve Casey. She'd made the addition possible by applying for the federal grant. First there was Andrew Carnegie, then there was the federal government. Once again, Traverse City would have to pay very little to enjoy a new library building.

Besides the new indoor space, the addition included a new paved entrance with a few off-street parking spaces. The need for library parking was already raising its head. The Cornwell addition would buy

The modern 1965 addition provided much needed space for expansion.

the library more time, but the narrow lot on Sixth Street could only hold so much. With the river on one side and Sixth Street on the other, there wasn't much more room to expand.

City leaders began quietly talking about demolishing the Carnegie building. Could the library gain more space that way? Library advocate and former trustee John Trezise remembered hearing about these early plans. "Jack Nelson told me that the city's plan for the library after the Cornwell addition was to raze the Carnegie building and replace it with a modern building that would effectively complete the Cornwell addition." Besides finding space, it was a case of out with the old and in with the new.

You're Under Arrest!

Soon after completion of the new library addition, Flaherty stepped down and moved out of town. By the end of 1966 the city library had a new director, Bernard Oppenneer. He didn't stay long. Next came Robert "Scotty" Olney from 1970 to 1979.

Bernard Oppenneer, library director 1966–1970.

Robert "Scotty" Olney, library director 1970–1979.

Olney was quite concerned about the number of overdue books that were never returned: 553 books in 1977. Fines were 5¢ a day, and fines capped at one dollar. He tried amnesty weeks, where patrons could return books without paying the fine. He tried phoning patrons, mailing notices, or sending Boy Scouts out to households as messengers. These methods took up a lot of time and still, many library books did not come back.

"We used to figure on losing $1,000 per year through books lost in circulation," said Olney. "Suddenly we've lost $2,000 in six months." His solution: make a lost library book a criminal offense.

Traverse City attorney W. Peter Doren agreed. He modeled the criminal ordinance after one in Troy, Michigan. With the new law, library patrons were subject to $25 fines or up to ten days in jail.

A patron would get three warning letters about an overdue book. Then, if the book was still overdue after four months, the city attorney would send an official letter: Return the book or face arrest!

Traverse City issued five arrest warrants for overdue library books from 1977–1979. The city attorney issued "dozens of letters."

The only trouble, Doren admitted, was knowing whether the person who checked out the book was an adult or a child. "We don't want to initiate legal action against a juvenile," Doren said.

"Any child who gets a letter from the city attorney should have his parents call and explain," reported the *Record-Eagle*.

The First "Friends"

Today's Friends of the Library was incorporated in 1982 but there was an earlier version before that. Back in 1971, Dorothy Hall founded the Grand Traverse Area Friends of Libraries. This was part of a national trend, and "Friends" groups were rapidly sprouting up during the 1960s and even before. By 1973, there were approximately 1,000 Friends of Library groups across the country.

Hall was a strong supporter of the arts and local libraries. Not only did she start the first local Friends group, but the next year, in 1972, she was elected president of the Michigan Library Association's Friends of the Libraries Division.

For a book-loving town like Traverse City, a Friends group was a natural option. The *Record-Eagle* announced the launch of the Grand Traverse Area Friends of Libraries in April 1971, featuring Mayor Jack Rokos buying a membership from Dorothy Hall as one of his first official acts in public office. Membership cost one dollar.

The group's aim was to support *all* libraries in the Grand Traverse region, from the city library and community libraries to public and private school libraries, and the college library. That meant 24 libraries all together. The Friends created a "library-pool" in Central Grade school, asking people to donate used books and magazines. Soon donated copies flowed in, including eight cartons of *National Geographic* magazines. The Friends distributed the materials to libraries in the area, particularly schools. They also staged "Lunchtime Book Review" talks to gather and discuss current books like the bestseller *Future Shock,* by Alvin Toffler. The group remained active during the 1970s and frequently attended professional training along with library staff.

Library Director Mike McGuire at his stand-up desk, late 1980s. McGuire was an energetic, earnest book lover and musician who from the beginning thought a library should be more than books.

I like to see a very lively library.
Screaming, no, but a modest amount of noise.
Mike McGuire

CHAPTER 7

The McGuire Years

MIKE MCGUIRE AT SIXTH STREET

Many people today who remember the Carnegie library on Sixth Street think of long-time Library Director Michael McGuire.

Mike McGuire grew up in the small town of Centerville, Indiana. His local library was tiny, dark, and not open every day of the week, so Mike rarely went as a child.

As a college student at Indiana University, Mike thought about law and political science, but got hooked on libraries after getting a student job at the university library. He graduated with a master's in library science.

McGuire moved to Traverse City to work at the library in 1975. "He became assistant director, then director," said his wife Nancy McGuire. "He never looked back." McGuire served as assistant director from 1976 to 1979 and director from 1979 to 2009.

At the time, city employees had to live in the city itself, so the McGuires lived in the neighborhood, initially in a house on Seventh Street, just a block and a half away from the Carnegie library. Living so close had its disadvantages.

"He was a bit of a workaholic," admitted Nancy McGuire. "He lived there most of the time." One night the security guards called in the middle of the night. Lights were on at the library, and there was a man in there, long after the library had closed. It turned out to be McGuire himself.

He brought the library home with him, too. McGuire read book reviews in the evening, and brought towels home since the Carnegie building didn't have laundry facilities. "We did laundry once a week. We'd wash puppets along with towels, and sometimes repair them," said Nancy. The family would also screen all the new film discs that came into the library, watching PBS documentaries and other films first to make sure they worked. They also helped clean discs that were returned dirty or smudged.

When McGuire started, the library was back to using cardboard library cards. "We got to make those at home," said Nancy. "The staff didn't have time to do that." The three McGuire children helped, and it was a family affair laminating the cards and punching them with a hole. They set up the laminating machine on the family dining room table. The no-card method introduced under Terese Flaherty didn't last.

The library was still losing 300 books a year when McGuire took the helm. The harsh criminal system of dealing with overdue books was still in place, but few people were actually sent arrest warrants, and it was obvious to McGuire that 5¢ fines didn't deter late returns. He suggested doing away with nickel-a-day fines.

"We are not a nickel and dime organization," said McGuire. People could either return the book or settle up with the library by paying the cost of the book.

McGuire wanted to draw people to the library, and always had a vision for enhancing book service, especially involving technology. He dreamed of the day when people could order books from home via "two-way cable television."

When NMC decided to stop hosting the innovative Traverse.net program in the 1990s, McGuire picked that up and gave Traverse.net a home at the library. Traverse.net was a free, public system of connecting to the internet that offered people email accounts ending in *@traverse.net*. McGuire also had a TV cooking show, called "What's Cooking at the Library" with Vicki Penney (later Carpenter). It aired in the 1990s on Channel 2, Traverse City's public access TV station (TCTV2). Librarian Margaret Braden (later Kelly) was his first guest. Channel 2 was originally hosted at NMC but moved to the library, part of McGuire's plan to drum up new library fans and reach out into the community.

McGuire was a talented musician. He'd studied music, played the trumpet, and performed with the troupe, *The Young Americans*. This group staged shows at Crystal Mountain and Shanty Creek every summer, and the performers waited the tables as singing waiters. His vision for the library was multi-media. McGuire introduced laser discs—large 12" diameter vinyl discs that played movies and were precursors to video cassettes and DVDs. In 1983, patrons could check out a laser disc player for $7.75 along with four laser disc movies such as: *The Black Stallion, West Side Story,* or *Super Memories of the Superbowl.* McGuire gathered the library's vinyl records, cassette tapes, and laser discs together and created a brand-new Sight & Sound department. Cassette players, slide projectors, and 16mm film projectors were also available. Soon McGuire added CDs (compact discs) to Sight & Sound.

Traverse City Public Library

322 Sixth Street — Traverse City, Michigan 49684 — (616) 941-2311

This library logo emphasized the "beyond books" role of audio-visual collections (film reel on left, laser disc on right behind books). Note the ripples representing the bay.

"Mike introduced CDs to the library early on," said Dawn Buchanan, who worked as McGuire's administrative assistant. "For a while, the Traverse City library had the best collection of CDs in the country!" Interlochen Public Radio thought so, too. "WIAA Interlochen used to come in to borrow CDs from our collection," said Buchanan. "They were so much better to play on the air."

This was unusual at the time. Many librarians shook their heads and said no when patrons asked for films and music. The role of libraries was shifting, but not everyone was ready to shift with them. Some thought libraries should only be for serious study, not entertainment. "It was a fairly new concept," said Buchanan. "A lot of libraries said: 'Oh, no. We just have books and magazines.'"

But McGuire persevered. He built up a robust music collection, with a wide variety of music styles, especially strong in jazz. Aaron Olson worked with McGuire for years and currently heads the library's Sight & Sound department. He credited McGuire's early vision for film and music: "He was a guy who knew AV [audio visual] was going to be an important part of the future." In 1980, McGuire added the library's first public computer: a TRS-80 microcomputer from Radio Shack. "Traverse City library enters the computer age," read the *Record-Eagle* headline. The article reported how the library's computer was loaded with something called "software." McGuire invited people to come in to the library to learn BASIC, an early computer programming language. The library also added a Polaroid camera available to check out.

"He wanted to show people that libraries are not just books... He wanted everything checked out," said Nancy McGuire. "Puppets, records...tax forms...most everything. He said: 'A library should be a place where people can find everything they need.' If you needed it, they could find it."

THE START OF TADL

When Mike McGuire stepped up as library director in 1979, one of the first things he did was conduct a patron survey to see who exactly was using the city library. The bounds of Traverse City itself were rather small. The region had grown, but technically "the city" was still just a few business districts and neighborhoods.

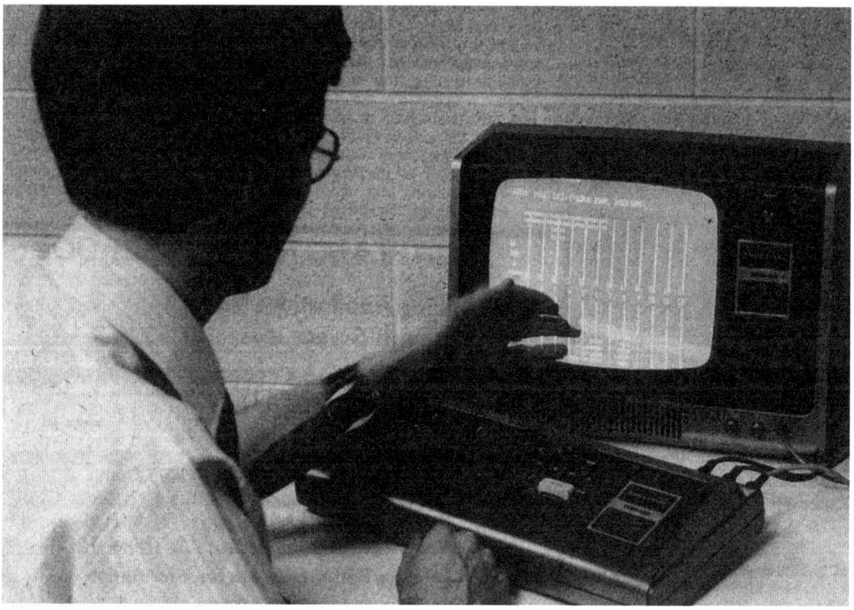

With 4k of memory, this Radio Shack TRS-80 computer took the Traverse City library into the computer age. Connection to the internet would still be years away.

The survey provided some stark answers: 45% of library users lived in the city, but 55% of them lived outside the city limits. County residents were flocking to the library, which was wonderful, but the city was expected to pay for it.

The library's budget in 1980 was $270,000, and 65–70% of that came directly from city taxpayers. Was this fair? It was true, the library did get $9,000 in state aid per year, in acknowledgement of its role in serving the surrounding area, and also another $20,000 from the government from local penal fines. Michigan's constitution directed a portion of local traffic court fines and other violations to fund local libraries. Any influx of funds helped, but it was really city taxpayers who were carrying the burden. Nearby townships like Peninsula had their own libraries, but still 225 Peninsula residents also held a library card at the Traverse City library. These neighbors got to use the library, but provided zero money. Long Lake and Garfield Township residents were also major city library users.

"Everyone was using the central library but not paying for it," explained Fred Nelson. "We wanted to spread that out and increase services."

McGuire set up a group to study the issue. Richard Burkhardt, Jack Nelson, Joe Muha, Ted Okerstrom, and Jim Tompkins formed the new Regional Library Services Study Committee. This was a joint city-county appointed commission, led by chair Joe Muha. The big question: What should we do about the library?

One idea was to combine with the NMC library. The college wasn't interested in that plan. There was also a small law library in town, housed in the county courthouse, and a medical library run by Munson hospital. Neither specialty library wanted to join a general collection.

Some people thought it was best to even things out by charging non-residents a fee to use the library, but McGuire didn't believe a fee was the answer. The city library had tried that for a while in the 1960s. Charging a non-resident user fee didn't feel right, and only added $2,000 to the budget.

Besides, McGuire at heart hated fees. He believed in access. Since becoming director, he'd gradually done away with library fines. It formerly cost 5¢ a day for an overdue book and 25¢ to reserve a book. "Fees can deny the use of the library to a segment of the population," he said. "And income from those fees didn't keep up with the cost of paperwork."

"Mike was thinking countywide," said Nancy McGuire. Mike McGuire and others wanted to form a district. The area had four community libraries scattered around the county by then: Fife Lake, Peninsula, Kingsley, and a new one forming in Interlochen. Would it be possible to cooperate and combine with them? Downstate, Jackson and other cities had successfully combined their county and city libraries into one district.

For McGuire, Muha, and others, the idea of a district took hold. Change the city library into what it really had been all along: a regional, district library for the Traverse area.

They decided to try it. On March 1, 1982, the city and county passed a resolution to create a regional library as a "one-year experiment." Both the city and county would cooperate to mutually fund the former city library. For just one year, Grand Traverse County would contribute $75,000 and the city would provide $200,000. Non-tax money from state aid and other sources made up the rest. The new entity was called the Traverse Area District Library (TADL) and would formally begin on January 1, 1983.

Department Heads of the Traverse Area District Library in 1983: Theresa Schaub, Children's Librarian; Mary Franklin, Circulation; Mike McGuire, Library Director; Marie Kulibert, Reference; Carol Hubbell, Library for the Blind and Physically Handicapped; and Gloria Crandall, Audio Visual.

While this temporary structure was in place, it was time to take the idea to the voters. McGuire and his group proposed a county-wide millage, something all local residents would support, the way the community had rallied to create and support NMC. That was the unknown question. Would Grand Traverse County residents support a district library the way they loved and supported the community college?

Unfortunately, the early 1980s were a difficult economic time for the region. "Reagan was president," said Joe Muha. "We were having an economic downturn at that time. It was hard for people to support new taxes."

Partly because budgets were tight, the Chamber of Commerce passed a resolution to save money by avoiding duplication of services. It was a time of consolidation everywhere. The city police merged with the county sheriff department by sharing one building, and the city and county fire departments also cooperated. "One of the logical places for this was the library," said Muha.

Muha helmed a joint commission made of city library board members Larry Murdza and Jack Nelson, city commissioner Phill Orth, plus county commissioners Elizabeth Edwards (later Rollert), Dick Fitch, and Will Rasmussen. They set a special election to vote on the district library proposal on September 13, 1983. The proposal asked for .6 mills.

This first vote to go before the people failed. It got passing votes only in Traverse City, plus Acme and Garfield townships. Mostly, county residents voted against imposing a new tax. Others, including some city commissioners who lived in the Old Town neighborhood near Sixth Street, did not like the idea of broadening the city library's mission. A city library was just fine, they said.

More important, several of the existing county libraries did not want to join the district. They feared loss of control, loss of small-town community spirit, and possible closure. Would the larger district change their hours? Remove their boards? Fire their staff? Deplete their funding? And worse—would a district board someday vote to close the smaller libraries?

A takeover sounded scary.

TADL was still nothing more than a name, with a tenuous funding agreement that would expire in a few months. Could they create something that would last and benefit the entire community?

TADL proposed going back to voters a second time, again with a millage request of .6 mills. To help this second vote succeed, McGuire and Joe Muha set out to talk to the county libraries. They found an immediate ally in John Trezise in Interlochen. Trezise was a retired executive from Ford who'd settled in Interlochen in 1982. He'd immediately joined his neighbors Sue and Bill Happ to revitalize the struggling Green Lake Township Library.

"We had a rudimentary library in Interlochen," said Trezise. "We occupied the old Town Hall. It was a terrible place. Bats and things in it."

The TADL officials offered a funding plan of 50–50. If the Interlochen library became part of the district, they would get half of the tax revenue raised from their township. The other half would go towards the main library in Traverse City to run the district. Besides sharing funding, the district would share their collection, training, and professional library services.

"At the time we had no revenue source, so it sounded to people like a good idea," said Trezise. "When the TADL people came to share taxes, we signed up immediately."

That was not the case when McGuire and Muha pitched the idea of the vote again to Peninsula Township. Unlike the other townships, Peninsula already enjoyed an exceptionally good tax base. What good could come of sharing?

"We were worried," said Ann Swaney, Peninsula Library board member for 12 years, from 1984 to 1996. "Peninsula Library was so well used by all the school children. It's also where we voted. It was a community hub. There was a lot of pride in community. Pride in our own library and we didn't want to give it up. We were totally content with how things were. We were worried we'd be forced to change our hours and not be able to do special events. Worried that they'd micromanage us," she said. "It turns out that was not the case."

Despite strong Peninsula opposition, some township residents came around. "Joe [Muha] came out and worked his charm," said Swaney.

Other county residents remained strongly opposed. A letter signed by Kingsley librarians Eileen Reamer, Lorene Sedlacek, and Dorothy Westrate came out against the millage. Others feared that if the millage didn't pass, the main library would have to charge user fees to out-of-city residents. That could discourage library users.

"In a free society, books should never be a luxury for the few," wrote Ruth Gamble, president of the local League of Women Voters, as she urged voters to vote yes.

The second vote to fund the library district took place on November 8, 1983, just two months after the first failed attempt. Nine out of thirteen townships voted against the millage, including Peninsula. In Fife Lake, only four people voted yes, and 150 voted no. That pattern was repeated in the sparsely-populated Union Township (which had no library), and Mayfield. The measure barely passed in East Bay, and voters approved it in Acme, Garfield, and Long Lake. Green Lake Township, home of Interlochen's library, still rejected the millage, but residents there rejected it by a much narrower margin (169 to 155), a big change in attitude.

Still, despite strong rural opposition to new taxes, the measure passed county-wide thanks to city residents who overwhelmingly voted to share the burden. The Traverse metro area voted in favor of it 2 to 1. Within the boundaries of Traverse City, 1,800 voted yes and 713 voted no. The millage won by a margin of only 298 votes county-wide. "It wasn't a mandate," the *Record-Eagle* reported.

"It was a squeaker," admitted Mike McGuire. Still, he had his district. The Traverse Area District Library was launched and funded, if not universally approved.

"We were forced to cooperate," said Marge Arney, Peninsula Township librarian. "I'm very disappointed that the voters of Grand Traverse County did not support the positions of three smaller public libraries. It's the same force attempting to consolidate everything," she said. "Consolidation takes away your personal pride." The citizens of Peninsula and Fife Lake were proud of what they'd built locally and did not want to participate. Both townships came out adamantly against the district millage

"It's simple," said Lorene Sedlacek, Kingsley Public Library director. "We didn't want it. We don't want to pay 6/10 mill for nothing and that's exactly what we'll get."

It was a rough start all around. Fife Lake not only voted against the district, it brought a lawsuit against TADL. Fife Lake felt forced into being part of a district. They wanted to control their own destiny and were pleased with their own set-up. "They had a nice little library at the time," said Swaney. Peninsula Community Library was also contemplating a lawsuit. The Peninsula library board met to decide whether to join Fife Lake's suit. They did not pursue it. "Our attorney told us to just watch and wait," said Swaney, Peninsula library board member at the time.

"There was a lot of fear that we would be closed," said Julie Gray, who worked for the Fife Lake library for thirty years and later became its director. "We were small and basically right on the county line."

The Fife Lake Township board vowed to "fight this unfair taxation," taking it all the way to the Michigan Supreme Court, if necessary.

In June 1985, Judge Karl Forester ruled against Fife Lake. They appealed, and lost again. Willing or not, Fife Lake would become part of the larger library district.

Building a District

Bringing four new community libraries into the fold was a tricky juggling act. It was not the same as creating branches. The community libraries were considered to be "member" libraries, each with its own independent library board and ability to hire its own library director.

Besides having their own boards, each member was invited to have representation on the TADL board. There were seven trustees. Getting the balance of power right was an early issue.

"They [The City Library Trustees] wanted it to be four city and three county," explained Fred Nelson. "I said: 'No, there's more of them. Let them have four votes! We want the county to pass it!' So they set the TADL board up to be three city and four county." Today TADL has five representatives from the county and two from the city, chosen by the county and city commissioners.

John Trezise was the Interlochen representative on the TADL board in 1983. For Interlochen, being part of the district was a godsend. It tripled Interlochen library's income in 1984. Besides their share of Green Lake Township's tax revenue from the millage, Interlochen received new access to state funding, plus half of neighboring Grant Township's library tax, since those residents were considered part of Interlochen's service area.

Although Interlochen now had plenty of operating money to run their library, they were so new they didn't have a building. The district was set up to share funds and services, but not to construct buildings. If a member library wanted to build or renovate, that was up to them.

Bill Happ took the lead in writing grants and asked the township for funding. He also headed the building committee. It would take nearly $100,000 for a "community center and library." The trouble was, many longtime locals feared that getting a library building would deplete township funds. "There was a loud and rude anti-library movement," recalled Trezise. One firefighter spoke up, concerned that funds would be taken away from the township fire department, suggesting "library supporters could go to the library for a book on how to extinguish the blaze when their houses were on fire."

In the end, the Interlochen library teamed up with a senior group called the Golden Fellowship. They shared a building and were able to open the doors in June 1985.

Not every member library was as pleased. Fife Lake was still disgruntled in the aftermath of their lawsuit.

"With Fife Lake fighting it in the courts, there was bad blood there," said former Fife Lake Library Director Julie Gray. "There was always that threat, or that feeling, that they'd close us down if they could. Because basically we were a financial draw on them."

A good formula for sharing district library funds took years to work out.

"We were getting a lot less than the other libraries," said Gray. Fife Lake had a low population and low tax base. On the flip side, the Peninsula library was outraged at how much of its tax base was redirected to TADL. Peninsula was receiving *less* money for its budget than before the district formed.

There was also growing resentment that the Traverse City library was the main focus, not the surrounding community libraries.

"We are like poor stepchildren," said Jane Hardwicke from the Interlochen library board. "We get whatever is left over."

"It seemed like a good idea at the time, but it isn't enough money," said Sucile Mellor, Kingsley librarian in 1993.

Funding woes often reached a crisis point. Although Interlochen was excited about new funds to start, they soon realized their share was inadequate. Patronage had shot up. So had costs. In 1993, the Interlochen library was struggling to fix its broken copy machine and had to cut back on janitorial staff, so library board members cleaned the toilets. Board members also dug into their own pockets to pay operating bills.

"It was not a happy arrangement in the beginning," said Ann Swaney. "We felt that all they wanted was our money."

"It took several years to work out a funding formula everyone accepted," said Dawn Buchanan, TADL administrative assistant, now retired.

For years, fights about funding dragged on. What was the fairest method of fund distribution? Some townships had a wealthier tax base. Some areas were big library users. Other communities had great need and could benefit from increased services. TADL's mission was to serve all residents in Grand Traverse County. Trustees finally settled on a funding formula that pleased most people and attempted to find a balance.

Besides the amount of money community libraries were allotted, there was uncertainty. TADL was often slow about administering contracts, and member libraries had to guess at the budget and prod the district to disburse funds.

TADL adjusted the funding formula again and again. As late as 2009, member libraries got nervous that the main library would close them down or underfund them. Funding disputes lasted for approximately fifteen years, and included a compromise that no township library would get less money than they had been receiving before. As time went on, the district concept began to click.

"For a while, it still felt like a city library," said Buchanan. Being a district and working together was new. "It took a little while for people to get used to thinking of it that way."

Patrons enjoyed having access to a wider collection of books and materials. Now everything in the district system could be checked out. In the days before easy inter-library loan, this opened up a vast array of materials. Member libraries also began to see tangible service benefits. In the 1980s, TADL added computers to member libraries, all paid for by the district. Technical support and training were taken care of, and smaller libraries learned how to operate professionally. TADL put plastic coverings on new books, and the computer system kept getting better and better. "TADL was fabulous. None of the member or branch libraries could have done it alone," said Bernadette Groppuso, who directed the Interlochen library from 1991 to 1998. "Having an actual tech department at TADL has just made all the difference." It was good to be part of a district.

There were benefits to remaining autonomous, too. Member status allowed for different styles of management. Since Peninsula was attached to an elementary school, they didn't charge fines for overdue

TRAVERSE AREA DISTRICT LIBRARY

The new district library tried out a tripartite banner recognizing the roles of the county and the city.

books. That was different from the district. "Our indie status allows us to serve our community," said Vicki Shurly, current director of Peninsula Community Library.

The four original member libraries shifted over time. Today there are three member libraries in the district (Fife Lake, Interlochen, and Peninsula) and two branches (Kingsley and East Bay). Kingsley moved from being a member to a branch in 1999, when the State of Michigan ruled that there could not be two overlapping district libraries in the same area. Kingsley, which had been set up as the "Kingsley District Library," was told they had two choices: 1) become a branch of TADL or 2) dissolve. Kingsley chose to become a branch. "Everybody was afraid TADL would just close them," said Groppuso. But in the end, "things went rather well for Kingsley," she said.

TADL is the only federated library district in Michigan. Other districts operate with main libraries and branches, but TADL has a unique system of member libraries, branches, and the central one. "It's a very convoluted system," said Fred Nelson. Although it works for northern Michigan, the state decided not to replicate Traverse City's system. "It's a unique animal," agreed Anne Magoun, a library advocate who was deeply involved in establishing the new Woodmere library. "There was never one like this before, and there'll never be another like it again."

And although there were growing pains, all's well that ends well.

"It turned out well," said Swaney. "It's evolved. We realized that the more we help each other, the better off we are. There's more for everyone." The district model gives every library more resources.

Millage for the district was easily renewed in a new vote in 1986. Voters agreed to extend the .6 mill tax, and this time the measure passed by more than 1,000 votes (3688 to 2503). What had changed? The district was working, and more and more people were using the TADL family of libraries.

Adult Department Reference desk in 1988 Carnegie Library. Book shelving in background contains fiction books on the top level and non-fiction below.

Library facilities are an essential part
of our nation's civic infrastructure.
American Library Association

CHAPTER 8

Outgrowing the Carnegie Library

CARNEGIE CROWDED

Meanwhile, the Carnegie building was getting crowded.

Books piled up on the floor and in offices. The work room for returned books was completely cluttered. "You could hardly walk around there," said Dawn Buchanan. "There were books on the tables. Books on the floors."

The freight elevator—the only elevator for the five floors—opened on to Director Mike McGuire's office. Staff workspace was scrunched behind the staircase. Library space was already cramped when McGuire added in the Sight & Sound department. Soon overcrowding could no longer be ignored.

"Parking was hopeless," remembered John Trezise, a former library board member. "Parking was especially difficult if there happened to be a funeral going on across the street." Perry Hannah's former mansion on Sixth Street had been transformed by the Jonkhoff family into a stately funeral home.

"[The library] wasn't welcoming. Not the sort of place you'd want to go," said Vicki Shurly, director of the Peninsula Community Library.

It seemed time to expand the Carnegie library again. However, things were different now. After the 1966 Cornwell addition was built,

A crowded library forced books to be stacked everywhere.

the Sixth Street area surrounding the library became designated as the Central Neighborhood Historic District. In 1979, it was added to the National Register of Historic Places. It wasn't so easy to slap an addition on anymore. Any new addition had to fit into the historic Victorian style. Also, Perry Hannah's original gift of parkland to the city meant that the land surrounding the library was officially "park" land. If the library wanted to expand and build on city parkland, they needed to obtain a 75% vote by city residents. Library board chair Joe Muha wasn't so sure it would work. "Try to get that many people to agree on anything," he said. Still, the library needed growing room. Becoming a district had helped the library grow. "If we expanded to a county-wide system, we needed to expand the library," Muha said. "It had a force of its own."

The library board first looked at buying the Christian Science church, located just west of the Carnegie building. The church building was for sale. There was mixed enthusiasm among the library board, but there was no question it was a prime site. If there was ever a chance to expand the original Carnegie building, this was it. The library signed a purchase agreement to buy the church property.

The sale never went forward after the discovery of contamination caused by a leaking underground storage tank. The library withdrew from the agreement and looked at new options.

At the same time, the aging Carnegie building needed a new roof and the heating system failed. "We spent $75,000 on that old building just to keep it functioning," said Trezise. "It began to get expensive."

"Instead of maintaining this dump, we ought to put our money into a new library," Muha told the other library board members. He appointed three trustees to look into the possibility: John Trezise from Interlochen, Jim Hunter from Traverse City, and Norman Crampton from Peninsula.

This early committee determined two things: 1) the Carnegie building was no longer adequate, and 2) the library was in the wrong location. It needed to be more central and with more parking. The library was a county library now, not just a city library, and it should be placed with good access for all county residents. It was time to build a new library.

The committee presented their findings to the TADL board. In the audience were people from Traverse City's Central Neighborhood who staunchly opposed such a move. Many of them had children who walked to the library. They were proud of the Carnegie library building and didn't want it abandoned for a modern one someplace else. Suzanne Antosh (later Connor) led the opposition and was an effective leader. "I'm telling you right now, we're going to fight you," she told Trezise.

McGuire and the board considered alternatives but could find no good options. They brought in library consultant David Smith from Hopkins, Minnesota, to help out. Smith recognized the Carnegie library's historic character, but pointed out its many liabilities: lack of space; awkward areas; multi-levels; inadequate parking; poor lighting, heating, and cooling; and outmoded electrical system. If you like the building, keep it as a branch or a museum, the consultant suggested.

"He validated our ideas," said Trezise. However, when these ideas were presented at a public meeting in May 1988, the atmosphere was charged. Residents from the Central Neighborhood showed up in force, and the meeting was described as rude and confrontational. Tempers rose. Neighbors called it a crime to close the Carnegie building. Proponents of a new library deplored the conditions.

Trezise yelled at one point: "You people are treating this beat-up old building as if it were the Sistine Chapel!"

Connor shot back: "You can bring somebody in from Minnesota or you can bring somebody in from Mars, but you can never justify taking away this building from the community!"

Historic Preservation

Traverse City at this time was experiencing its own growing pains. The old city landmarks were aging, mall developers were moving in, and there was great pressure to knock down the old buildings and replace historic sites with the new.

You people are treating this beat-up old building as if it were the Sistine Chapel!

"The town was looking tired," said Carol Hale. A teacher, long-term city commissioner and former mayor, Hale had moved to town with her husband Jan in 1970. "The city courthouse was under threat and the Opera House hadn't been open in fifty years," she said. She moved into a historic home on Sixth Street and got involved in local politics and historic preservation.

In the mid-1980s the city planned to tear down the old courthouse. They were already building a new courthouse next to it and wanted to expand the jail. County officials saw no reason to keep the old building.

"Why preserve it?" asked Hale, incredulously. "All you had to do was look at it." She campaigned for its preservation. Many fellow residents agreed, and the old courthouse was saved, renovated, and turned into extra storage and court offices. The basement housed the 86th District Court, the first floor held the 13th Circuit Court and offices for Probate Court and Friend of the Court. The top floor was used for storage and a community law library.

The City Opera House was in peril about the same time. Bill and Gretchen Votruba owned the building and donated the Opera House to the city, but it took many years to raise enough money to restore it to its former glory. Central Grade School was another beloved local landmark that residents rallied to save. It served as the city's only public high school until 1960. Remnants of the old high school chemistry lab and auto shop still remained. "Central has been in jeopardy many times," said Hale.

Then there was the range of historic buildings left behind on the former State Hospital grounds. From 1885 to 1989, Building 50 and its associated buildings served as a psychiatric hospital for mentally ill patients from around Michigan. When the State Hospital closed, the stately towered buildings remained, along with 450 acres of land near the heart of the city. The State had plans to sell it off piecemeal to maximize income. That plan would have resulted in big box stores at the Commons and around Silver Lake Road up to West Junior High School. It wasn't until visionary builder and preservationist Ray Minervini stepped up in 2000 that the vision changed to saving and restoring the buildings. Minervini's company created a "Village" concept, the Grand Traverse Commons, and kept the open land as parkland.

As mayor pro-tem, Hale herself helped stop demolition of one of the outlying buildings. Traverse City residents had been promised that the State wouldn't tear down the buildings, but when she stopped by one morning "there was a wrecking ball and a bulldozer." There was also a line of Michigan State police and Traverse City police facing off. The State had jurisdiction over the land as State property, but the city still required a building permit before any demolition. The police standoff ended mid-morning.

Public libraries were celebrated by the United States Post Office in 1982, when a first-class letter could be sent for 20¢.

Hale sensed rising pressure against local landmarks, and she and many others spoke up for preservation. "The courthouse, the Opera House," Hale said. "And then there was the library."

Suzy Antosh Connor lived on Sixth Street half a block away from the Carnegie library. She was president of the Central Neighborhood Association and later a city commissioner for five years. She'd been active in helping residents rally to save Central Grade School, and now, as their representative, tried her best to let their voices be heard.

"It was the typical experience of a freight train rolling through," said Connor. The library board appeared to have already made up its mind about moving sites and constructing a new building before they came to the people. "People in the neighborhood had a much more historic perspective," she explained. Connor and others were especially interested in preserving the Carnegie library building, not just preserving the structure, but keeping it open as a library.

At one of the meetings, Connor attempted to educate the library board about the history and heritage of their own library building. She outlined the original mission of Carnegie's library program. "To think we were chosen as one of the sites back in the day. ...It's just amazing," she explained. "It's hard to say we love libraries. We love libraries so much we're willing to bond for one...and then turn your back on the Carnegie mission and the Carnegie philosophy."

"This wasn't just about the Central Neighborhood. Not NIMBY [Not In My Backyard]" she said to the library board. "It's what you lose when you turn your back on history. About understanding our heritage. We were chosen to host a Carnegie building. Not everyone was chosen."

"These old buildings just eat money," was the answer.

"We have obligations to see that money is spent on library services."

That was the mindset in the 1980s and 1990s. Old buildings were full of contamination. It might have asbestos. It would have lead paint. It was always better to build new on a new site rather than fix up the old. One possibility was to remove the 1960s flat-roofed Cornwell addition and replace it with something better that could be built into the hill. Although there was some support for this, the library board did not pursue it. Many citizens felt the library board was giving lip service to the idea of improving the library at the Carnegie site.

"Currently, the library board seems intent on a shiny new library at the Civic Center," said Linda Smyka in a letter to the *Record-Eagle* editor in 1989.

Meanwhile, the Board of Education was talking of demolishing Central Grade School, the heart of Central Neighborhood on Seventh Street. Neighbors cried foul, and gathered en masse at a school board meeting, which was held in the school cafeteria. The school board gave citizens two minutes to speak, but Connor had another plan. She asked supporters to bring flowers.

"We *packed* the cafeteria with flowers in vases," said Connor. "Every flat surface was covered in flowers."

"Well, I guess we know whose funeral this is," said Vern Oxender, the school superintendent.

Connor used her designated two minutes to involve the community. "Please, all the teachers here stand. Everyone with a child at Central, please stand. Everyone who went to school at Central, stand." By the end, almost everyone in the room was standing in a room filled with flowers. Partly as a result of this huge demonstration of support, Central Grade School was allowed to stay open. It remains an active elementary school of 635 students (2019–2020 school year) to this day.

"The State was decommissioning the State Hospital property," said Connor. "Along with Vern Oxender's push to pull out of Central Grade School, and Mike McGuire's emphasis on leaving the Carnegie building." All three issues were happening in the early 1990s.

We're not looking for a fight. We're looking for solutions.

Traverse City residents who valued historic landmarks or lived in historic houses were ready to take a stand. Opposition to moving the library took a different form, however. "We're not looking for a fight," said Connor. "We're looking for solutions. And real solutions might mean a new library elsewhere."

Maybe the library *did* need a new location. The narrow strip of parkland on Sixth Street had all sorts of limitations, and parking was a nightmare both for patrons and neighbors. But if the library district went to voters for money, they should build in funding for the Carnegie building too.

"We aren't the bad guys, but we have some concerns," said Hale.

"If you are truly librarians, if you are truly committed to the concept of public education and public availability of resources, you can't turn your back on the Carnegie library You have to have a solution before you move," maintained Connor and other neighbors. "The bond proposal should include something to fund the needs of the Carnegie building."

The main concern was: what to do about the Carnegie building? What about making it a branch library? Would it still have a life if the library moved out? What would that mean for the people of Traverse City and Old Town neighbors?

Connor, Smyka, and others went door to door, handing out copies of the *Cobblestone Crier*, the Central Neighborhood Association newsletter. The newsletter posted library board meeting dates and encouraged neighbors to speak up. Once again, Sixth Street was the center of a fight between Traverse City residents, and the library was in the middle of it.

GRAND PLANS

Two weeks after the Minnesota consultant unveiled his recommendation to close the Carnegie library, the TADL board met to decide what to do. They met in Fife Lake.

Connor rented a bus to make the 29-mile trip. She filled the bus with 25 Carnegie building supporters and packed the meeting. It certainly seemed to many that the library board was purposefully making it difficult for citizens to reach the public meeting. The location was unfortunate. The TADL board regularly rotated meeting locations throughout the county, trying to be considerate of member libraries. June 9, 1988 was scheduled to be in Fife Lake.

Under intense public pressure, the library board unanimously voted to keep the Carnegie library open.

A promise was a promise. Still, they needed a new library. McGuire and the board changed tacks. What if they could have both? Keep their promise—keep the Carnegie building open and functioning as a library—but also construct a new building.

With this in mind, McGuire hired architect Rick Skendzel. If they couldn't expand to the church lot or move to a new site, they'd just have to make the current Carnegie building better. Skendzel drew up plans that proposed doubling the size of the Carnegie building.

The trouble with making the Carnegie building the main library, however, was that after this, there could be no more expansion. The site was skinny and bordered by the river. If this wasn't big enough, there was no more room to grow at Sixth Street.

"We plan not just for today, but for the next fifty years," said library board member Jim Hunter. "No further enlargement could ever be made."

A new plan emerged. During 1988, the library board came up with two options: 1) expand Carnegie to 40,000 square feet and build a new, small 8,000 square-foot branch in Garfield Township; or 2) build a big new main library of 40,000 square feet and keep the Carnegie building as a branch. It would take $5 million to do either.

The board flung itself into seeking a site for the small-or-large new building. There was a good potential site where the Burke Flexo-Products building was located on five acres. It was located on the southwest corner of South Airport and Park Drive and was owned by Dr. John Spencer. Burke was known for its Flexo-Lure line of plastic fishing lures, including plastic worms. Another possible five-acre site on South Airport was located east of US 31 across from the Faith Assembly of God Church.

Main libraries are cultural centers and should be located in the cultural center of the county.

As time went on, some in the city grew worried. All the library board's efforts seemed to be focused on the new library. Had they forgotten their promise to stay true to the Carnegie building? Besides that, all the sites being looked at were south of town, contributing to sprawl. South Airport might be closer to the geographic center of the county, but it certainly wasn't near downtown.

"Main libraries are cultural centers and should be located in the cultural center of the county, just as governmental centers and courthouses are," said architect Bob Cornwell, then on the planning commission.

Timing of the bond got pushed back as library board members argued about sites and finally reached a compromise. An even more ambitious plan emerged. The library bond request that was placed on the March 19, 1991 ballot was a sweeping proposal to increase library capacity. It proposed a slate of three major building projects:

1) double the size of the Carnegie building by adding 30,000 square feet on the north side, building into the hill, AND
2) build a large, new branch, 20,000 square feet in size, in either East Bay or Garfield Township, AND
3) construct *three* smaller branch buildings in Kingsley, Peninsula and somewhere in the northeast, in either Acme or Whitewater Township

Whew! Instead of $5 million, this comprehensive bond project would cost $7.9 million. At the same time, TADL asked for 1.3 mills in operating costs. The total cost was 2.6 mills, more than four times the previous millage request from 1983.

Much changed at the Carnegie Library over the decades but not storytime, here offered by then Children's Librarian Martha Vreeland, in 1984.

"[If this fails,] we'll just continue to get worse," said McGuire. "We can't put a 400-pound man in a size 12 shirt."

Although the stakes were high, no one was actively campaigning on behalf of the library. Fred Nelson, newly appointed to the library board, succeeding his father, approached McGuire about the upcoming election. "I'm happy to help on the campaign," he said. "What are you going to do?"

"We're not going to do anything really," replied McGuire.

Shocked, Nelson went home and discussed the situation with his wife, Marcy Manseau, who was experienced with state and local political campaigning. "Well, then, they're going to lose," said Manseau. "Because if you don't campaign, you don't win." Nelson agreed: "You can't go for an election on faith."

We really went down in flames.

"Library millage fails by large margin," reported the *Record-Eagle* in 1991. The loss was more than a 3 to 1 ratio.

"We lost. Miserably," said Martha Vreeland. "We really went down in flames."

"It sort of passed in town," said Nelson. "The rest of them hated us."

"The vote failed. It failed miserably," agreed Trezise. "Even in the Central Neighborhood it only passed by five votes. That was the end of it."

The library board retreated. In the face of such strong opposition, it didn't seem likely that the library could win support for a new site. "We kind of gave up," said Trezise, later reflecting that the 1991 proposal had been a terrible idea.

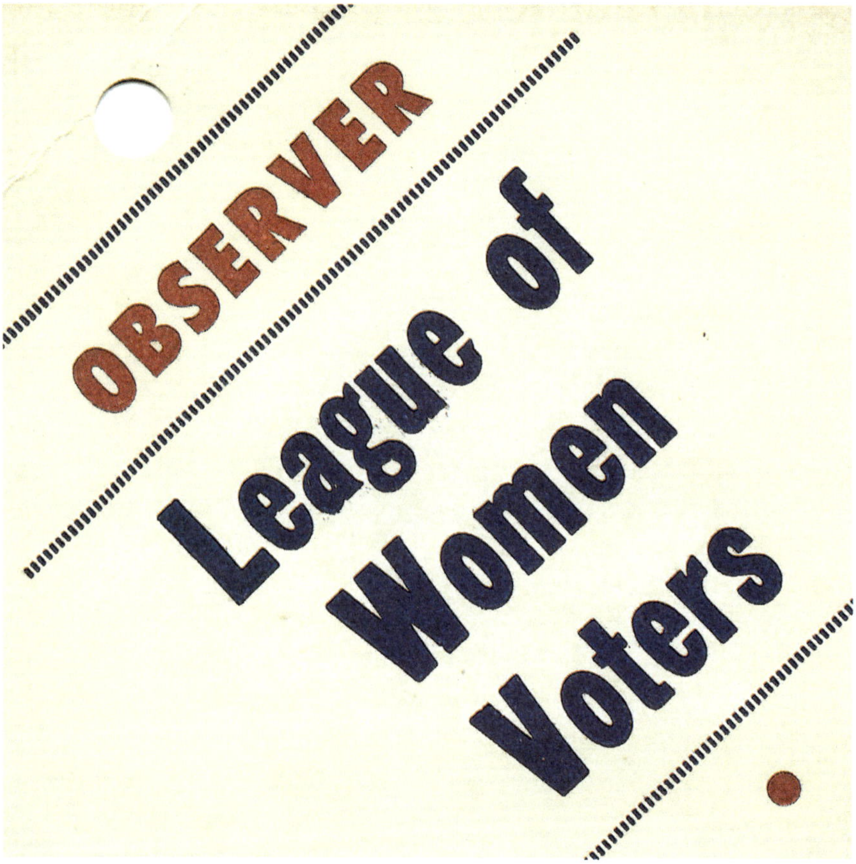

League of Women Voters members often attended library board meetings as observers, wearing an identification tag.

Whatever the cost of our libraries, the price is cheap compared to that of an ignorant nation.

Walter Cronkite

CHAPTER 9

Rallying for the Library Again

A BRANCH FOR EAST BAY

While library trustees and citizens were debating the merits of building a slate of new library buildings, an unexpected opportunity cropped up in East Bay Township. The township had built a new town hall and moved into it in 1991. This left the old town hall near the corner of Hammond and Three Mile roads vacant. Did the library want the space?

It was easy to say yes. East Bay Township had been asking for a branch library for some time. In fact, they'd petitioned the TADL board in 1988 but were turned down.

"We don't consider it a dead issue by any means," said John Porter, East Bay Township Supervisor at the time. "We feel library services are needed on this side of town."

TADL voted to open a "temporary" branch in East Bay. The township had already partially renovated the old hall and offered to donate use of the building. The library board approved $110,000 to set up the branch. The idea was to serve patrons on the east side of the county in this spot temporarily until a new $2.4 million permanent branch home could be built as part of the bond package.

The East Bay branch of TADL continues to operate in the old town hall today.

Friends of the Library

Even before the millage failed, McGuire realized the library needed more friends. More people had to love the library, come to the library, and appreciate what the Traverse Area District Library meant to the community. Why not start a Friends group?

The 1970s Grand Traverse Area Friends of Libraries had faded away, but there was a continuing need, and "Friends of the Library" groups remained popular around the country. These were separate nonprofits made up of library fans who could raise money, buy additional books, stage events, and generally drum up passion for libraries. What Traverse City needed before going back to the voters was a Friends group.

New retirees like Jim and Ruth Hunter and Ward and Evelyn Parr agreed. The Parrs moved up from Birmingham where Evelyn Parr had been active with the Birmingham Friends group. "When we moved to Traverse City, I was surprised that the library had no Friends and thought it ought to," said Ward Parr.

Together with Eldon and Dorothy Henricks, the Hunters and Parrs created the local Friends of the Library group, which incorporated in 1982. Bob Hughes was also an early member and kept the group grounded with sound financial advice. "Bob Hughes was a godsend!" said Jody Clark.

The new Friends of the Library got in touch with a Friends group in Oregon, and learned from their mistakes. The Oregon Friends had gotten in a spot of trouble because they hadn't paid taxes. Hughes made sure that Traverse City's Friends filed all the right papers to become a proper 501(c)(3) organization. They were joining good company. By 1980 there were 2,000 Friends of the Library groups across the U.S.

At first the Friends met in private homes, but later held meetings in a small room in the basement of the Carnegie building. "The room would get packed," said Jody Clark, long-term member of the Friends. "We had speakers, talked about books. It was an attempt to bring people into the library and see it as a community place."

The Friends were busy. They held more than 300 programs during their first year, starting with a bookmark contest and moving on to a used book sale which brought in $700. They used the money to buy a second video laser disc player and film strip projector for the library.

Jim and Ruth Hunter were dedicated supporters of libraries, guiding the Friends of the Library (later Friends of TADL) for many years.

Soon they were offering a free weekly movie series, showing early 1980s films like *Coal Miner's Daughter*, *Ordinary People*, and *On Golden Pond*.

Friends of the Library members initially paid $3 a year to join, an amount that gradually rose to $20 annual dues. Members met monthly and took turns serving on the 12-member board. Still, over time, it was an effort to get people excited about libraries. Sports were king, and sticking up for libraries often involved a clash of cultures. "Hockey was big up here," said Clark. "Football, basketball, any sports thing. Hockey mothers made money hand over fist. If the library tried [fundraising], we got something small."

During one membership drive, an irate farmer stood in the lobby, snapping his suspenders. "I'm totally against you!" he cried. "I'm mad my wife got the kids involved." He was obliged to wait while his family attended Story Time. His children were regular library users and checked out the maximum number of books.

Still, money quietly accumulated in the Friends' coffers, and more people joined the group. The Friends took over publication of a newsletter that Mike McGuire and Marie Kulibert had started, originally named *025.52*, an oblique reference to libraries, using the Dewey Decimal system. The newsletter was later renamed *TADL Tales,* and editor

TADL Tales was a newsletter started during the McGuire years, with Jody Clark as long-time editor.

Jody Clark expanded *TADL Tales* to include activities at member and branch libraries. The Friends threw strawberry ice cream socials and picnics, plus invited speakers to present travelogues. Soon there was not just a Friends group, but even a Junior Friends group for children, which Rhonda Estes formed in 1988. The Junior Friends formed to help brighten the dreary atmosphere in the aging library and was active for about three years. The Junior Friends wore bright yellow T-shirts with a picture of bumblebees busily dusting bookshelves.

"I remember how dusty and drab looking the children's department was," said Estes, a new local resident at the time. "We met on Saturday mornings. I led art projects, and the children…donated their time to dust, wash shelves, alphabetize and clean books." They hung the children's artwork on the walls and ceiling to make the area look more cheerful.

Now the library had Friends. Would it be enough?

League of Women Voters

The official "Friends" group wasn't the only organization rallying behind the library. Another quiet, effective group of supporters was forming, too: a Library Committee through the League of Women Voters.

"The League of Women Voters was the spark," said Fred Nelson. "They were all bright people with an ability to organize and persuade."

"Judy [Halsted] was really a mover and shaker. I give her a ton, a ton of credit," said Diane Viskochil, former library trustee. "She was very political and could influence people."

"Women's influence and choice to be active in education, and therefore libraries, runs through the entire history of Traverse City," said historian Peg Siciliano.

The League's serious involvement began when Betty Parker formed a committee to study the needs of the public library in 1985, around the time the library district formed. Parker's husband, Ken Parker, was a journalist for the *Record-Eagle*, and Betty herself was an English teacher and an avid theater director at Old Town Playhouse. They had three children and their home was full of books.

The League was the perfect place for Betty Parker's energies. The new Library Study Committee was made up of about 17 women, most of whom were teachers, retired teachers, and retired librarians. Some had worked at the University of Michigan library, others in school libraries or public libraries out-of-state. These were women who knew how to research and, like their Ladies' Library Association counterparts a century before, they were a band of women absolutely devoted to expanding education and access to education.

"The names that stick in the history books tend to be male," said Peg Siciliano. "But…there were numerous women working behind the scenes that were also contributing to these efforts. And women, especially early on, tended to work in groups, not as individuals."

This logo for TADL was used throughout the 1990s.

"We started it. Very definitely," said League member Anne Magoun. "The League of Women Voters prepared to get this off the ground. It was a group of ladies. The Ladies' Library Association in 1869, and in 1995, another group of women did it again more than a hundred years later."

The League of Women Voters indeed would have been familiar to many of the members of the Ladies' Library. It arose out of the women's suffrage movement and was founded in 1920, six months before the 19th Amendment was finally ratified. The League was a direct descendent of the National American Woman Suffrage Association, which was led by Susan B. Anthony, and later by Carrie Chapman Catt. The women who'd pushed for voting rights formed the League as a "mighty political experiment" to help women navigate their new civic responsibilities. On the national level, the League included leaders like Eleanor Roosevelt.

In Traverse City, a local League began in 1924, but it faltered and disbanded after its young president, Sadie Bartak, died of illness at age 48. The chapter attempted to re-start in 1950 during the McCarthy era, but was quickly attacked as "too pink or red," and shut down again. It wasn't until 1960 that the Traverse City League of Women Voters got properly established.

Whenever the League set up a study committee, they truly sank their teeth into the topic. The League's two main functions have always been to 1) provide nonpartisan, non-biased voter education and 2) advocate for chosen causes. Before choosing a project, League members thoroughly study and vet the topic. In this case, they wanted to know: was the current library adequate to meet the needs of today's residents?

"One of the things that impresses me about that organization is when they choose to get involved in something...they seriously study the issue," said Peg Siciliano. "It's only after they do all that really

League of Women Voters Library Committee in 1996: (front row from left) Ruth Gamble, Frances Spedding, Judith Halsted, Ellie Long, Arline Howe; (back row) Anne Magoun, Pat Trezise, Betty Parker. (See 147 for all committee members)

serious, hard work that they choose to take a position. Once they take a position, then they will decide: *Well, what can we do?*"

"They really knew we needed a new library long before the staff realized it," said Martha Vreeland, who was TADL assistant director at the time.

Betty Parker's new Library Study Committee met monthly at members' homes for soup study sessions. The host made soup, and others contributed bread, fruit, and cookies. Betty Parker made a good onion soup and a tasty tomato gazpacho. The women investigated standards for a public library in a town of Traverse City's size. How much square footage was needed? The answer: 39,000 square feet, nearly twice what Traverse City had. What's more, in ten years that number would be 55,000.

A Determined Force

One of the members of the League's library committee was Judith Halsted. A determined woman, trained in library science at the University of Illinois, Halsted and her family moved to Traverse City in 1974. She'd grown up in a small town with a Carnegie library, but also knew how impressive a modern library could be. One of the first things Halsted did was visit the local library.

"I walked into the library on Sixth Street for the first time. It was horrible!" Halsted recalled. "There were books stacked on the floors, alongside the shelves, because the shelves were full. *The city fathers are certainly working on this*, she said to herself. *I'll wait and see what happens.*

What happened was nothing. The Sixth Street library grew more tired, crowded, and decrepit. Halsted settled in as school librarian at Pathfinder School and watched and waited. Finally, she could stand it no longer.

"If someone wanted to do something about the library," Halsted asked her neighbor, friend, and League member, Helen Sullivan, "where would she start?"

"You need to meet Betty Parker," Sullivan told her, and arranged a lunch date.

"You need to meet John Trezise," Betty Parker told her over lunch at the Omelette Shoppe. And that was the beginning of it.

Halsted met Trezise at the Park Place Hotel for coffee. He was still involved with Interlochen's library and had served eight years on

TADL's board. Trezise connected her with journalist David Hacker and *Record-Eagle* publisher Frank Senger.

At the time, Halsted wasn't working and her two sons were in high school and college. She'd just published a book called *Some of My Best Friends are Books.* Although she'd been deeply involved in helping her Unitarian Universalist congregation construct a new building, that was her main experience in leading any kind of public campaign. She wasn't one of the League's leaders either, but she had passion and a deeply rooted conviction.

"I very much thought: *this is what I need to be doing now*," said Halsted.

When Betty Parker stepped down as chair of the League's Library Committee, Halsted took over as the new chair. By August 1994, the League changed the study group name from the Library Study Committee to the Library Action Committee. They'd done their due diligence. It was time to take action. The standard public approach had failed; the city fathers Halsted had been waiting for had still not done their part. It was up to grassroots citizens.

Championing the library became Halsted's cause for the next several years.

"Much of my usefulness [came] from nine years of meeting with the League of Women Voters," said Halsted. "We had already thoroughly envisioned what needed to be done...so we understood where the barriers were."

Next, Halsted and her team at the League developed a plan of action. They outlined a timeline laying out all the steps from July 1995 to election day in 1996. Together, they formulated a structure for a citizens' coalition, complete with an executive committee, steering committee, advisory committee, and subcommittees.

Halsted put an April 1995 public meeting on the calendar. They'd meet in the Carnegie basement for a kick-off event to build public support for a new library.

"She was the spine of this whole thing," said fellow League member Magoun, referring to Halsted. "She has a quiet vision but makes things happen. She was totally focused. She does one thing at a time and nothing deters her. She's meticulous in everything she does and that includes relationships."

Library Ambassadors

Relationships were key. Bitterness over the creation of the library district still rankled in outlying communities, so League members set out to rectify that. They knew they'd have to win the support and trust of member libraries and their patrons if they were to gain a better facility for the main library. This job would take time and patience. There were so many nested layers of control in the TADL system, so many relationships to navigate.

Ellie Long spearheaded the League's efforts to reach out to member libraries and quietly get them on board. Long was a petite powerhouse of focused energy. She was a retired college instructor who'd spent a lifetime championing civic ideas in her own gentle but insistent way.

Under Long's and Halsted's direction, League members became ambassadors. They attended local library board meetings month after month, driving out to Fife Lake, Kingsley, Interlochen, and Peninsula in the snow, listening, learning, and patiently conveying member library concerns back to the TADL board.

"One of my good supporters...was the League of Women Voters," said Julie Gray, Fife Lake's library director during that time. "Ellie Long supported me *so* well through all that."

Change did not come overnight. But gradually trust took root. The League embarked on a concerted, multi-year task of reestablishing good relationships.

Citizens For Libraries Co-chairs Judith Halsted and Dick Rosser championed better library service for the entire county.

In a democracy, everyone needs access to information, and it should be free.

Karen Nielsen

Chapter 10

Citizens for Libraries

Finding a Champion

If someone wanted to do something about the library, where would she start?

Judith Halsted pushed forward to find out. Downtown Development Authority head Bryan Crough helped her out. Crough was a member of the League of Women Voters, and arranged for a meeting with someone who knew a lot about capital campaigns, Jay Zrimec, a chief fundraiser for Munson Hospital. Crough, Halsted, fellow League member Anne Magoun, and Zrimec all sat down together in a booth at Minerva's in the Park Place Hotel.

"Don't you think it's shameful that a community that takes such pride in itself has such an inadequate library?" asked Crough.

"How do we do this?" Halsted asked.

"You need a champion," replied Zrimec. "Nothing happens without a champion."

That was easy enough to say, but who could best champion the library's cause? Halsted knew she was a diligent behind-the-scenes worker. Who could they find to be the out-in-front champion?

Almost the next week, they knew. A letter to the editor appeared in the *Record-Eagle*, signed by a Dick Rosser. "Our local library system can only be described as pathetic! It would be barely adequate in size for a town of 10,000, with a main building that is an antique," Rosser wrote. "I suggest that you, the editors, start with an investigative series to get to the root of the problem." Many of the League library committee members read it. *Really*? thought Magoun. *Who is this guy?*

It was the beginning of a new groundswell of grassroots support.

New Friends in Newcomers

While Halsted was quietly working behind the scenes with the League, a newcomer, Dick Rosser, had moved to town.

Shirley Murray, League member, avid reader, and retired elementary school teacher, met him first. She volunteered on the greeting committee at the Presbyterian church in Traverse City, and when Rosser walked in on his first Sunday in town, he encountered Murray.

"Have you been to the TC library?" he asked her.

"I'm afraid I have," said Murray.

"For a city this size, *that's* the library?"

Rosser had recently stopped in at the Carnegie library by chance. He'd been showing visitors around Traverse City and was driving down Sixth Street, when his friends said: "Oh, that's a cute library." So they went in. But when Rosser entered the outdated, gloomy building, he was stunned. At first, Rosser assumed what he was seeing was merely a branch library. *Where's the main library*? he wondered. He soon discovered his mistake. Could it be? That was the main library for a population of 60,000? The next Sunday he went to church.

"This place is a civic disgrace!" he told Murray, meaning the dark and crowded library. "I'm appalled."

Murray was struck by Rosser's energetic personality. She'd been deploring the state of the library for years, and sharing her concerns with friends like David and Barbara Hacker. Now here was a man who could spark change.

"I saw right away what Dick Rosser's personality was. He was a person who liked to be in the center of things...I could tell he was *itching* to do this. It was right up his alley," said Murray. If she could couple him with behind-the-scenes thinkers like Judith Halsted and David Hacker, who was a Pulitzer Prize-winning journalist, it would be just the thing.

After church that day, Murray and her husband invited Rosser and the Hackers to lunch at Minerva's at the Park Place Hotel.

"I just knew these...people would be a catalyst for the new library happening," Murray said. "This was a connection that was meant to be."

Hacker worked for the *Detroit Free Press* as its "up north" reporter. He also wrote for the *Prime Time News*, a publication he started with Anne Stanton. "Hacker was a listener. He always had a notebook in his pocket. He couldn't go to a restaurant without interviewing the waitress," Murray recalled.

Rosser, in contrast, was an executive, in-charge man. He'd held a string of leadership jobs. He was a retired colonel in the Air Force, dean of faculty at Albion College, past president at DePauw University, and president and CEO of the National Association of Independent Colleges and Universities in Washington, D.C. Then he moved to Traverse City. "He had ten honorary degrees and so forth," said Murray. "He was a person used to being the head of things."

Ironically, Rosser wasn't a regular library patron. "Dick Rosser had never been to a library to check out a book," said Murray. "He always bought his books...But he was a big supporter of libraries. [It was] an egalitarian idea."

After the *Record-Eagle* published an editorial pointing out the need for a new library, Rosser wrote back. In his letter to the editor on April 10, 1995, Rosser admitted to being a newcomer in town, and not privy to local politics. He wrote:

> *I read with great approval your March 28 editorial calling on our community to recognize the sad state of our regional library.... I then waited several days to see forthcoming letters to the editor. But so far, nothing.*
>
> *The sad state of the library system is all the more glaring because of the amazingly rich cultural life we have otherwise. I simply can't believe this is because of indifference. The editorial notes that there are now more than 20,000 active card-holders.... We need to organize the 20,000 card-holders and other potential friends of the library system....Let's turn a community embarrassment into a marvelous addition to our beautiful region.*

Judith Halsted and the Library Action Committee had found their champion.

Halsted wrote back to Rosser in a public letter to the editor, urging him to join the League's efforts and help "carry Andrew Carnegie's legacy honorably into the next century."

The time was right for strong citizen action. They had all the ingredients: leadership, research, passion, and a team of enthusiastic volunteers. Rosser and many other men and women teamed up with the League of Women Voters and together they formed a new organization: Citizens for Libraries (CFL), a group dedicated to giving Traverse City a brand-new, state-of-the-art library.

Citizens for Libraries Forms

The Citizens for Libraries got its start on June 7, 1995 at the Bowery, a popular informal restaurant later known as the Jolly Pumpkin. The restaurant was located on Old Mission Peninsula behind Bower's Harbor Inn (now Mission Table).

League members Judith Halsted and Anne Magoun met with David Hacker and Dick Rosser to discuss how to expand the League's library groundwork into something more. "We'd like to think about forming a citizens' group," wrote Hacker in his invitation. "Organizing efforts to get something done in terms of upgrading the library for the Twenty-first Century." The twenty-first century was less than five years away. Four years ago, the library millage had failed spectacularly. How should they do it? "There are a lot of toes out there and we want to step carefully," advised Hacker. Who should they involve?

"David Hacker whipped out a piece of paper and started writing down names," said Magoun. "They were all men."

"You haven't mentioned a single woman!" Magoun protested. "This is how women get written out of history," Magoun reflected later. "Women have always been movers and shakers." Hacker quickly amended his list and added twenty more names, including Helen Milliken, former Michigan First Lady; Shirley Okerstrom, from the NMC board of trustees; and Mayor Linda Smyka.

Citizens for Libraries was something new: a citizens' grassroots organization, separate from the League of Women Voters. The League had laid the groundwork, though, and League library committee members chaired or co-chaired every committee.

Dick Rosser and Judith Halsted became co-chairs of the Citizens for Libraries. It was an unusual, but effective, combination. Halsted knew libraries and locals. She was quiet and reserved, highly organized and filled with dogged grit. Rosser was flamboyant, funny, a seasoned leader and public speaker. "He was a short fellow, bubbling over with energy," said John Trezise.

Library Director Mike McGuire was enthusiastic about all the new help. In his "Director's Ramblings" in September 1995, McGuire instructed library staff to do all they can to help. "Hey there, hi there, ho there. There sure is a lot going on," he began. "The Citizens for Libraries (a group of energetic and dedicated citizens) is bound and determined to build a new main library for the community. Can't argue with that. This group needs and deserves our support and assistance. Our response to any request is, 'Yes, we can do that.'"

Now the library had Friends, lots of friends. Maybe it was time to try the millage again.

GETTING TO WORK

As Citizens for Libraries recruited more library-loving volunteers, they also drafted a set of working assumptions, including these: the need was dire, timing for the millage had to be 1996, and the cost should stay under $7.9 million. That was the cost of the first, failed millage request. On top of this, any plan needed to include a new role for the beloved Carnegie building.

"If we are not successful with this effort," the group concluded, "it may be years before there is another opportunity."

Timing was certainly critical. The current tax millage supporting library operations would expire in December 1996. The library would have to go before voters in 1996 in any case. Why not include a request for a new building then, too? Besides, the economy had improved since the last millage defeat in 1991. It might just work.

As for educating citizens and mobilizing voters, that would take enormous effort and outreach. "We have a much harder sell than we thought," commented Henry Morgenstein, retired NMC instructor, during an early meeting of the Citizens for Libraries.

"It's a certainty that tomorrow's library is going to be a communications or media center, and not just a collection of books, magazines, and card catalogs," wrote David Hacker to Rosser in the summer of 1995. "The revolution is enormous and Traverse City is such a go-slow community that we have to orchestra[te] change with all the precision and speed of a snail undergoing a brain operation."

In November 1995, Citizens for Libraries brought in Christine Hage, director at the Rochester Hills Public Library, to speak at Northwestern Michigan College. Rochester Hills had recently built a new 70,000 square-foot library. Hage gave a talk called "Building Better

Libraries," sharing all the ins and outs of the building project, from calculating the space needed to the importance of hiring an architect with library experience.

Slowly, the steps to bring a new library building to Traverse City were coming into focus.

OPPOSITION

Not everyone was in favor.

"So many people said 'no, we don't read,'" said Shirley Murray. "It took a lot of convincing."

Funding a library was also a hard sell in the 1990s. It was the dawn of the internet and electronic books. The World Wide Web burst into popular life. By 1995, the first widely popular search engine, Yahoo!, made the web accessible to regular users, and companies like eBay and Amazon began. Many people were convinced that libraries would go the way of the dinosaurs as the digital era exploded.

"'Oh, libraries won't exist anymore,'" people told Michele Howard, current TADL director, who was then in library science school at the University of Michigan. "People were convinced that libraries were going to go away. Librarians knew. Ha! See you in twenty years!"

"People thought libraries were a dead institution," recalled Vicki Shurly. "People thought...no one was going to check out a book. No one was going to read [books] when you could get anything with the World Wide Web."

"There was a lot of that talk, about libraries being obsolete," said Fred Nelson. "They said: 'You don't want to build a library because everything's going to be digital!' In the 1990s, some people sincerely believed digital was going to take over."

Oh, libraries won't exist anymore.

"Why do we need a new library?"

"Why not just use a vacant shopping center? Or a warehouse?"

"Why not just use the college library?"

Politics also hampered efforts. Many people remained disgruntled about how member libraries had been treated within the district. One upset donor gave $1,000, then asked for the money back. "I think Fife Lake was the most opposed," said Diane Viskochil, citing concerns from Fife Lake, Kingsley, and Peninsula. "They were all upset because they didn't think we should put a big library in Traverse City."

Adding to that, Traverse City had never really had to face up to the full price of constructing a main library building before. The Ladies' Library Association had privately funded two library buildings, but the city had always relied on outside saviors. First, Andrew Carnegie's philanthropy, and then the federal government's library grant program in the 1960s. The city itself had only footed the bill for one-third the cost of the 1965 addition. The task seemed daunting. The cost was sure to be in the millions. It was a problem of money and mindsets.

But the Citizens for Libraries group was determined. "David Hacker was a great convincer," said Murray. "He's the kind of person who could engage people. He was a natural born interviewer. He knew how to interview and ask questions and listen to people."

It was also key to show people the *inside* of the library. From the outside, the Carnegie building still looked impressive and gorgeous. What could possibly be wrong?

AN AGING CARNEGIE LIBRARY

Things were getting worse at the central library on Sixth Street.

"The carpet is what I remember most," said Carol Hale. "It was green and held together by duct tape. I took my boys to preschool story hour. Everyone sat on the floor on that mangy carpet."

Paint was also peeling. "The color on the walls!" exclaimed TADL librarian Sandy Robey. "It was the color of little plastic baby dolls, pinkish-orange. It was ghastly."

"Our magazines were in a closet," said Katheryn Carrier, TADL librarian who began working at the Carnegie library in 1987. "We couldn't keep back issues." Financial records were stored in a bathroom, and there were traffic jams at the circulation desk.

Adult fiction was located upstairs in the mezzanine with a steep metal staircase leading to it.

"All the fiction was upstairs in the round part and not accessible to anyone with a disability. Staff had to run up the stairs," said Martha Vreeland, who was assistant director at that time. "You couldn't browse." Fiction was up above and nonfiction was below.

"It was very dark because the shelves covered the windows," said Fred Nelson. "Shelves were up against the windows because there was nowhere else to put them."

"We had more books than we had shelves," said Robey. "So Martha [Vreeland] went out and bought plastic dish pans." The dish pans became extra "shelves." They were filled with books and sat about on the floor. "I was always crawling around on the floor," said Robey. But too much time near the carpet gave Robey bad allergies. She went to her doctor.

"Where do you work?" he asked.

"The Library."

"You have to quit your job. There's all sorts of book dust there and the carpet's a million years old!"

All the fiction was upstairs...not accessible to anyone with a disability.

She didn't quit. Books continued to overflow. Library pages, whose task was to re-shelve books, didn't know what to do. One library page was resourceful. "She checked out about twenty books because she couldn't find room for them and took them home!" said Vreeland.

Some of the shelf-crowding was purposeful. "We stopped weeding books because we wanted it to look overcrowded," McGuire confided to Ann Swaney, NMC librarian.

The bookshelf situation was so crowded that Don Pratt, TADL board president, took to storing the overload in his garage, twelve miles away. Library staff made sure to note the location in the card catalog.

"The card told you 'Pratt's garage,'" said Grace Rudd. "Don could find it."

League of Women Voters member Ellie Long helped conduct a survey of library patrons early in 1996.

The library catalog itself took up a fair amount of space. There were three long rows of wooden drawers holding the card catalog. Even though it was the mid-1990s, there was only one public computer.

There were so many books, however, the weight load of books upstairs in the mezzanine threatened the building's structure. The bookshelves downstairs became part of the support system holding the ceiling up. It was also not air-conditioned. "It got so hot up there, we'd sometimes close the department," said Vreeland.

Downstairs had its own problems. There were stairs, but no regular elevator. "The elevator was a freight elevator," said Vreeland. "You had to have staff take you up or down." "It was a hand-operated elevator. You didn't punch a button, someone had to operate it," said Dawn Buchanan. Staff had to pull a gate across each time they operated the elevator and it could stop between floors. The freight elevator came up in the reference area, and downstairs it opened right into staff offices where they worked, wedged in behind the staircase and in the hallway. Staff shared one computer.

The basement housed Sight & Sound, plus staff work areas and space for children's Story Time. "Down in the basement there was a big trash can sitting on the table catching a drip. It sat there forever. For *years*," said Robey.

Navigating the different levels of the building and the 1960s entrance with double glass doors was challenging, too, especially for a librarian with a cartload full of books. "The dropbox for returned books was outside. Outside on the sidewalk," explained Robey. "I spilled books over countless times. It was so awkward getting full carts through those doors. It was a tough library to work at."

"The condition of Carnegie was so wretched. People referred to it as the dump," said John Trezise, former TADL board member. "There was no good place to sit around and read. It was just hopeless."

"We did not have the room to function," said Fred Nelson, "If not for the spectacular staff, it wouldn't have functioned at all. We had 16,000 square feet and thirteen off-street parking spots."

One winter, part of the roof collapsed. "Ice broke the ceiling," said Vreeland. "Water came gushing down the stairs like a waterfall."

It was high time for a new library building.

For those who couldn't see it in person, Citizens for Libraries took their show on the road. David Hacker and Shirley Murray co-chaired the public relations committee. Hacker was the main speaker, but he often put slides in upside down or in the wrong order, so Murray handled the slide projector.

The slides started off showing state-of-the-art buildings around town. The refurbished Park Place, expanded facilities at Munson hospital, and the brand-new Visitor Center. Then Hacker showed Carnegie's front door.

"You can't even *use* the front door anymore," Hacker exclaimed. "You must go in through the wing and enter a labyrinth. The whole building is a disaster for the disabled."

Then he showed pictures of Carnegie's crowded inside. Stacks of books piled on the floor. Sight & Sound "filled to the gills" with bins and temporary shelving.

"Every book added requires a book to be thrown away!" he fumed.

"That was the picture that really convinced people," said Murray. "No room on the shelves for books. And so many books were shoddy looking."

He showed pictures of staff workspaces. Jill Bert, the storyteller, in an airless basement. Dawn Buchanan, administrative assistant, in a cubbyhole under the stairs. Martha Vreeland, assistant director, with her hands over her face, embarrassed to be showing the library's storage room. He pulled in slides from libraries with similar service populations: Livonia, Lake Orion, and Midland in Michigan. Libraries elsewhere, like Delaware, Ohio. Even Cadillac had a better library. People were shocked by the contrast.

"No other community project could make a bigger improvement or benefit more people," Hacker proclaimed. "We rest our case."

Together Hacker and Murray went to the senior center, men's groups, church groups, and Parent Teacher Organizations and showed slides of the deplorable conditions of the old library building. Dick Rosser sometimes spoke at meetings, too.

"When Rosser would show up he'd get raucous and enthusiastic. He was entertaining," said Trezise. "Active, arm waving. He made big promises. Sometimes over the top. He was overpromising, but effective."

A Reluctant Board

Although citizens were getting fired up and organizing to support the new library, the library board wasn't so sure. The failed millage from 1991, just four years before, still rankled. The board had retreated and it was difficult to rouse them.

"The board seemed kind of quiet," said Martha Vreeland. "They'd been burned."

League of Women Voters representatives began regularly attending board meetings, speaking up for libraries and presenting their hard-earned data. They came armed with statistics and research, telling the board exactly how big a library should be for a city of this size.

"Our present library facilities, designed to serve the small town of Traverse City 90 years ago, are now woefully inadequate for a county-wide, heavily professional population of about 65,000 people," said Judith Halsted. Halsted attended every TADL board meeting.

"They had done the homework. You like to speak to people's hearts, but you also need to talk about brass tacks," said Peg Siciliano. "They were able to do that."

It was hard to say no to such a determined set of women. League members not only attended TADL board meetings, but invited McGuire and the library trustees, one or two at a time, to their own Library Action Committee meetings, held in private homes. Though the trustees never stayed for soup dinner, these were intimate meetings, and often transformative, letting board members and League members get to know each other better. "What are your priorities? Why did you join the board?" the women asked. The last question for the visitor was always: "What can the League of Women Voters do to help you achieve your goals?" Library board members began to realize that the library truly meant something to the community, and that this quiet but unwavering group of women was about to do something big.

Every book added requires a book to be thrown away!

The board began to turn around. That change also accelerated as the make-up of the TADL board shifted. Fred Nelson helped recruit new board members like John Welch, who knew the financial side and could be a good listener, and Doug Brown, an astute administrator at Munson Medical Center. Frank Senger, publisher of the *Record-Eagle* also joined the board, and Diane Viskochil, a Traverse City foreign language teacher, who brought new passion, insight, and energy.

"Citizens for Libraries seriously pushed the board," said Welch. "The board had to catch that enthusiasm."

Despite their recent failure, the new TADL board grew energized again about the idea of a new library building. Community support never seemed stronger, and the most vocal opposition had died down. Suzy Connor, who'd effectively elevated historic preservation and Central Neighborhood concerns, moved out of town for family reasons. Many people still cared about historic preservation, but opposition to moving the library was not as well organized.

More and more people began to agree with Carol Hale: "Get rid of that mangy carpet and move somewhere else!"

Site of the future Woodmere Library at the north end of Boardman Lake, near the train depot. Other landmarks are the Wastewater Treatment Plant, where the lake flows into the Boardman River, and Cone Drive Manufacturing directly across the lake. Trains were still active there in the early 1960s.

I'd move to Traverse City just for the library!

Mariel Magoun

CHAPTER 11

Finding a New Home

SITE SELECTION

Where should Traverse City put a new library? Downtown? At the Commons? In the center of the county? Some people suggested putting the main library out on Old Mission Peninsula.

The question of siting fell to a volunteer committee that included Bryan Crough, Ted Kidd, Fred Nelson, and John Trezise. Twelve sites were considered, most of them vacant. Just like the Great Site Fight nearly a hundred years before, various sites were proposed and championed, but selecting a site this time proceeded in a cooperative, orderly manner.

"Being a city fellow," said Nelson. "I really wanted the library in town."

Downtown was a popular option. Downtown advocates, like Bryan Crough of the Downtown Development Authority, hoped the new library would be located on a downtown street, like State Street, or on West Bay where the coal-fired power plant stood. The power plant was still partially functioning, but perhaps they could buy it and remove it. "Everyone was thinking about the beautiful view of the bay," said TADL board member Diane Viskochil. But being an active industrial site, it might well bring contamination issues, and there was limited space for parking at the bay. Years later, the power plant was demolished and the land was turned into the Open Space. The State Street location became a parking structure.

Others thought Tenth Street would be a good location, near McGough's feed store. Brown's lumberyard was going out of business next door, which made the property available, and the site overlooked the river. Still, the lumberyard site did not have great visibility; it was hidden back in a corner, off the main streets. Later that site became Oryana Community Co-op.

Being near the Boardman River was an attractive option, however. There was a beautiful spot at the top of the hill on Park Drive, south of South Airport Road that might do. It had a building already with good vistas of the river, but the river frontage was expensive. It was not very accessible either. There was no stop light to reach the site and safely cross South Airport.

The Commons was a popular suggestion, but also divisive. Some people thought it should only be kept as open parkland. Why clutter up the Commons with a large building and parking area? The Commons location also involved considerable red tape. The land had protective covenants that meant inevitable delays, and realistically, it would take years to be able to build there. The library hoped to break ground quickly, as soon as the spring of 1997.

Some suggested putting the library over by Oleson's grocery store on Three Mile Road, because that location was the center of the county's population.

"The geographic center of the U.S. is in western Nebraska!" pointed out Nelson. "But no one moves the U.S. capital out there."

While the site committee was examining Traverse City locations, some member libraries asked, "Why can't the library be built in Interlochen? Or Fife Lake or the Peninsula? Then Traverse City people can go *there*."

Walkability was a main factor. Neighborhood children could currently walk to the Sixth Street library. Where could they put the library that would still be walkable?

Another in-town choice was the old Traverse City Iron Works property at the corner of Cass and Lake streets. It was a central location, but it was pricey. And then there was an old abandoned factory site on Woodmere Avenue near the railroad tracks.

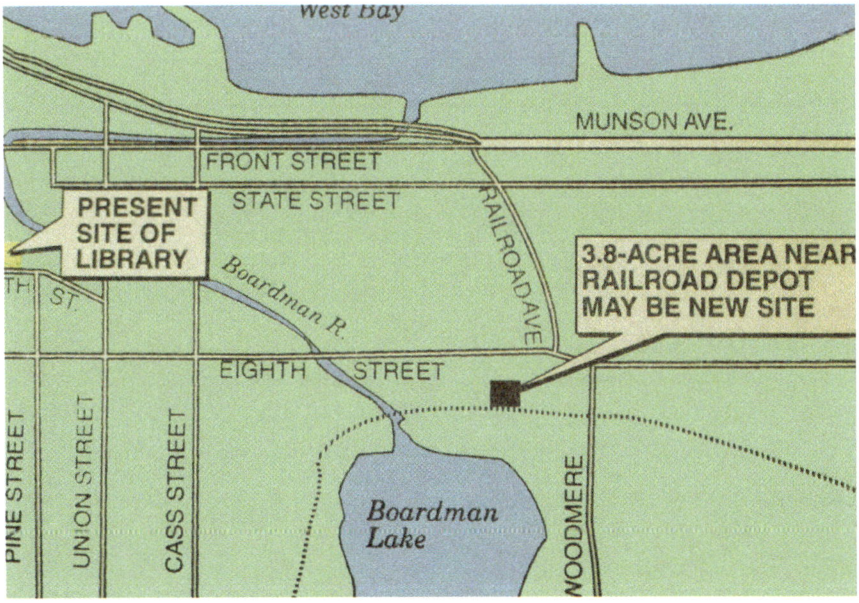

Map showing location of proposed Woodmere library site, as shown in the *Traverse City Record-Eagle,* March 1, 1996.

"The Woodmere property was a third of the price, and bigger!" said Nelson. "And just about geographically the center of town."

Woodmere was a gritty, industrial part of town. A grain elevator had been there over the years. Remnants of the building were still there, but mostly it was vacant, unused land. Factories used to occupy the land, sited next to nearby train tracks, including the Beitner Chair Factory, which made dowels, curtain rods, spindles, and chair bottoms. Originally, the land in that area had been used by Henry Hull for his sawmill for the Oval Wood Dish factory. A hundred years ago, men had pushed logs with gaff hooks right there on Boardman Lake. The site where they wanted to put the library was an old lumber yard, now more of a junkyard.

They picked this piece of property that was like a railroad yard.

"They picked this piece of property that was like a railroad yard," said Martha Vreeland. "It had loading ramps on it and so on."

"At the time it did not seem like a good location. It was run down," said Dawn Buchanan.

But there was potential. The site selection team had a vision to transform the area.

Part of this vision had been started years before. Fred Nelson remembered his father often talking about the land around Woodmere. "There's a lake there," Jack Nelson would say, discussing the city's potential with friends like Frank Power. "We should be able to do something with this other than an industrial park." Those conversations stuck in Fred Nelson's mind: *there was a lake, a magnificent lake, right near the heart of the city. What a beautiful place for a library!*

"It basically came down to Woodmere and the downtown area," said Trezise. Woodmere was essentially vacant land. The price was much more affordable, and there was plenty of space for both parking and a library building.

Gosh, thought Nelson. *There's enough room to do what we want!* The site team already knew they needed a lot of parking, and downtown sites all had limited parking. "You can't expect people to come into town from Grawn on foot," said Nelson.

Every site had a drawback, and the Woodmere site had two detractions. One was the sewage treatment plant that sat nearby at the head of the lake. The other was accessibility. While it was visible and accessible by car, being right on a main road, the location wasn't very walkable. At the time, there was no TART trail system to connect it to neighborhoods. Still, perhaps that would come.

Woodmere offered empty land. Affordable, roomy land in town. Perhaps siting the library on Woodmere could also give a redevelopment boost to the whole area, including nearby Eighth Street. And although it looked like a junkyard now, it had a prime location: next to Hull Park, just a few feet away from the sparkling waters of Boardman Lake.

Woodmere Site

If Henry Hull could have looked into the future, he would have been astounded to see that he "won" the great Library Site Controversy after all. Nearly a hundred years later, the new district library settled next to Hull Park on Woodmere Avenue.

What happened was this. After the Beitner Chair Factory closed and Oval Wood Dish factory moved to New York, the old factory sites were knocked down. The city of Traverse City bought Henry Hull's factory site in 1926. By then Hull had died, and his estate owned the property. The industrial landscape made way for new open space and public recreation. For years, residents flocked to the area for Fourth of July celebrations, and it became a popular place for picnics and Boy Scout campouts. This open parkland was officially named Hull Park in 1930.

When the library site selection team came looking, they weren't thinking about Hull's old fight with Perry Hannah. Hull's original choice had been Cass Street, after all, not his factory site. In 1996, the Hull Park region was not attractive. It was an abandoned area with an unsavory rcpuation.

But time had a way of evening things out. The Traverse Area Community Sailing program moved in. The Depot area blossomed, and Hull Park was rejuvenated to become beloved parkland again. In 2019, the city spent more than $4.7 million to revitalize Eighth Street.

"The Woodmere library became one of the anchors that helped turn Boardman Lake into the southern recreation anchor of Traverse City," said Peg Siciliano.

Bus Tour

In January 1996, the League of Women Voters and TADL Board President Don Pratt organized a bus tour to visit other libraries around Michigan. This type of "go see" trip was standard practice for the League. Whenever they chose a topic to study, members would research first, then go out and visit in person. They particularly wanted library staff to go. Many of staff had been working for years at the library under substandard conditions and had never seen a modern library.

"Most of the staff didn't realize the potential," said Dawn Buchanan. While Citizens for Libraries included newcomers who'd lived in cities with grander library facilities, most of the local staff had grown up in small towns with similar Carnegie libraries.

The tour would help Traverse City library staff see what was *possible*.

So on Monday, January 8, they loaded up two vans of library staff, board members, and Citizens for Libraries members, and set off downstate for a library bus tour. Twelve staff and five volunteers went on the overnight trip. They visited five libraries in two days, libraries that had been recommended as tour stops by Christine Hage, the Rochester Hills library director. The new library at Rochester Hills was one of the stops, plus Midland, Lake Orion, Bloomfield, and Livonia. Many of these libraries had open designs, completely different from the dark recesses in the Carnegie building.

"They were light and bright," said Halsted. "Larger space, more space in the aisles and between the stacks, and very happy staff." Some had used-book gift shops and cafés.

"No one had their carpet taped together," said Martha Vreeland. "Instead they had *art*. The buildings were so beautiful, big, clean, and fancy."

Jody Clark was impressed with the Bloomfield Township library and got ideas from the Friends of the Library there. "It made our staff realize what they could do. What they could reach for," she said.

Staff also got inspired by touring other libraries' children's areas. One library had a wooden rowboat among the books. "Oh, we need one of those," the Traverse City visitors said. The Lake Orion children's area also had an aquarium, rocking chairs, a play pen, and lots of parenting materials. Staff were also impressed with puppet theaters they saw in children's areas, and decided to include one themselves.

In contrast to the Traverse City library, which functioned, but scraped by, the libraries they toured were attractive and bursting with patrons and programs. "A functioning library is just fine," said Fred Nelson. "But it doesn't attract people."

The Traverse City tour participants marked down their impressions, making notes in 22 categories. "We had a checklist," explained Halsted. "We rated everything, such as the circulation area: 105,000 square feet in Midland, 200,000 volumes..." Categories included visibility, youth area, rest rooms, book return, security, loading docks, meeting rooms, and more. Lake Orion had a noisy heating system. Midland had an excellent book repair room. Rochester Hills had a drive-up window for book pick-ups. The Traverse City staff was turned loose with cameras.

One tip the group learned was that it was not enough to pass a millage to *build* a library building. They also would need a library operating millage to support it. One of the libraries on the tour had done just that: constructed a beautiful new building with no additional money to support it. "It turned out to be a real problem," said Katheryn Carrier.

Judith Halsted and Don Pratt organized the bus tour, but not everyone went. "Mike would not consider closing the library for the trip," said Anne Magoun. "Mike stayed home and ran the library." Still, with much of the staff away on the bus tour, the library would be shorthanded. An eager group of about 12 volunteers stepped in and took 4 to 6-hour shifts, answering the phone, reshelving books, and assisting patrons. They also learned how to operate the clumsy freight elevator.

The bus trip was so successful that later they staged a second tour with stops at northern Michigan libraries in smaller towns like Charlevoix, Petoskey, and Walloon Lake. After each bus tour the staff came back energized, their eyes sparkling with new ideas.

"It opened our eyes about what libraries were doing," said Halsted.

DESIGNING THE WOODMERE LIBRARY

Woodmere Avenue was the chosen site. Although it didn't look like much at the moment—bare ground with tall grass growing up—everyone hoped this rough, industrial site on Boardman Lake would soon host a modern library.

"We're all about lakes up here, and that lake is available on the whole side of the building," said Halsted. "People just fell in love with that site."

The TADL board hired architect Joe Huberty, of Engberg Anderson Design Partnership, headquartered in Milwaukee. Huberty specialized in designing libraries. The library architect would help make sure that the building really worked well for library purposes, but it was also important to have a local architectural firm on the team. Engberg Anderson selected AAI from Traverse City. AAI architect Bob Holdeman and Bill Williams of Engberg Anderson worked with Huberty to come up with the design concept. Holdeman developed the form and general aesthetics for the building, and AAI partner Bob Sommerville was active during the construction stage.

"The input from the public was through a rather intense process called a 'design charrette,'" said Holdeman. "Much of the original design concepts from the process resulted in what we have today."

Fred Nelson was part of the design charrette, which took place in May 1996. When he first saw the proposed layout, the library's staircase was much narrower. "This will not do," remembered Fred Nelson. "It's got to look grand. We wanted the light and the view."

One drawback was that there could be no basement. The water table was too high. Instead of a basement, the architects created an attic, a third floor for storage, not accessible to the public.

Soon a vision for a new library building began to emerge. It would have a clock tower to look like a train station, connecting the library visually to the railroad depot next door. The new library would retain echoes of the Carnegie design, including a "bump" out towards the water. And, the crowning glory, a panoramic view: a whole panel of windows overlooking the lake.

Library staff had big ideas for the children's department. Although there was currently no full-time children's librarian, they knew that was coming. They envisioned a large children's room with display cases, a community room, and space to show videos for children.

Meanwhile, the Friends of the Library were looking at their role. What could they contribute? For years, they'd been charging $20 membership dues and additional donations came in. The small amount in their bank account had risen dramatically. "Bob Hughes said, 'You have to do something with the money.' It was in the tens of thousands by the time he really roared," said Jody Clark.

The Friends of the Library contributed $5,000 toward construction of the third floor attic storage room, and also purchased kitchen appliances for the new community room. The large community room (later the McGuire Room), was rated for 160 people and equipped with a real kitchen. The third floor attic was primarily a place to store books, particularly donated books for the annual used book sale. "We'd been storing boxes of books in our homes and we were really tired of it," said Jody Clark. The floor had to be reinforced to hold the weight of all the books. The Friends soon took over the job of hosting the library's annual used book sale. They also paid for setting up a small Friends of the Library gift shop under the library staircase.

TRAVERSE AREA DISTRICT
LIBRARY

During the design process, there was much discussion about the placement of hands on the new clock logo. There are still no hands on the clock.

"So many people were working together," said Vreeland. "The Friends researched coffee pots!"

When the design team decided on having a clock tower, it made sense to incorporate the clock face as part of the library's logo. It was distinctive and attractive, and it tied the library to its railroad-dominated site history. But they fretted over what time the clock's hands should point to. "They never could decide," said Karen Nielsen, who worked on the Get Out the Vote campaign. "To this day, I'll bet there's no hands on [the logo.]"

McGuire worked closely with the architect. They chose art glass made from pressed glass over the circulation desk. "They held out for Italian blue tiles on the outside trim," said Nancy McGuire. "It mirrored the lake so well." Inside, the color scheme was blue and green, too, to fit the northern lakes and forest.

Diane Viskochil joined the library board in 1991. A French teacher at the high school, Viskochil applied for the board position because the library had limited hours and she knew students and working parents needed more access and she wanted to do something about it. "The library was not open on Sundays and had very limited evening hours, too." She was one of few women on the board, and also one of the younger members. When it came time to design the new Woodmere library, Viskochil jumped right in with her ideas, often clashing with older board members.

"I envisioned a computer lab," she said. "[They] thought that was stupid. [I said,]'I don't think you get it. Computers are going to be necessary and you're going to need a lab.'" The board was already in discussions with a computer company to purchase two public computers. "They thought two computers were enough for a big huge library!" said Viskochil.

Some of the older board members were gravely concerned about offering computers. They were worried patrons would use the computer lab to go on porn websites. Viskochil knew otherwise. Computers were entering schools, computers were essential for school work, and she knew library users would need a quality computer lab. "We needed to go into the 21st century," said Viskochil. In the past, McGuire controlled the library's public computer. "You would go to Mike and he would look stuff up for you."

Attitudes on the board were based on faulty societal assumptions, too. "Why would kids in high school or poor people need to use a computer?" some asked. Or: "If people want computers, they can buy them at home."

After some heated discussions, a large room upstairs was included in the design for public computing. Thanks to Viskochil and vocal support from trustees like Frank Senger and Fred Nelson, the board relented and placed an order for twenty computers, instead of two.

"It turns out to be one of the most popular features of the new library," said John Welch.

Another design struggle arose over parking. Parking had been limited—almost desperate—for years on Sixth Street. Now there was a chance for 125 parking spaces, but with increased patronage, wouldn't the new library need more? Viskochil and others pushed to buy additional land across the railroad tracks. The landowner was willing to sell, but the purchase stalled. At the time, the board did not think they needed any more parking.

"The biggest debate, surprisingly, was the drive-through," said library board member John Welch. "They'd never heard of such a thing! Why would you have one? Well, it would be nice to pull up and drop off books." Viskochil, Welch, and others successfully advocated for a book return drive-through, which was originally designed also to have a drive-through window for book pick-ups.

When Viskochil's modern ideas were dismissed by the board, League members and Citizens for Libraries spoke up. Some of the board were "old school." "They didn't take questions or suggestions from females very well," said Viskochil. But Citizens for Libraries leaders, like Ellie Long, consistently attended board meetings. In fact, Long attended every single one. "There was Anne Magoun and there was Judy [Halsted]," said Viskochil. "They would bring up those same points during public question time. They were very supportive of me."

Viskochil was involved on the decoration committee, which included furnishings. Together with McGuire, Dawn Farley, Vicki Carpenter, and Beth Bynum, she picked out items like the carpet, tables, and chairs.

"The chairs!" said Nancy McGuire. "Mike loved the chairs. They were big and nice and comfy. You could just curl up and read."

Some items didn't have to be purchased. The library placed some original round tables from the Carnegie building in the new genealogy area.

The committee chose a carpet that would be sturdy, with blue-green tones and orange wave-like flecks. Here again, Viskochil's years of teaching came into play in a practical way. Carpets in local schools, in contrast, often showed every bit of lint with their red and black color scheme.

"It's a very natural area," said Vicki Carpenter. "There's water and trees, and we pulled in the blues and greens and different shades of browns—sort of an earth sense, but not too earthy. And we tried to make it fun, too, and use leaves in the patterns and fabrics." They also used cherry wood for interior design as a nod to the local cherry industry.

Then there was the kitchen. The board wanted a community room, but hadn't considered including a kitchen behind the scenes. After years of making crêpes, nachos, and enchiladas with high school language students, Viskochil knew a community room needed a kitchen. "You're going to want to have coffee, cookies," she said. "And you need a way to clean those dishes and towels. You're going to need a washer and dryer, dishwasher and sink."

Finally, there was the roof. Viskochil was tired of public buildings leaking.

"I worked in four schools in this district, and all of the roofs leaked. We put cherry buckets under them. Big, white cherry buckets all over the place to catch the leaks." She suggested a copper roof, the type she'd admired on trips to Quebec.

"Diane, do you have any idea how much copper costs?"

"No."

"You're not from around here, are you? You have a champagne pocket book."

Copper was too expensive, but the library did get a metal roof. There are no leaks, though ice dams remain a problem.

We get to build a library once every fifty years around here, so let's build one that will be viable.

The new library would be 58,000 square feet, nearly four times bigger than the old Carnegie building, even with the addition. It seemed overly big to some locals.

"We get to build a library once every fifty years around here," said Viskochil. "So let's build one that will be viable."

The library board wasn't the only one involved in designing the library. Library staff knew what they wanted and had many ideas to contribute after their bus tour, and the design was also opened up to the public through a special design committee. Names were chosen randomly.

"My name was chosen from the phone book," said Barb Berry, also a long-term League of Women Voters member. "Twenty people came to the public input."

The public offered feedback on the community room and computer lab. They suggested making the community room bigger, to fit

Although librarians in other districts warned against odd "architectural features," the Woodmere library ended up with an architecturally interesting, large hole in the middle of the second floor.

more people. Berry was very pleased to be involved. Not only was she a League member, but also a school librarian. "I'd visited lots of libraries and knew Carnegie was not it. I knew what a library should look like."

One peculiar feature of the Woodmere library design was the "hole in the floor." The architects liked the idea, but the librarians weren't so sure. Why give up precious floor space by inserting a great big open area above the circulation desk? Besides, noise would travel straight up from the ground floor to the second floor.

Katheryn Carrier remembered advice from fellow librarians on the bus tour: "Don't let the architects sell you an architectural feature," they warned. Many libraries had been burned by agreeing to big, open staircases. "We still ended up with a hole in the floor," she said. "The architect assured us [the hole] could be covered over at some point."

"There were supposed to be two holes," said Sandy Robey. "'Let's just have one,' somebody said. 'Because the sound will come up.'" That's just what it did. Staff strung flags across the opening to dampen the noise, but upstairs reference librarians still scurried to answer the phone when it rang downstairs, and ground floor chatter rose to disturb patrons reading in the comfy armchairs above.

More than twenty years later, the library's strategic plan calls for removing the "hole in the floor."

LEAGUE OF WOMEN VOTERS GRAND TRAVERSE AREA LIBRARY COMMITTEE

(participation varied between 1993 and 1999)

Ronnie Alff
Barb Berry
Dorothy Crocker
Peg Featherstone
Marianne Fields
Ruth Gamble
Judy Halsted
Arline Howe
Pat Laarman
Ellie Long
Anne Magoun
Darlene Miller
Shirley Murray
Betty Parker
Anne Rock
Grace Rudd
Frances Spedding
Ruth Taylor
Pat Trezise
Martha Vreeland
Jane Watts

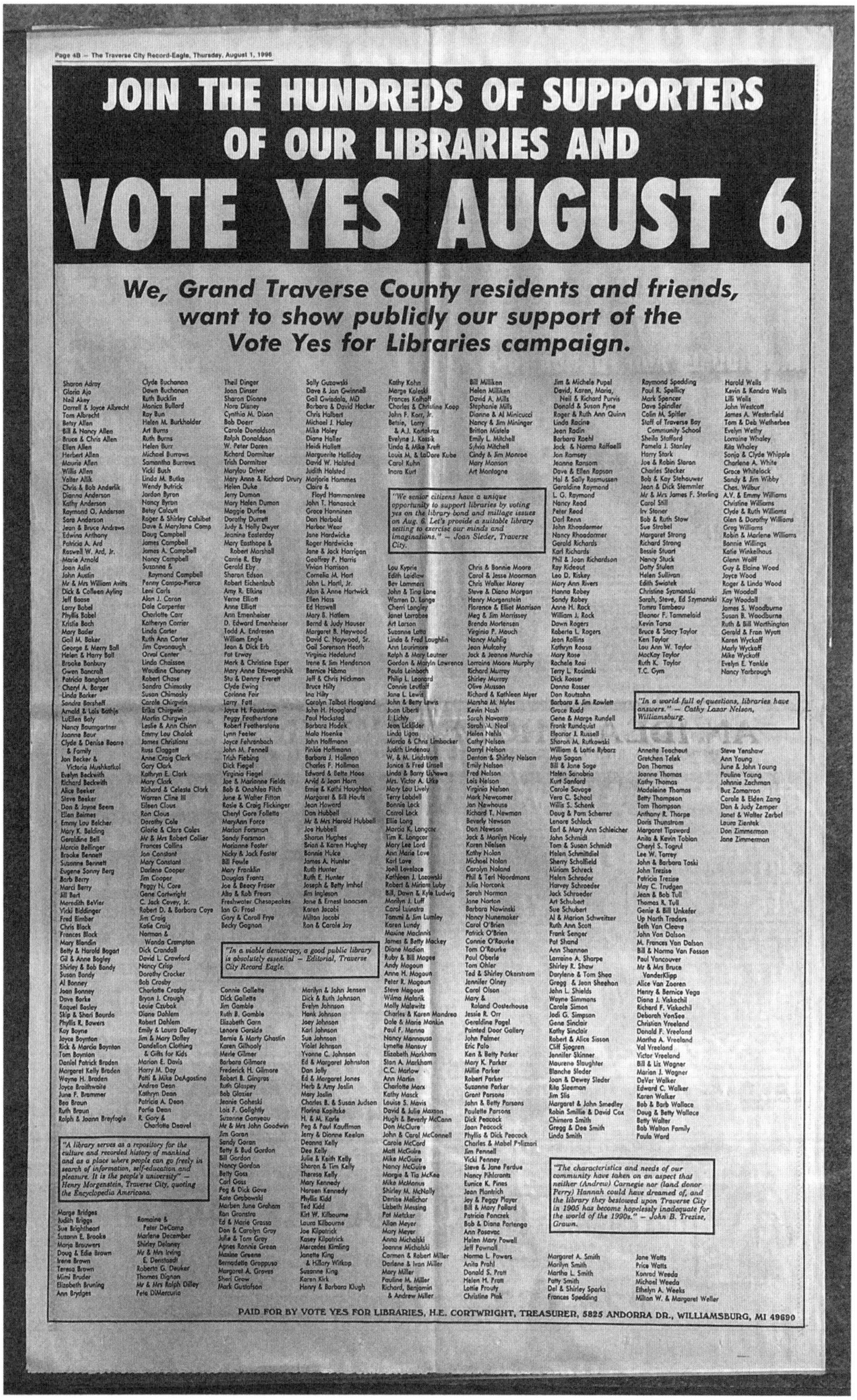

Page 4B — The Traverse City Record-Eagle, Thursday, August 1, 1996

JOIN THE HUNDREDS OF SUPPORTERS OF OUR LIBRARIES AND

VOTE YES AUGUST 6

We, Grand Traverse County residents and friends, want to show publicly our support of the Vote Yes for Libraries campaign.

Sharon Adray
Gloria Ajo
Neil Akey
Darrell & Joyce Albrecht
Tom Albrecht
Betsy Allen
Bill & Nancy Allen
Bruce & Chris Allen
Ellen Allen
Herbert Allen
Maurie Allen
Willis Allen
Valter Allik
Chris & Bob Anderlik
Dianna Anderson
Kathy Anderson
Raymond O. Anderson
Sara Anderson
Jean & Bruce Andrews
Edwina Anthony
Patricia A. Ard
Roswell W. Ard, Jr.
Marie Arnold
Joan Aslin
John Austin
Mr & Mrs William Avitts
Dick & Colleen Ayling
Jeff Baase
Larry Babel
Phyllis Babel
Kristie Bach
Mary Bader
Gail M. Baker
George & Merry Ball
Helen & Harry Ball
Brooke Banbury
Gwen Bancroft
Patricia Banghart
Cheryl A. Barger
Linda Barker
Sandra Barsheff
Arnold & Lois Bathje
LuEllen Baty
Nancy Baumgartner
Joanne Baur
Clyde & Denise Bearre & Family
Jon Becker & Victoria Mushkatkol
Evelyn Beckwith
Richard Beckwith
Alice Beeker
Steve Beeker
Don & Jayne Beem
Ellen Beirnes
Emmy Lou Belcher
Mary K. Belding
Geraldine Bell
Marcia Bellinger
Brooke Bennett
Suzanne Bennett
Eugene Sonny Berg
Barb Berry
Marci Berry
Jill Bert
Meredith BeVier
Vicki Biddinger
Fred Bimber
Chris Black
Frances Black
Mary Blandin
Betty & Harold Bogart
Gil & Anne Bogley
Shirley & Bob Bondy
Susan Bondy
Al Bonney
Joan Bonney
Dave Borke
Raquel Bosley
Skip & Shari Bourdo
Phyllis R. Bowers
Kay Boyne
Joyce Boynton
Rick & Marcia Boynton
Tom Boynton
Daniel Patrick Braden
Margaret Kelly Braden
Wayne H. Braden
Joyce Braithwaite
June F. Brammer
Bea Braun
Ruth Braun
Ralph & Joann Breyfogle

"A library serves as a repository for the culture and recorded history of mankind and as a place where people can go freely in search of information, self-education and pleasure. It is the people's university" — Henry Morgenstein, Traverse City, quoting the Encyclopedia Americana.

Marge Bridges
Judith Briggs
Sue Brightheart
Suzann E. Brooke
Marja Brouwers
Doug & Edie Brown
Irene Brown
Teresa Brown
Mimi Bruder
Elizabeth Bruning
Ann Brydges

Clyde Buchanan
Dawn Buchanan
Ruth Bucklin
Monica Bullard
Ray Bun
Helen M. Burkholder
Art Burns
Ruth Burns
Helen Burr
Michael Burrows
Samantha Burrows
Vicki Bush
Linda M. Butka
Wendy Butrick
Jordan Byron
Nancy Byron
Betsy Calcutt
Roger & Shirley Calsibet
Dave & MaryJane Camp
Doug Campbell
James Campbell
James A. Campbell
Nancy Campbell
Suzanne & Raymond Campbell
Penny Campo-Pierce
Leni Carls
Alan J. Caron
Dale Carpenter
Charlotte Carr
Katheryn Carrier
Linda Carter
Ruth Ann Carter
Jim Cavanaugh
Orval Center
Linda Chaisson
Waudine Chaney
Robert Chase
Sandra Chimosky
Susan Chimosky
Carole Chirgwin
Erika Chirgwin
Martin Chirgwin
Leslie & Ann Chinn
Emmy Lou Cholak
James Christians
Russ Claggett
Anne Craig Clark
Gary Clark
Kathryn E. Clark
Mary Clark
Richard & Celeste Clark
Warren Cline III
Eileen Clous
Ron Clous
Dorothy Cole
Gloria & Clare Coles
Mr & Mrs Robert Collier
Frances Collins
Jon Constant
Mary Constant
Darlene Cooper
Jim Cooper
Peggy N. Core
Gene Cortwright
C. Jack Covey, Jr.
Robert D. & Barbara Coye
Jim Craig
Katie Craig
Norman & Wanda Crampton
Dick Crandall
David L. Crawford
Nancy Crisp
Dorothy Crocker
Bob Crosby
Charlotte Crosby
Bryon J. Crough
Louie Czubak
Diane Dahlem
Robert Dahlem
Emily & Laura Dalley
Jim & Mary Dalley
Dandelion Clothing & Gifts for Kids
Marion E. Davis
Harry M. Day
Patti & Mike DeAgostino
Andrea Dean
Kathryn Dean
Patricia A. Dean
Portia Dean
R. Gary & Charlotte Deavel

Romaine & Peter DeCamp
Marlene December
Shirley Delaney
Mr & Mrs Irving E. Denstaedt
Roberta G. Deuker
Thomas Dignan
Mr & Mrs Ralph Dilley
Pete DiMercurio

Theil Dinger
Joan Dinser
Sharon Dionne
Nora Disney
Cynthia M. Dixon
Bob Doerr
Carole Donaldson
Ralph Donaldson
W. Peter Doren
Richard Dormitzer
Trish Dormitzer
Marylou Driver
Mary Anne & Richard Drury
Helen Duke
Jerry Dumon
Mary Helen Dumon
Maggie Durfee
Dorothy Durrett
Judy & Holly Dwyer
Jeanine Easterday
Mary Easthope & Robert Marshall
Carrie R. Eby
Gerald Eby
Sharon Edson
Robert Eichenlaub
Amy R. Elkins
Verne Elliott
Anne Elliott
Ann Emenheiser
D. Edward Emenheiser
Todd A. Endresen
William Engle
Jean & Dick Erb
Pat Erway
Mark & Christine Esper
Mary Anne Ettawageshik
Stu & Denny Everett
Clyde Ewing
Corinne Fair
Larry Fatt
Joyce H. Faustman
Peggy Featherstone
Robert Featherstone
Lynn Feeter
Joyce Fehrenbach
John M. Fennell
Trish Fiebing
Dick Fiegel
Virginia Fiegel
Joe & Marianne Fields
Bob & Onahlea Fitch
June & Walter Fitton
Rosie & Craig Flickinger
Cheryl Gore Follette
MaryAnn Force
Marian Forsman
Sandy Forsman
Marianne Foster
Nicky & Jack Foster
Bill Fowle
Mary Franklin
Douglas Frantz
Joe & Beecy Fraser
Alta & Rob Frears
Freshwater Chesapeakes
Ian G. Frost
Gary & Caroll Frye
Becky Gagnon

"In a viable democracy, a good public library is absolutely essential — Editorial, Traverse City Record Eagle.

Connie Gallette
Dick Gallette
Jim Gamble
Ruth B. Gamble
Elizabeth Garn
Lenore Garside
Bernie & Marty Ghastin
Karen Gilhooly
Merle Gilmer
Barbara Gilmore
Frederick H. Gilmore
Robert B. Gingras
Ruth Glaspey
Bob Glazier
Jeanie Goheski
Lois F. Golightly
Suzanne Gonyeau
Mr & Mrs John Goodwin
Jim Goran
Sandy Goran
Betty & Bud Gordon
Bill Gordon
Nancy Gordon
Betty Goss
Carl Goss
Peg & Dick Gove
Kate Grabowski
Marben June Graham
Ron Granstra
Ed & Marie Grassa
Don & Carolyn Gray
Julie & Tom Gray
Agnes Ronnie Green
Maxine Greene
Bernadette Groppuso
Margaret A. Groves
Shari Grow
Mark Gustafson

Sally Guzowski
Dave & Jan Gwinnell
Gail Gwizdala, MD
Barbara & David Hacker
Chris Halbert
Michael J. Haley
Mike Haley
Diane Haller
Heidi Hallett
Marguerite Halliday
David W. Halsted
Judith Halsted
Marjorie Hammes
Claire & Floyd Hammontree
John T. Hanasack
Grace Hanninen
Don Harbold
Harbor Wear
Jane Hardwicke
Roger Hardwicke
Jane & Jack Harrigan
Geoffrey P. Harris
Vivian Harrison
Cornelia M. Hart
John L. Hartl, Jr.
Alan & Anne Hartwick
Ellen Hass
Ed Haswell
Mary B. Hatlem
Bernd & Judy Hauser
Margaret B. Haywood
David C. Haywood, Sr.
Gail Sorenson Heath
Virginia Hedelund
Irene & Jim Henderson
Bernice Hibma
Jeff & Chris Hickman
Bruce Hilty
Ina Hilty
Carolyn Talbot Hoagland
John H. Hoagland
Paul Hockstad
Barbara Hodek
Mato Hoenke
John Hoffmann
Pinkie Hoffmann
Barbara J. Hollman
Charles F. Hollman
Edward & Bette Hoos
Arvid & Jean Horn
Ernie & Kathi Houghton
Margaret & Bill Houts
Jean Howard
Dan Hubbell
Mr & Mrs Harold Hubbell
Joe Hubbell
Sharon Hughes
Brian & Karen Hughey
Bonnie Hulce
James A. Hunter
Ruth Hunter
Ruth E. Hunter
Joseph & Betty Imhof
Jim Ingleson
Jane & Ernest Isaacsen
Karen Jacobi
Milton Jacobi
Ron & Carole Joy

Marilyn & John Jensen
Dick & Ruth Johnson
Evelyn Johnson
Hank Johnson
Joey Johnson
Karl Johnson
Sue Johnson
Violet Johnson
Yvonne C. Johnson
Ed & Margaret Johnston
Dan Jolly
Ed & Margaret Jones
Herb & Amy Joslin
Mary Joslin
Charles B. & Susan Judson
Florina Kapitzke
H. & M. Karle
Peg & Paul Kauffman
Jerry & Dianne Keelan
Deanna Kelly
Dee Kelly
Julie & Keith Kelly
Sharon & Tim Kelly
Theresa Kelly
Mary Kennedy
Noreen Kennedy
Phyllis Kidd
Ted Kidd
Kirt W. Kilbourne
Laura Kilbourne
Joe Kilpatrick
Kasey Kilpatrick
Mercedes Kimling
Janette King & Hillary Witkop
Suzanne King
Karen Kirk
Henry & Barbara Klugh

Kathy Kohn
Marge Koleski
Frances Kolhoff
Charles & Christine Koop
John F. Korr, Jr.
Betsie, Larry & A.J. Kortokrax
Evelyne J. Kossik
Linda & Mike Kreft
Louis M. & LaDore Kube
Carol Kuhn
Inora Kurt

"We senior citizens have a unique opportunity to support libraries by voting yes on the library bond and millage issues on Aug. 6. Let's provide a suitable library setting to exercise our minds and imaginations." — Joan Sleder, Traverse City.

Lou Kyprie
Edith Laidlaw
Bev Lammers
John & Tina Lane
Warren D. Lange
Cherri Langley
Janet Larrabee
Art Larson
Suzanne Latta
Linda & Fred Laughlin
Ann Laurimore
Ralph & Mary Lautner
Gordon & Marlyn Lawrence
Paula Leinbach
Philip L. Leonard
Connie Leutloff
Jane L. Lewis
John & Betty Lewis
Joan Liberti
J. Lichty
Jean Licklider
Linda Ligon
Marcia & Chris Limbocker
Judith Lindenau
W. & M. Lindstrom
Janice & Fred Linsell
Linda & Barry Lishawa
Mrs. Victor A. Litke
Mary Lou Lively
Terry Lobdell
Bonnie Lock
Carrol Lock
Ellie Long
Marcia K. Longcor
Tim K. Longcor
Mary Lee Lord
Ann Marie Love
Karl Love
Joell Lovelace
Kathleen J. Lozowski
Robert & Miriam Luby
Bill, Dawn & Kyle Ludwig
Marilyn J. Luff
Carol Luinstra
Tammi & Jim Lumley
Karen Lundy
Maxine MacInnis
James & Betty Mackey
Diane Madion
Ruby & Bill Magee
Andy Magoun
Anne H. Magoun
Peter R. Magoun
Steve Magoun
Wilma Malarik
Molly Malewitz
Charles & Karen Mandrea
Dale & Marie Mankin
Paul F. Manna
Nancy Mannausa
Lynette Mansuy
Elizabeth Markham
Stan A. Markham
C.C. Marlow
Ann Martin
Charlotte Marx
Kathy Masck
Louise S. Mavis
David & Julie Maxson
Hugh & Beverly McCann
Don McClure
John & Carol McConnell
Carole McCord
Matt McGuire
Mike McGuire
Nancy McGuire
Margie & Tia McKee
Mike McManus
Shirley M. McNally
Denise Melichar
Lizbeth Messing
Pat Metzker
Allan Meyer
Mary Meyer
Anna Michalski
Joanne Michalski
Carmen & Robert Miller
Darlene & Ivan Miller
Mary Miller
Pauline M. Miller
Richard, Benjamin & Andrew Miller

Bill Milliken
Helen Milliken
David A. Mills
Stephanie Mills
Dianne & Al Minicucci
Nancy & Jim Mininger
Britton Mistele
Emily L. Mitchell
Sylvia Mitchell
Cindy & Jim Monroe
Mary Monson
Art Montagne

Chris & Bonnie Moore
Carol & Jesse Moorman
Chris Walker Morey
Steve & Diana Morgan
Henry Morgenstein
Florence & Elliot Morrison
Meg & Jim Morrissey
Brenda Mortensen
Virginia P. Mouch
Nancy Muhlig
Jean Mulcahy
Jack & Jeanne Murchie
Lorraine Moore Murphy
Richard Murray
Shirley Murray
Olive Musson
Richard & Kathleen Myer
Marsha M. Myles
Kevin Nash
Sarah Navarro
Sarah M. Neal
Helen Nehls
Cathy Nelson
Darryl Nelson
Denton & Shirley Nelson
Emily Nelson
Fred Nelson
Lois Nelson
Virginia Nelson
Mark Newcomer
Jan Newhouse
Richard T. Newman
Beverly Newson
Don Newson
Jack & Marilyn Nicely
Karen Nielsen
Kathy Nolan
Michael Nolan
Carolyn Noland
Phil & Teri Noordmans
Julia Norconk
Sarah Norman
Jane Norton
Barbara Nowinski
Nancy Nunemaker
Carol O'Brien
Patrick O'Brien
Connie O'Rourke
Tom O'Rourke
Paul Oberle
Tom Ohler
Ted & Shirley Okerstrom
Jennifer Olney
Carol Olson
Mary & Roland Oosterhouse
Jessie R. Orr
Geraldine Pagel
Painted Door Gallery
John Palmer
Eric Palo
Ken & Betty Parker
Mary K. Parker
Millie Parker
Robert Parker
Suzanne Parker
Grant Parsons
John & Betty Parsons
Paulette Parsons
Dick Peacock
Joan Peacock
Phyllis & Dick Peacock
Charles & Mabel Pelizzari
Jim Pennell
Vicki Penney
Steve & Jane Perdue
Nancy Pihlcrantz
Eunice K. Pines
Jean Plantrich
Jay & Peggy Player
Bill & Mary Pollard
Patricia Ponczek
Bob & Diana Portenga
Ann Posavac
Helen Mary Powell
Jeff Pownall
Norma L. Powers
Anita Prahl
Donald S. Pratt
Helen H. Pratt
Lottie Prouty
Christine Ptak

Jim & Michele Pupel
David, Karen, Maria, Neil & Richard Purvis
Donald & Susan Pyne
Roger & Ruth Ann Quinn
Linda Racine
Jean Radin
Barbara Raehl
Jack & Norma Raffaelli
Jon Ramsey
Jeanne Ransom
Dave & Ellen Rapson
Hal & Sally Rasmussen
Geraldine Raymond
L. G. Raymond
Nancy Read
Peter Read
Darl Renn
John Rhoadarmer
Nancy Rhoadarmer
Gerald Richards
Karl Richards
Phil & Joan Richardson
Ray Rideout
Leo D. Riskey
Mary Ann Rivers
Hanna Robey
Sandy Robey
Anne H. Rock
William J. Rock
Dawn Rogers
Roberta L. Rogers
Jean Rollins
Kathryn Roosa
Mary Rose
Rochele Rosi
Terry L. Rosinski
Dick Rosser
Donna Rosser
Don Routzahn
Barbara & Jim Rowlett
Grace Rudd
Gene & Marge Rundell
Frank Rundquist
Eleanor J. Russell
Sharon M. Rutkowski
William & Lottie Rybarz
Mya Sagan
Bill & Jane Sage
Helen Sanabria
Kurt Sanford
Carole Savage
Vera C. School
Willis S. Schenk
Doug & Pam Scherrer
Lenore Schlack
Earl & Mary Ann Schleicher
John Schmidt
Tom & Susan Schmidt
Helen Schmittdiel
Sherry Scholfield
Miriam Schreck
Helen Schroder
Harvey Schroeder
Jack Schroeder
Art Schubert
Sue Schubert
Al & Marion Schweitzer
Ruth Ann Scott
Frank Senger
Pat Shand
Ann Shannon
Lorraine A. Sharpe
Shirley R. Shaw
Darylene & Tom Shea
Gregg & Jean Sheehan
John L. Shields
Wayne Simmons
Carole Simon
Jodi G. Simpson
Gene Sinclair
Kathy Sinclair
Robert & Alice Sisson
Cliff Sjogren
Jennifer Skinner
Maurene Slaughter
Blanche Sleder
Joan & Dewey Sleder
Rita Sleeman
Jim Slis
Margaret & John Smedley
Robin Smillie & David Cox
Chimera Smith
Gregg & Dee Smith
Linda Smith

"The characteristics and needs of our community have taken on an aspect that neither (Andrew) Carnegie nor (land donor Perry) Hannah could have dreamed of, and the library they bestowed upon Traverse City in 1905 has become hopelessly inadequate for the world of the 1990s." — John B. Trezise, Grawn.

Margaret A. Smith
Marilyn Smith
Martha L. Smith
Patty Smith
Del & Shirley Sparks
Frances Spedding

Raymond Spedding
Paul R. Spellicy
Mark Spencer
Dave Spindler
Colin M. Spitler
Staff of Traverse Bay Community School
Sheila Stafford
Pamela J. Stanley
Harry Stark
Joe & Robin Staron
Charles Stecker
Bob & Kay Stehouwer
Jean & Dick Stemmler
Mr & Mrs James F. Sterling
Carol Still
Irv Stoner
Bob & Ruth Stow
Sue Strobel
Margaret Strong
Richard Strong
Bessie Stuart
Nancy Stuck
Dotty Stulen
Helen Sullivan
Edith Swiatek
Christine Syzmanski
Sarah, Steve, Ed Szymanski
Tamra Tambeau
Eleanor F. Tammelaid
Kevin Tarsa
Bruce & Stacy Taylor
Ken Taylor
Lou Ann W. Taylor
MacKay Taylor
Ruth K. Taylor
T.C. Gym

"In a world full of questions, libraries have answers." — Cathy Lazar Nelson, Williamsburg.

Annette Teachout
Gretchen Telek
Don Thomas
Joanne Thomas
Kathy Thomas
Madeleine Thomas
Betty Thompson
Tom Thompson
Anthony R. Thorpe
Doris Thunstrom
Margaret Tipsword
Anita & Kevin Tobian
Cheryl S. Togrul
Lee W. Torrey
John & Barbara Toski
John Trezise
Patricia Trezise
May C. Trudgen
Jean & Bob Tull
Thomas R. Tull
Genie & Bill Unkefer
Up North Traders
Beth Van Cleave
John Van Dalson
M. Frances Van Dalson
Bill & Norma Van Fossan
Paul Vancouver
Mr & Mrs Bruce VanderKlipp
Alice Van Zoeren
Henry & Bernice Vega
Diana J. Viskochil
Richard F. Viskochil
Deborah VonSee
Christian Vreeland
Donald F. Vreeland
Martha A. Vreeland
Val Vreeland
Victor Vreeland
Bill & Liz Wagner
Marian J. Wagner
DeVer Walker
Edward C. Walker
Karen Walker
Bob & Barb Wallace
Doug & Betty Wallace
Betty Walter
Bob Walton Family
Paula Ward

Jane Watts
Price Watts
Konrad Weeda
Michael Weeda
Ethelyn A. Weeks
Milton W. & Margaret Weller

Harold Wells
Kevin & Kendra Wells
Lilli Wells
John Westcott
James A. Westerfield
Tom & Deb Wetherbee
Evelyn Wethy
Lorraine Whaley
Rita Whaley
Sonja & Clyde Whipple
Charlene A. White
Grace Whitelock
Sandy & Jim Wibby
Chas. Wilbur
A.V. & Emmy Williams
Christine Williams
Clyde & Ruth Williams
Glen & Dorothy Williams
Greg Williams
Robin & Marlene Williams
Bonnie Willings
Katie Winkelhaus
Glenn Wolff
Guy & Elaine Wood
Joyce Wood
Roger & Linda Wood
Jim Woodall
Kay Woodall
James S. Woodburne
Susan B. Woodburne
Ruth & Bill Worthington
Gerald & Fran Wyatt
Karen Wyckoff
Marty Wyckoff
Mike Wyckoff
Evelyn E. Yankle
Nancy Yarbrough

Steve Yenshaw
Ann Young
June & John Young
Pauline Young
Johnnie Zachman
Buz Zamarron
Carole & Elden Zang
Don & Judy Zemper
Janet & Walter Zerbel
Laura Zientek
Don Zimmerman
Jane Zimmerman

PAID FOR BY VOTE YES FOR LIBRARIES, H.E. CORTWRIGHT, TREASURER, 5825 ANDORRA DR., WILLIAMSBURG, MI 49690

Citizens for Libraries / Vote YES for Libraries showed community support for the ballot issues just days before the August 6, 1996 election.

A library is more than an organized collection of books and reference materials. It is one of the last free places devoted to public discourse. In a viable democracy, a good public library is absolutely essential.

Record-Eagle editorial 7/24/1996

CHAPTER 12

Vote YES For Libraries!

COMMUNITY FUNDRAISING

The price tag for a new library was big. Despite everyone's best efforts, it appeared that the figure would surpass $8 million. How could Citizens for Libraries make that number more palatable? Of course, tax dollars would have to provide most of the funds, but private contributions could help. If Citizens for Libraries could show voters the extent of their enthusiasm—by donating dollars—that might help the millage pass.

"We were trying to keep the millage as low as possible," said Guy Wood, a local book seller with a library science degree who co-chaired the fundraising committee. If private fundraising brought in enough money, they could shave off the millage amount, hopefully making the millage palatable for tax-averse voters.

With this in mind, the Citizens for Libraries set an ambitious goal of privately raising $2 million. Dick Rosser had extensive experience with private university fundraising, which involved appealing to well heeled alumni and corporations. Fundraising for a public resource was different, especially for a newcomer in town.

"I guess it seemed like a good number at the time," said Wood. The fundraising goal was eventually whittled back to $1 million.

Ken Parker started the ball rolling with fundraising. His wife, Betty Parker, had been the chair of the League's Library Action Committee, and Ken was an active advocate. "Ken said: 'Let's raise some money. I'll pledge $1,000,'" remembered John Trezise. "Then he got all his friends to contribute at least $1,000 to the cause. He got about 15 to 20 people to do this, so he contributed $15,000 to $20,000 to the cause immediately...He was very persuasive. Ken was a charming guy."

Ken Parker (center) was determined to make the first donation to the TADL Building Fund, and he knew how to draw publicity to this cause.

Wood and others solicited private donations from Traverse City acquaintances and local businesses. No one had much fundraising experience, but they had enthusiasm, and named different giving levels the "Andrew Carnegie Circle" and the "Perry Hannah Circle." All the funds went directly to the library, and McGuire kept track of donations in a special fund. The largest donation came from the Oleson Foundation, which donated a generous $100,000 gift.

In the end, the Citizens for Libraries fundraising team raised $350,000. Not close to their original $2 million goal, or even the updated $1 million, but enough to demonstrate strong support. "We were hoping to get enough money to lower the millage, but it did demonstrate support within the community for a new library," said Wood. "People were willing to pay money above and beyond paying taxes."

LIBRARY EVENTS

"There was tremendous need," said John Welch, library board member. "The question was would the community be willing to write the check?"

The final cost was pretty big: $8.5 million. "That's a huge number when you're used to dealing with a little library on Sixth Street," said Welch.

Citizens for Libraries staged events to drum up new friends, including "Tea at the Cinema," held at the Bay Theater in Suttons Bay. Volunteer Paula Leinbach organized a High Tea with "slivers of tea sandwiches and a spot of tea" catered by Cuppuccino's. They screened Jane Austen's *Sense and Sensibility*, and promised a "jolly good affair."

Another creation was the Books N Moore character. Citizens for Libraries public relations co-chair David Hacker developed the little mascot figure for ads and brochures, and Vicki Carpenter dressed up as a live mascot in a Books N Moore costume designed by Pinkie Hoffman, complete with book pages, gloves, hat, and giant puffy shoes.

Books N Moore mascot draws attention to benefits of libraries at low cost to residents.

"My arms were outstretched in the costume perpendicular to my body in the shape of a 'T,'" remembered Carpenter, who paraded as Books N Moore in the Children's Parade at the Cherry Festival. The theme for the Children's Parade that year was Little Golden Books, which fit in nicely. "Librarians are ageless" proclaimed a sign carried by Marly Wyckoff (later Hanson), as she walked among a host of library supporters dressed up

Library staff member Vicki Penney gamely dressed in costume as a walking, talking book to draw attention to library services.

in period costumes, some pushing strollers and others on rollerblades. As Books N Moore waved at children and danced around, librarians pretended to check out books for people along the parade route.

The Friends of the Library held two picnics at the empty Woodmere site geared to get families excited about the new children's department. The first picnic was a bit of a flop. Eager volunteers decorated the site with cardboard cutouts of Pooh and Piglet walking hand in hand, and announced a gathering called "A House at Pooh Corner," but didn't provide food. "This is dumb," complained one parent. "We don't have anything to eat." The next time, the Friends invited food trucks to come, which resulted in a much happier crowd.

Support grew and grew. Within a few months, Citizens for Libraries had 400 volunteers, and by election day, they had recruited 1,000.

On March 10, 1996, Citizens for Libraries held a fun-filled "literary gala" kick-off for the new library campaign, complete with bagpipes. It was held at the Sixth Street library.

Marly Wyckoff dressed up as Miss Wait, the original Carnegie building librarian, reprising her role from the 90th anniversary of the Carnegie building held the year before. Only a year before, the celebration (coincidentally also held on March 10) focused on the past. Library staff and fans had organized a staged reading and dressed in period costumes borrowed from Old Town Playhouse. Dean Robb had read Mayor Elisha Fulghum's dedication speech from 1905, dressed in

Fred Nelson as Library Trustee Elvin L. Sprague and Dean Robb as 1905 Mayor Elisha Fulghum exchange quips on the 90th anniversary of the dedication of the Sixth Street library. Library Director McGuire, Miss Alice Wait (Marly Wyckoff), and historian Larry Wakefield appreciate the humor.

a dashing white suit. Library board president Fred Nelson had donned long tails and black top hat to portray his counterpart Elvin L. Sprague. Even babies had come dressed in vintage clothes and bonnets.

This time, in 1996, the focus was broader. Along with Marly Wyckoff dressed as "Miss Wait," acknowledging the past, director Mike McGuire portrayed the present, and two young patrons, Konrad Weeda and Lily Prentice, represented the future. Citizens for Libraries asked people to look around at the aging building and envision a bright, modern, spacious library.

"The first load of books was brought by horse-drawn cart," said Wyckoff, as Miss Wait. "I really think it's time to pack up the books again."

"It was a hit," said Magoun. "It was well attended…and at the same time it was showcasing how bad the library was."

A day or two before the big event, however, the group hit a snag. Chuck Judson, their attorney, called. Since Citizens for Libraries was set up as a 501(c)(3) nonprofit, it wasn't allowed to get involved in political fundraising.

Citizens for Libraries members sprang into action and formed a new political arm. "Oopsie! We had to scramble and immediately get a PAC going," said Magoun.

The new PAC (Political Action Committee) was called: Vote YES for Libraries.

Vote Yes!

Anne Magoun grew up loving libraries. The first library book she checked out as a child was *The Secret of the Rosewood Box*, by mystery writer Hellen Fuller Orton. Her library in East Lansing shared a building with a police station, so it wasn't glamorous, but even so, when she moved to Traverse City as an adult, she was not impressed with its worn-out library.

"It was rather dingy, not just crowded, but past its prime," said Magoun. She had been a League of Women Voters member in Connecticut and had learned a lot about advocacy strategies through her work there. Betty Parker invited her to join the Library Committee, and Magoun became one of the leaders in Citizens for Libraries.

When it came time to promote the millage, Magoun knew they would need the best local leaders in town. Karen Nielsen had worked on a massive and successful $54 million bond proposal to build a second public high school. The school bond to build West Senior High School passed in June 1995. This was practically unheard of in Traverse City. School millage requests rarely passed. Now Nielsen was heading up the campaign for another school millage request, which looked like it was headed for success, too. Nielsen would be the perfect person.

"We need you, Karen. Can you help us?" Magoun asked.

Nielsen was raising two children, running an accounting business and taking college classes for an accounting degree. She'd just finished helping with an exhausting school millage campaign and was ramping up for another one with an election date set for June 1996. But Nielsen was an avid reader and adored libraries. She supported the idea whole-heartedly.

"Fill me in."

She joined the Steering Committee and learned how the League had laid the groundwork. The Citizens for Libraries group was now rallying the community and had the technical aspects like sites, experts, and architects covered. But the group knew nothing about passing a millage. Nothing at all.

"Karen was at the pinnacle," said Magoun. "She knew people. She knew the process, she was smart, she was reliable."

"Traverse City was notorious for turning down millages," said Nielsen. Property taxes were already steep for many homeowners, especially older residents trying to stay in their homes. "People were not opening their pocketbooks for anything. Even road millages were defeated."

Yet Nielsen and hundreds of school supporters got recent school bonds to pass. Could she work her magic for the library? The trouble was, time was short. The school millage campaign was June; the library's election was slated for September.

Just a few months before the election? thought Nielsen. *That's insane. A tall, tall order. This was about the last thing I needed.* But Nielsen was an enormous book-lover who devoured books, ranging from physics to history.

"We need to take a shot," Nielsen said. She agreed to head the new Get Out the Vote Committee, along with co-chair Margaret Braden, a TADL librarian, who helped organize volunteers.

Nielsen was self-taught on how to run a millage campaign. She followed her father's mantra: "Figure it out, Karen." When Citizens for Libraries contacted Nielsen, they were summoning not just experience, but determination.

As a girl, Nielsen was a student activist. She attended high school in the 1960s, during an era when girls were told not to join science classes because only boys could be doctors. Girls shouldn't take up class space. Like many schools, her high school in Midland would not allow girls to wear pants. She organized a strike her senior year. After that, girls could wear pants to school.

She also cut her teeth on fundraising and community organizing early. When the Midland school board cut music and drama extracurriculars in her high school, Nielsen showed up at a school board meeting.

"These are important. If we raise the money, will you reinstate the programs?"

"Yes," replied the school board. "If you do it in 28 days." The task was for students to raise $113,000 in a month. "Make sure you have a method of giving back the money," warned the school board. "We don't think you can do it."

Nielsen got busy. "I went to all the chicken lunches," she said. "Rotary, Elks, service clubs." Teachers allowed her to skip classes, telling her she was learning more with her fundraising work. Within a month, Nielsen and her classmates had surpassed the goal and raised $126,000.

"If you can do good, you should," said Nielsen. "You gotta try...If you want something good, you have to go out and work for it. Don't expect someone else to do it."

This was the type of grit and determination Citizens for Libraries was hiring. Of course, they weren't actually hiring her. Nielsen was a volunteer, and although she'd worked miracles in the past, she'd never run a millage campaign in a single summer.

Then the time frame shortened. Citizens for Libraries and the TADL board had drafted a timeline based on holding the vote at a September Special Election. Waiting until the regular November election didn't seem wise. What if they lost? Then there would be no time to recoup and reorganize before the end of 1996. On December 31, 1996, the library operating millage would automatically expire. They needed a buffer before the end of the year, so a September election date seemed perfect.

When the September election date appeared in the *Record-Eagle,* local township clerks were outraged. What a waste of money! Calling a special election was uncalled for, they said, and imposed additional hassle on local townships. The clerks opposed any election in September (today Michigan election law does not allow September elections).

The library board held an urgent meeting. The next regularly scheduled election was the August 6, 1996 primary. That was so soon! It was already April. Could they possibly be ready in time? They decided they'd have to try it.

"They were really late," said Nielsen. "But I had the bones of what had to be done in my head."

One of those ingredients was a database. Nielsen had developed a database of local voters over the years. This was slow, painstaking work. She'd paid for a list of registered voters, then built a massive database, identifying likely "yes" voters, and filling in their phone numbers.

"In those days we had phone books," said Nielsen. One by one, volunteers looked up names in the phone book and entered the phone number. Sometimes they collected phone numbers through word-of-mouth, asking people "Who do you know who knows…?"

"The library was lucky," admitted Nielsen. "I'd developed a database identifying yes voters…If I hadn't had that, it would have taken me months and months to get phone numbers." Nielsen took this existing voter database and merged it with a database of TADL cardholders to create a library database. "The core was the database," said Nielsen.

Not only did she have a voter database in place, but Nielsen had a ready stable of engaged volunteers who were veterans of the recent school millages. Volunteers made thousands of calls on landlines.

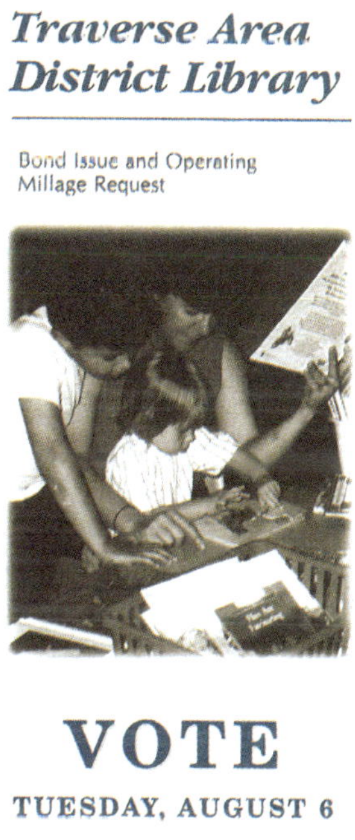

Still, even in the lead-up to the election, some TADL board and staff members remained skeptical. The last failed millage kept haunting them.

"We've tried this before," they said. "It never worked."

But the last time they hadn't had grassroots groups like Citizens for Libraries, the League of Women Voters, Vote YES for Libraries, and Friends of the Library on their side. Nor had they had the tenacity of Judith Halsted, Dick Rosser, and Karen Nielsen.

"When you believe in something, you can do it," said Nielsen. And she believed in libraries. "In a democracy, everyone needs access to information and it should be free."

Just like her days of chicken lunches back in high school, Nielsen and the Vote YES for Libraries team spoke to anyone who would listen. They sent out a mass mailing to every registered voter. Nielsen designed the brochure, and volunteers held "labeling parties" to stick on address labels.

David Hacker suggested writing the brochure himself. After all, he was a Pulitzer prize-winning writer.

"Tell me how you're going to sell this to people," said Nielsen.

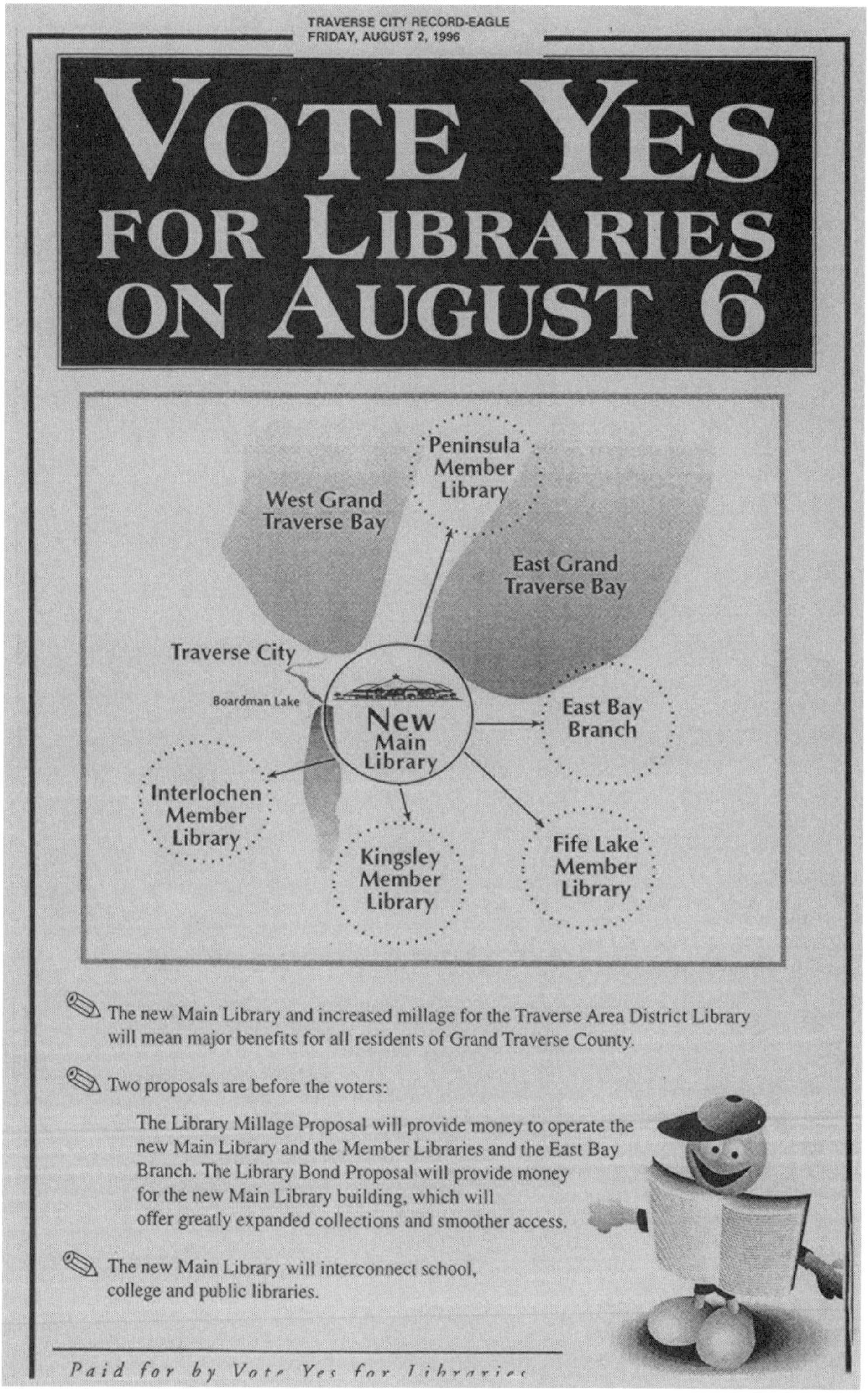

1996 ballot proposals promised big advantages to library services within the district system.

Hacker's version was too long-winded. "No, no," said Nielsen. "It's got to be one piece of paper, front, back. Date of the election, what you're asking for, and why you're asking for it. One paragraph." The brochure had to have a picture, preferably of an adorable child, and the text written at a sixth-grade reading level. That's how you reach voters, she said. Nielsen included the group's Books N Moore cartoon mascot, but encouraged Hacker and others to put their opinions in letters to the editor and *Record-Eagle* forum pieces. This was the place for waxing eloquent:

> *A library is as deeply religious as the Vatican and the ceiling of the Sistine Chapel, as devout as the call to worship from the bells of a Muslim minaret; a library is the worship of civilization's progress (and lack of it); a library also is as secular—devout if you will—as the Constitution of the United States and its Bill of Rights.*
>
> David Hacker, Life Accounts column in *Prime Time News and Observer,* August 1996

Letters to the editor in support of the library flooded in. "Time for a new library," the headlines read, "Let's look to the future," "Library needs overhaul," "Do something about it," "Library opens the world," "Warehouse won't do," and "Vote yes for libraries." Volunteers poured out letter after letter, like this one:

> *This summer we observe the fifth anniversary of our fine museum. On Aug. 6 we will have an opportunity to vote for the fine, spacious library we need and deserve. May we have the wisdom to bring home a YES!*
>
> Marcia Bellinger, downtown business owner

"A century ago, Andrew Carnegie stepped up and gave this nation its system of so-called 'free' libraries," wrote David Hacker in another guest column. "But then it was up to the communities to pay for their operations. That's what tax millages are for." He urged people to support a new building and operations. "The Carnegie Library was built at a time when people walked or traveled via horses to the library." We have the Dennos Museum, he reminded readers, plus Munson Medical Center, a new governmental center and a modern tourist and convention center, "[but] a library built only 40 years after the Civil War ended."

LIBRARY
Fast Facts

The Traverse Area District Library system covers Grand Traverse County and Elmwood Township, and has 22,000 users served by the Sixth Street main library in Traverse City, the East Bay branch, and member libraries on Old Mission Peninsula, Interlochen, Kingsley, and Fife Lake.

★

The Sixth Street main library is used by more area residents of all ages than any other public building in the area.

★

The main library was last expanded in 1965. Between 1965 and 1995, the population of Grand Traverse County nearly doubled, and continues to grow.

★

In 1965, 80,000 items were checked out. In 1995, circulation has grown to 500,000 items, a six-fold increase.

★

In Grand Traverse County, library funding at present costs a family living in an average-priced home only $23 a year: the price of a night out at the movies and less than the cost of one new hardcover book.

★

Every year, Americans visit their libraries 3.5 billion times and check out an average of six books. More children take part in summer reading programs than play Little League baseball.

CITIZENS FOR LIBRARIES

QUESTIONS
and Answers

Why does the Grand Traverse Community need to upgrade its main library?

The district's Sixth Street library was built in 1905 and was last expanded and modernized 30 years ago. The main library is far too small for our community's present and future use.

Why not expand the present facility?

The site is too small for expansion. Parking space is grossly inadequate.

What will happen to the Carnegie Library building?

The TADL board, city officials, and Citizens for Libraries are studying ways to preserve this architectural treasure and find new uses for it compatible with library purposes.

Where would a new library be located?

Traverse City is the cultural core of this area. Our sense of community and neighborhood focuses the site search in or near downtown.

How would a new library be funded?

Bond issues, operating millages, and private gifts. How much will be needed depends on the size of the new facility and the kinds of modern services the community wants. Member libraries also may need more money for operations and physical improvements.

How can I help?

For information, call 922-9696.

Statistics and Q&A about Traverse area libraries in 1996

The naysayers were writing, too, though not in such numbers. "Reject all millages and bonds," wrote one resident, voicing the concerns of many. Would the Traverse City region support paying for a library?

Thankfully, all the relationship-building with outlying community libraries paid off. Community libraries mobilized for the new millage. Interlochen sent out postcards and rallied teachers. Volunteers reached out for endorsements from local banks, schools, garden clubs, and township boards. Citizens for Libraries produced blue buttons saying "Vote YES for Libraries," plus bumper stickers, and TV, newspaper, and radio ads. "Your Public Libraries—the best bargain around!" they touted. Everywhere, volunteers and library staff got into the action. The Reference department staff held button-making parties. Volunteers sold Vote YES buttons downtown at Traverse City's summer Friday Night Live community street parties every week, taking $1 a button, or any donation. All summer there were events, including a picnic downstairs in the library basement. It was a big crowd. Martha Vreeland brought a Potter's bakery cake with blue frosting that turned everyone's mouths and tongues blue.

Were they ready? Blue tongues or not, the vote was approaching. Only a few days to go.

The Vote

Near election day, the phone calls ramped up. On election eve itself, the plan was to personally call more than 12,000 voters. That's where the voter database really came in, and Karen Nielsen knew the importance of setting up a community phone bank.

"If you send a list home with volunteers, they get distracted by kids, dog walks," said Nielsen. "You don't get compliance. If you bring people together in a group, there's more enthusiasm and they're more convincing on the phone."

She also knew human nature. If people sign up to help, you typically get 60–80% who show up.

Neilsen got local businesses like banks, realtors, and insurance companies to donate office space for a phone bank. These phone banks were scattered around the city, so each space had a phone bank captain. Nielsen was at "Command Central" at Old Kent bank downtown (now Fifth Third). Volunteers called people before the election to persuade them, with the biggest push of calls on election eve. They even called on election day to remind voters and catch stragglers. If a registered voter hadn't made it to the polls by late afternoon, they got a phone call from a Traverse City neighbor. "We need you to vote before the polls close."

So many people were eager to help the library that they had to open up a new floor of phones. "I had 105 or 110%! Extra people showed up," said Nielsen. "'Can my husband help?' We were running out of phones." More than a hundred people volunteered on election eve, and there were so many helpers, volunteers were able to finish the call list in only an hour and a half.

Election day wasn't all about phone calls. Vote YES for Libraries recruited 24 high school students to hold banners at ten intersections around Traverse City. The student helpers were paid with donations towards their senior fundraiser. Election day involved poll watchers, too. These trained volunteers stood at polling precincts and kept track of who had voted and who had not. They couldn't determine which way people had voted, just that they had voted. Poll watchers made lists and forwarded them on to the phone banks.

Nielsen cast her vote for the library at the fire station, then hurried to Command Central.

On election night, August 6, 1996, Citizens for Libraries gathered together for a watch party down in the basement of the Carnegie library. As the results from each township came in, Dick Rosser grew more and more excited. When Green Lake Township posted its results, Rosser asked John Trezise, "You think this means it's going to pass?"

"Yes, I do," replied Trezise.

The library millages both passed by more than 60%. Voters approved up to $8.5 million for construction of a new main library and up to 1.1 mills for twenty years to fund operating costs for all the libraries in the district. The bond to build the new library passed by a nearly 2 to 1 margin. Halsted wrote to supporters: "With your help—all 1,000 of you—there were more than 10,000 'yes' votes for the new main library and the operational millage increase, and only some 6,000 'no' votes. This was a land-slide by any measure."

Shirley Murray was delighted, especially since three townships that had never before approved a library or school millage voted in favor of the library millage. "That was one of our biggest achievements," she said. "I like to think it was all those trips out to those areas."

Only two townships voted against the library millage, Whitewater and Paradise. These townships were not wealthy and were fairly distant from the city. Library fans had won over the rest.

After two years of non-stop volunteering, Judith Halsted could finally relax. "She was very calm and very direct and very stick-to-it-ive," said Viskochil. "Very driven. She was the leader. She is the reason that the library got built."

"It consumed my life for three months," said Nielsen. "For me it was a Blitz. Dig in, do it, done. We did it!"

Traverse City had $8.5 million for its new Woodmere library.

Disbanding

Two days after the vote, Citizens for Libraries voluntarily disbanded. Dick Rosser wasn't so sure this was a good idea. He started talking about all the other projects the group could take on. But everyone else was adamant: the group was done.

"We saw it as a campaign, with a beginning and an end," said Anne Magoun. "This was a group that was put together for one purpose, and that was to get a new library in town."

Together the library board and the Friends of the Library would shepherd TADL through its next phase. There was no need for another group. Citizens for Libraries had accomplished their goal, and it was time to go. The political arm, Vote YES for Libraries, likewise disbanded, transferring their remaining funds, $1,176, to the library building fund.

"Citizens for Libraries and the League of Women Voters deserve a heck of a lot of credit," said Nielsen. "They built momentum for years. They put people together to make it happen. A small group of dedicated people generally makes most anything happen…the power of the few."

The American Library Association agreed and honored the Friends of TADL with their Baker & Taylor Award in national recognition of their role in shaping the new Woodmere library. The Grand Traverse Area League of Women Voters was also praised in the American Library Association's *Public Libraries* magazine in recognition of their dedicated efforts on behalf of TADL.

Like the Ladies' Library Association, the Citizens for Libraries had played their part at a critical time, paving the way for others to follow.

Eight-year-old Konrad Weeda, the youngest donor to the building fund, breaks ground for the new library with Judith Halsted and Dick Rosser. Looking on are TADL Board Members John Welch and Fred Nelson.

Books are my family.

David Hacker

Chapter 13

Welcome to Woodmere

Groundbreaking

There were still many details to work out, from dealing with zoning restrictions to debating exactly how much parking the library needed, but the next major event was a groundbreaking ceremony and celebration. On Sunday, May 4, 1997 the public was invited to "Family Day" at the future site.

"It was a party out in the weeds!" said Martha Vreeland.

The loading ramps were gone by then, but the site was still empty. A field of possibility filled it instead. A clump of balloons marked the future library's front door, and balloons were staked out, outlining the perimeter of the future building's walls.

"It's big," Mike McGuire told gathered citizens. "It's going to serve this community well."

All the Citizens for Libraries committees were there, plus library staff, League of Women Voters, and Karen Nielsen's Vote YES for Libraries! volunteers.

"John, did you ever think you'd see the day?" Joe Muha asked John Trezise, both former library board members.

"The library-to-be is *our* dream, *our* success," said David Hacker. "What distinguishes this remarkable accomplishment is that most major

TADL board members (from left) Doug Brown, Shirley Mesch, Don Pratt, John Welch, Fred Nelson, Diane Viskochil, and Frank Senger ceremoniously break ground for the Woodmere library.

public works projects are dreamed from the top down…In every sense, this was a grassroots, community-inspired success."

Whole families came for the groundbreaking picnic, and there were balloon animals and rides on an antique fire engine for the children. Library board members posed with hard hats and shovels for the media. When it came time for the actual groundbreaking, the seven library board members donned bright green hard hats and dug into the soil with golden shovels. Then others took a turn, including Halsted and Rosser. The groundbreaking group included Judy Baltz, representing the Library for the Blind and Physically Handicapped, and eight-year-old Konrad Weeda, the youngest donor to the library capital campaign.

Then the bulldozers and cement mixers moved in to prepare the ground and build a foundation. A foundation that had been laid by library advocates for more than a hundred and thirty years.

CARNEGIE GOODBYE

It took eighteen months to construct the new building, beginning in July 1997. Until the clock tower was built, workers topped the library roof with a small fir tree. Lights and landscaping were added, book shelves went in, and a crane raised the six-foot diameter clock to the cupola.

At the same time, it was time to say goodbye. The people of Traverse City loved the Sixth Street library, and generations had memories of walking among the stacks there.

"There's such love for that Carnegie building," said librarian Margaret Braden. "Mike McGuire compared it to an old sweater…you love it, it's full of holes, doesn't quite keep you warm anymore, but it's hard to get rid of."

The night the library left the old Carnegie library building, library board and staff hosted a small ceremony. Dawn Buchanan's husband, Clyde, brought his bagpipes, along with Bob Braveheart, another local piper.

"Mike hated bagpipes, just *hated* them," said Dawn Buchanan. But McGuire was outvoted and put up with the pipe music for the sake of the rest of the staff. It was tradition to have bagpipes to mark the library's landmark events and anniversaries. "The night we closed off the old library and shut everything down…Clyde was up in the balcony [with his pipes]," said Dawn Buchanan.

It was a fitting tribute to the old Scotsman, Andrew Carnegie. While Clyde Buchanan stayed up in the balcony, Braveheart ceremoniously walked down through the stacks of the old Carnegie library in his green tartan kilt, ending up by the stately front door. Beside him, his young son Gabe beat a solemn tattoo on the drums.

McGuire thanked people as they emerged from the Carnegie building and finally shut the door as the crowd walked out into the snowy night.

GRAND OPENING

"It was a spectacular opening," said board member John Welch. "On time, on budget. Unheard of."

It took about two weeks for the library to complete the actual move. Most of the moving, including the books, was done by professional movers. During that time, the library was briefly closed while library staff arranged books and materials in each department.

On January 9, 1999, the library hosted a grand pre-opening gala party for donors. Most of the men dressed in black tie, including Mike McGuire, and many guests rented tuxedoes for the occasion. Women arrived in fancy dresses, high heels, and stylish boots. The party was in winter, after all, and it was a snowy night.

"The opening party was the worst snow storm of the year, but people showed up," said Martha Vreeland.

They certainly did show up. The library's pre-opening gala was no small party. Some estimates said there were close to 2,000 people. McGuire officially reported 1,200 guests—a figure that strained the building since it was rated for no more than 863. Guests flocked in and packed the library.

Again, McGuire tried to resist having bagpipes included.

The Woodmere building dedication included a ribbon-cutting ceremony on the staircase landing (from left) Judith Halsted, Dave Maxson, Jeff Kroesing, Doug Brown, Fred Nelson, Dick Rosser, Mike McGuire, and Frank Senger.

"We're not in Carnegie anymore!" he protested.

"I insisted," said Fred Nelson. "Clyde was the bagpiper. We had a string quartet, too."

The string quartet was made up of local high school students, including the McGuires' daughter Erin who played the violin. Fruit and other hors d'oeuvres were served in the atrium near the staircase, with wine from local wineries and dessert from the Underground Cheesecake Factory.

League of Women Voters leaders Judith Halsted and Betty Parker, "unsung heroes who quietly get things done."

Many guests were seeing the library for the first time, and others were still marveling at what they'd collectively accomplished.

"Oh, it was gorgeous," said NMC librarian Ann Swaney. "When I walked in and saw that stair going up to the heaven of adult reading." Above the open stairway hung a 28-foot-long metal mobile sculpture called "Secrets of the Pond," donated by local artist Will Case.

Library supporters had planned a small ceremony with speeches for the gala, but in the end, only McGuire spoke briefly. With more than a thousand people crowding around food and drink, the library was so loud nobody could hear anything. An agitated McGuire cancelled the rest of the program. Postponement was not a problem, for there were more events to come.

The next day, the library opened to the public. Then in April 1999, there was a formal dedication that included a ribbon-cutting ceremony. Library board, volunteers, and staff cut a red ribbon on the stair landing. Guests gathered at the base of the grand stairs for speeches. Michigan Supreme Court Justice Betty Weaver presented the keynote. Mike McGuire gave remarks, along with the Honorable Jim

McCormick, TADL board member Frank Senger, Dennis Fedorinchik of Hallmark Construction, and Friends of TADL President Art Burns. Citizens for Libraries was represented by Dick Rosser and Judith Halsted, who both spoke.

"Over ten years ago, a small group of women from the League of Women Voters met to discuss the needs of our public library," Halsted began. "This is truly a citizens' library," Halsted told the crowd. "Many communities build libraries, but what happened here, what makes this an unusual story, was the grassroots groundswell that carried the community along to the voting booths—that was extraordinary. This is your library. Enjoy, and thank you."

It was the culmination of years of effort. Though as Halsted reflected on the earlier ribbon-cutting, it didn't seem quite right that she had been the only woman among the ribbon cutters. Women had been at the heart of the library for so long.

"All the unsung heroes," as Nielsen put it. "Who quietly get things done."

There were also people to miss. Dick Rosser had moved away before the library was completed, but returned for the grand pre-opening gala. David Hacker was not present. Hacker had spoken at the groundbreaking, but was not well, and died in March 1999, soon after the new building opened.

Despite these deep losses of library friends, the library they'd helped create was bustling to life. In the Youth Services area, the brand-new children's department, storyteller Jill Bert greeted families with her story bear Brown Sugar in his basket. A giant, huggable Winnie the Pooh was also there to meet children. Delight was palpable. Young patrons scrambled into the new wooden rowboat and tried out the puppet theater.

The New Library

The new main library officially opened to the public on January 10, 1999. Soon after the library opened, a man walked up the grand stairs and approached the reference desk, where Sandy Robey was working.

"How in the world did this town get such a fantastic library?" he asked.

"We voted for it and paid for it."

"I am so stunned," he said.

After seeing a downstate library's similar boat on their bus tour, TADL staff wanted one for children in the new Woodmere building.

"When you get up there on the second floor it's just priceless," said Fred Nelson.

"The minute it opened, the patronage skyrocketed," said John Trezise. "It became the great hub for all kinds of people."

Mike McGuire proudly toured visitors around the new facility. "He was in seventh heaven," said Nancy McGuire. "He just loved it. He gladly gave them a tour—every little nook and cranny." The sheer size was impressive. "Director McGuire always said the building was like two football fields stacked on top of each other and the adult reference desk on the second floor was about the 50-yard line," said Vicki Carpenter, TADL administrative assistant.

New patrons joined and hundreds became card-holders for the first time. Grand Traverse County was discovering what a library could be.

"People overlooked it before Woodmere," said John Welch. "Called it a charming little library."

"Our library is like a gift to the people," said Martha Vreeland. "This one, especially, because the people have given it to themselves. We're going to make it sing."

Jill Bert and her buddy, Brown Sugar, were well-known as storytellers at both the Sixth Street and Woodmere libraries. This photo is from early days at the Woodmere location.

In anticipation of increased patron use, the staff had doubled prior to the move to the new building. Thanks to the twenty-year operating millage, TADL was able to add these positions.

One to arrive was Bernadette Groppuso, who moved from being Interlochen library director to becoming head of the main library's children's department. She was given a free rein to build up the children's collection. Theresa Schaub had started a quality collection, but now there were resources to work with.

"When we moved into the children's department, he [McGuire] gave us such a wonderful budget. He said it was basically 'shop until you drop,'" said Groppuso. The children's department upgraded books, replaced shabby copies, and made sure they had copies of all the Newbery and Caldecott award winners and Newbery Honor books. They also began to invest in audio books, enjoyable for all, but especially important for children who had difficulty reading text.

"Reading can improve if they listen to a book," Groppuso explained. "Their vocabulary shoots up."

And, they had a story room. A designated room just for children's programming where children could gather each week for Wigglers' Story Hour with Brown Sugar, Jill Bert, and other story tellers.

At first, tweens were lumped into the children's area, but they soon spoke up and demanded their own space. The new separate Young Adult Department was stocked with young adult books, computers, music, and resources of interest to teenagers.

Woodmere Library staff try out the new wooden train in 2001. (L-R) Charlotte Sanders with baby Sophie Swanker, Sandy Robey, Marly Hanson, Jim Cavanaugh, Marie Kulibert, Carol Kuhn, Margaret Braden, Larry Fatt, and Katheryn Carrier.

This beautiful archway was constructed as the welcoming entrance to TADL's Children's Garden.

Renewal is not just inovation and change. It is also the process of bringing the results of change into line with our purposes.

John W. Gardner

Chapter 14

Community Growth and Change

Children's Garden

The idea of a Children's Garden came from Susan Kuschell, a member of the Friendly Garden Club. Kuschell grew up gardening in England and was passionate about flowers and fresh vegetables. She suggested a "hands-on" children's garden outside the children's area of the library. At the time, there were few public gardens in the region. The Friendly Garden Club designed and maintained a flower garden at the Open Space in Traverse City, but the idea for a Botanic Garden was still in the dreaming stage. The Botanic Garden at the Historic Barns Park was not established until more than ten years after the Children's Garden.

"We've always needed a children's garden in Traverse City," said Susan Kuschell, when the library opened. She believed kids belonged in the garden, and children needed gardening to be healthy.

Mike McGuire was enthusiastic. Kuschell toured the Meijer Gardens in Grand Rapids and consulted with the director of Michigan State University's children's garden. Soon a walk through storybook garden came to life behind the main library, designed with the help of local landscape architects, Dean Connors of Borealis Design and Russ Clark of R Clark Associates.

From the beginning, it was important for the garden to be accessible to all. A grant from the Kellogg Foundation assured this, and the Grand Traverse chapter of the Michigan Council of the Blind and Visually Impaired offered funding to create a Scent and Touch garden designed with the blind in mind. The Scent and Touch garden contained aromatic plants such as rosemary, lavender, sage, and lemon balm, plus low-thorning roses and the delightfully fuzzy lamb's ear. The name of each garden area was also written in raised letters and braille on glass mosaic markers throughout the Children's Garden.

The garden walk began with the Moon Garden and led into a Storybook Theme Garden, the Touch and Scent Garden, Bird and Butterfly Garden, and Rose Garden, ending with a sundial. One of the most beloved features was a Willow House, a cozy hide-out made entirely of live willow trunks, trained to bend over and form a roof. The cuttings were originally taken from a National Champion black willow that grew in the Historic Barns Park. The Willow House was redone twelve years later when it became too thick and woody, this time using clippings from a Norwegian pussy willow.

The Frog Prince stands guard amidst roses in the Children's Garden.

Besides all the plants, whimsical statues were scattered throughout the garden, including a rotund frog from the "Frog Prince" in the Rose Garden, fairies, and a giant metal sculpture of a turtle named Grandpa Ted. Grandpa Ted was named during a contest sponsored by the Friends. Many of the art pieces, including Ted the turtle, were donated by the artists. Peg Jonkhoff donated the butterfly chair. Barb Nowinski, assistant library director, was the driving force behind having a fish pond, so a Pond Garden was added, along with the bow of a boat for children to climb in.

Friends of the Library member Jody Clark encountered a "reading train" on her travels, and, given the Woodmere library's location right next to the train tracks, an outdoor reading train seemed like a perfect fit. Sam's Club Associates donated the wooden train for the Children's Garden, and an Amish craftsman from St. Johns, Michigan built it.

About two years after the Walkthrough Garden sprang to life, the Children's Garden expanded to create a *real* children's garden—twelve rows of raised beds where children could get their hands in the soil and do gardening. Families and groups such as day camps, therapy groups, and the Women's Resource Center adopted plots and came to plant seeds, water, pick flowers, and harvest their own vegetables. This area, called the Community Learning Garden, was expanded to include a pavilion and greenhouse, called the Edna Rosenfield Greenhouse. For many years there was a working pizza oven made of local clay—a great hit with annual harvest parties.

The Children's Garden attracted many partners, including Friends of the Library, Friendly Garden Club, Optimist Club, Rotary Club, Grand Traverse Regional Community Foundation, Michigan State University Master Gardeners, the city, and TADL itself. MichCon made a significant gift of $75,000. Susan Kuschell was the passionate force behind the garden for twenty years until her death in 2018. Her daughter Emily Kuschell stepped in as director for a year. Another daughter Sarah (Kuschell) Masak became director in 2021.

During the 2020 COVID-19 pandemic, the Community Learning Garden grew and harvested 1,000 pounds of fresh vegetables, which it donated to local food bank programs. Future plans include a Farm Camp and community skills in soil and compost, medicinal plants, growing, cooking, and food resiliency.

"My mother believed in community," said another of Susan's daughters, Holly T. Bird. "She thought this was such a good platform for different nonprofits to come together and grow this sense of community."

The Grand Traverse Area Children's Garden is a separate 501(c)(3) organization with a five-person board tasked with managing the gardens. The land is technically part of the library and Hull Park.

"It's a place of healing and safety and inspiration," said Kimberly Conaghan, the garden's director in 2020. "We welcome children of all ages."

CARNEGIE RENAISSANCE

"I still can remember hearing the library doors close," said Peg Jonkhoff. "Gulp."

While the library settled comfortably into its new home on Woodmere, the original Carnegie building sat empty at first. According to Andrew Carnegie's gift stipulations, the library had to give the building back to the city. The idea was to restore and reuse the building as a history center. Several nonprofits were interested. The trouble was, although the new main library had a healthy operating fund for its services, the Carnegie building had no such operating revenue.

"You have to have a plan for operating it," said Suzanne Connor, who had initially raised concerns about preservation. "To this day, that remains a concern."

Back in 1998, the city was anxious to find new occupants, and a coalition of historical groups was eager to explore options. The Friends of Con Foster Museum led the partnership. The museum had been housed in a city-owned building in Clinch Park by the bay (now the Bijou Theater), but needed more room to display their collection.

Friends of Con Foster Museum proposed moving to the Carnegie building and teaming up with other organizations with a similar historical mission. They could collaborate on programs and fundraising and draw more people to visit. The Grand Traverse Pioneer and Historical Society also stepped up. The Grand Traverse County Historical Society had been originally founded by Leon Titus' younger brother Harold in 1924, and later merged with the Pioneer Study Center in 1985 (today it's known as the Traverse Area Historical Society). They'd been renting extra storage space downtown, but humidity led to mildew problems and they needed a more professional, temperature-controlled environment for their collection of documents and artifacts.

The Maritime Heritage Alliance joined in, along with the Railroad Historical Society of Northwest Michigan, Grand Traverse Rock & Mineral Club, and the Women's History Project of Northwest Michigan. They were all local groups with no room to roost. Now they could work together.

The new venture was called the Grand Traverse Heritage Center.

"We didn't want it torn down," said Judith Halsted. "We didn't want it bulldozed for a parking lot. We wanted to leave the building and use it." Citizens for Libraries had a committee called Carnegie Renaissance. This had been a priority from their very first feasibility meeting at The Bowery restaurant in June 1995. "First," read the agenda, "find positive uses for the Carnegie Building."

Many people disagreed. Why keep an old library building past its use? The library had a new home. It would be better for the city to tear it down, they argued. Keeping this old one will just turn out to be an expensive liability.

First, find positive uses for the Carnegie Building.

But the Carnegie building was much beloved, and on the outside at least, still beautiful. Making it a museum and history center would continue its original mission: community education.

"It's a treasure of our community," said Ann Hoopfer, director of the Con Foster Museum. "It should be kept. It should be used."

"Keep it useful, but not commercial," urged Fred Nelson.

The city agreed, on one condition: renovate the building. This had to be accomplished as soon as possible. The Carnegie building was not up to code to reoccupy.

Massive, heartfelt renovations began in 1999.

"This was a huge community effort," said Peg Jonkhoff. The Jonkhoff family was heavily involved, partly because of their interest in historic preservation and partly because of their proximity: they owned Perry Hannah's former house on Sixth Street, which they ran as a family business. Peg Jonkhoff co-chaired the Carnegie restoration campaign, along with Frank Senger.

Peg Jonkhoff and Frank Senger, Co-chairs of the Heritage Center Capital Campaign, in 2000.

There was so much to be done. The original slate roof had been removed in the 1950s, but the new roof leaked. The Heritage Center redid the roof and added extensive structural support in the attic to support snow load. The floor was stripped of its old pea-green carpeting and refinished, revealing gorgeous maple planking.

"It was all there," said Hoopfer. "It was only covered up…It was sort of like unwrapping a present."

Then there were the ceilings. The soaring, 18-foot-high ceilings had been covered up and were still obscured by 1960s dropped ceilings with fluorescent light bulbs. It was time to take those down and restore the ceilings to their former glory.

Once the mezzanine was removed, painstaking efforts, including the reconstruction of this plaster rosette and chandelier, were taken to restore this early 20th century "ornament to the city."

The original ceiling had rosettes set in plaster. "Most were destroyed with the wiring and pipes, all the fluorescent bulbs," said Hoopfer. "Ray Minervini sent his son Jeff and a crew over. They restored the plaster ceilings and walls."

Jeff Minervini made a rubber mold from one of the remaining complete rosettes. Then he and his crew poured new plaster rosettes. They restored the decorative frieze around the ceiling and added three coats of new plaster.

"Oh! It was absolutely gorgeous," said Hoopfer. Hoopfer added in period light fixtures, huge chandeliers she found at Odom's Re-Use store. The chandeliers, which had originally come from a downstate high school auditorium, fit the new ceiling perfectly.

One of the biggest endeavors was to install a new heating and air-conditioning system. Having a good ventilation system with excellent humidity controls was essential for properly storing and displaying artifacts and historical documents. The Heritage Center invested in a complex HVAC system with eleven pumps costing more than $700,000.

The entire renovation cost $1.4 million, paid for by a passionate community fundraising drive, along with contributions by the history nonprofits. The city contributed $45,000 for an architect, and the rest came from local fundraising. The Grand Traverse Heritage Center was lucky to have a powerful trio of women who took on the Carnegie restoration campaign: Peg Jonkhoff, Marsha Smith, and Jeanne Snow. Smith directed Rotary Charities, and Snow led the Grand Traverse Regional Community Foundation. Generous gifts flowed in from the community. The new kitchen was named after Ida and Jim Tompkins's daughter, Mary Ann Galic, and the new board room was named the Reynolds-Jonkhoff Board Room.

"Every dollar raised for the capital campaign went through the Foundation, and along with Jeanne's expertise and encouragement...$1.4 million plus was raised and it was a huge success," said Jonkhoff, a major player in the renovation efforts.

To keep costs down, Hoopfer recruited a work crew from the jail, and many local businesses, including the Minervini plasterers, donated their labor. Local builder Mike McMaster coordinated a 50-plus person crew of carpenters, electricians, drywallers, and painters. The restoration team added a kitchen, reconfigured the stairs, and stripped paint off the woodwork. Hoopfer did most of the paint stripping herself.

"All the woodwork was painted a s--t brown," she said. "But there was hardwood underneath. Oak."

Finally, they painted the walls off-white with a slight blush pink tone. Having a slightly warm pink tone was supposed to be best to show off exhibits.

When they finished, the Carnegie building was sparkling, revitalized, and alive with hope. *It will be a museum for the next hundred years,* thought Hoopfer proudly.

Then they moved in. The Con Foster Museum set up its eclectic collection, from a bark wigwam to newspapers from the 1800s, in the main Carnegie building. The Maritime Heritage Alliance, Pioneer and Historical Society, and others all had their own offices, mostly in the basement of the Cornwell addition. Hoopfer, the city's sole paid staff person for the Con Foster Museum, became director of the new Grand Traverse Heritage Center. For a reception desk they used Alice Wait's original library desk from the Carnegie library days.

"It was appropriate that the building that was almost a museum itself should be a museum," said Dawn Buchanan, who'd worked in the Carnegie building for years when it was a library.

The Grand Traverse Heritage Center opened to the public in June 2002.

"The library was the centerpiece of our neighborhood," said Carol Hale. "To have it come back as something for the public is just excellent."

The Grand Traverse Rock and Mineral Club set up in the basement, hosting Rock Swaps and turning a storage room into a workshop with grinders for the lapidaries. The Maritime Heritage Alliance trained volunteers on knot-tying in preparation for work aboard their historic wooden schooner *Madeline.* The Railroad Historical Society took over floor space in the Cornwell addition each December for its popular Festival of Trains, which showcased model trains. During the fall, the Heritage Center hosted "Heritage Days" for local schools. Fourth graders from five counties got to see historical reenactments and watch old-fashioned skills like flintknapping, spinning, and rug hooking. Heritage Center staff and volunteers dressed in period costumes

Grand Traverse Heritage Center dedication (from left) Rich Brauer, John Matz, Zeke Fleet, Ann Hoopfer, Joan Bonney, Ken Taylor.

from different eras, and children got to roll up their sleeves and participate, such as trying out Civil War-era games or doing laundry with a wringer and wash tub.

Steve Harold led Friends of Con Foster, which eventually merged with the Pioneer and Historical Society. Unfortunately, the Con Foster Museum was the only organization that had a steady income. They received a $50,000 annual operating stipend from the city. This proved not to be enough, and the other nonprofits struggled to contribute and maintain their programs.

The Grand Traverse Heritage Center remained open for 12 years. Eventually funding struggles forced the history center to close its doors in 2014. The city declared the history center was not a "core city service," and balked at continuing to contribute to the building's maintenance. The Con Foster Museum closed, its partner nonprofits scattered, and the museum collection was placed in storage.

The Carnegie building was at a pivot point again.

Then in 2015, the Crooked Tree Arts Center moved in and made the old library its new home. The Petoskey-based group set up a new art center in Traverse City and re-opened the Carnegie doors to offer watercolor, photography, and other classes for children and adults. It also hosted lectures, music, and art exhibitions. At first they used just the Cornwell addition, then in 2018 Crooked Tree signed a seven-year lease with the city to move into the historic Carnegie section and use the entire building. Crooked Tree still hosts the annual Festival of Trains organized by the Northern Michigan Railroad Club, and the city uses the building as a voting precinct.

"It was our library until 1999," said Jonkhoff. "It's still educating. I'm just so happy. I believe in repurposing," she added. "Many towns don't even have a Carnegie library anymore. Just a memory."

The old library building at 322 Sixth Street remains a vibrant community center, now with a focus on the arts. And the heartfelt restoration of the building remains.

"All that renovation is still here," said Peg Siciliano. "It's a beautiful restoration of a historic building."

The American Library Association annually sponsors a "Banned Books Week."

No person is your friend who demands your silence
or denies your right to grow.
Alice Walker

Chapter 15

Privacy and Censorship

The Patriot Act

After McCarthyism (see page 71), libraries enjoyed a period free from major censorship and surveillance from about 1954 to 2001. Then, after the September 11, 2001 terrorist attacks, libraries were in the government spotlight again. In the wake of 9/11, Congress rushed through the USA PATRIOT Act. Designed to stop terrorist threats, it contained a controversial "library records provision" in Section 215. Librarians were forced to turn over patron records to the FBI upon request, so the government could see what books a person had checked out. They were also put under a gag order so librarians could not warn patrons or talk to anyone, including the media, about FBI requests.

"That was a red flag to any red-blooded librarian," said Ann Swaney. "Libraries rebelled." The Library of Michigan in Lansing invited all Michigan library staff to attend a teleconference scheduled for December 2002, entitled "Safeguarding Our Patrons' Privacy: What Every Librarian Needs to Know About the USA Patriot Act and Related Anti-Terrorism Measures."

If no records existed, federal agents could not see them. TADL hosted a public meeting about the Patriot Act, which attracted a capacity crowd in the community room. For years, librarians and the American Library Association fought for patron privacy rights.

The Patriot Act went against the Library Bill of Rights. The American Library Association staunchly defends the rights of libraries to provide open access to books and ideas, and to keep patron records private. Libraries are supposed to provide information from all points of view—including, or even especially—conflicting opinions. "Libraries should challenge censorship," the Library Bill of Rights states. "Libraries should…resist abridgement of free expression and free access to ideas."

In 2013, the extent of the government's surveillance became exposed by whistleblower Edward Snowden. Snowden's leaks of classified information spurred a new look at surveillance and privacy laws. Section 215 of the Patriot Act expired in May 2015.

BANNED BOOKS

"Mike had a vision that was very public-oriented," said librarian Martha Vreeland. "He would serve anyone who walked in. He stood up for that. Mike would say: 'We don't refuse to buy a book because someone doesn't want it in the library.'"

For example, when one of the library staff separated out children's books about human sexuality, Mike McGuire stepped in. The staff member was a devout Catholic and didn't want those books out on the shelves. "She'd been holding things back, deferring to parents," said Vreeland. "Mike made her see she had to put out everything she had. Mike said: 'Anyone should be able to find out anything they need.'" That included kids, too.

"We had some 'banned books' at Peninsula Community Library," said Ann Swaney. "It was Old Mission School parents complaining. We just moved them behind the desk so they could still be checked out when requested. One may have been a Judy Blume book."

In 1981, the TADL library board reported that a patron complained about the content of the book *The Art of Maurice Sendak*. Maurice Sendak is the author and illustrator of the beloved children's book *Where the Wild Things Are*. Sendak's picture book *In the Night Kitchen*, featured illustrations of a naked little boy, which shocked many people at the time.

"We have to re-order *Heather has Two Mommies*," said Michele Rudd, current TADL children's librarian. "People hide picture books they disapprove of, or check them out and never bring them back."

Frequently banned children's books in 2020 in the U.S. included *The Hate U Give* (anti-police), Harry Potter books (witchcraft, spells), *The Absolutely True Diary of a Part-Time Indian* (poverty, alcoholism, racism), *Captain Underpants* (inappropriate, violence), *Thirteen Reasons Why* (suicide), *George* (transgender child), and the picture book *Tango Makes Three* (a penguin with two fathers).

Adult titles that are frequent targets include: *The Kite Runner* (Islam, sexuality); *To Kill a Mockingbird* (racism); and *Fifty Shades of Grey, The Glass Castle,* and *The Handmaid's Tale* (all for sexuality).

Privacy remains a central tenet of library service. In 1983, Michigan passed the Library Privacy Act. This was largely due to the rise of HIV and public perception about people with AIDS.

"People would worry that if people found out they were reading a book about HIV that they would be fired from their job," said Library Director Michele Howard. "That's no one else's business and that's protected by law."

TADL today remains a staunch defender of patron privacy and free access to books and information.

Woodmere Library from lakeside: the half-rotunda or "bump" is reminiscent of the Sixth Street library "bump."

The very existence of libraries affords the best evidence that we may yet have hope for the future of man.

T.S. Eliot

Chapter 16

The Modern Library

At the Helm

Mike McGuire settled into the new Woodmere library with joy. He was hardly ever at his desk.

"Mike also liked to walk around the library facility at least once an hour to interact with staff and library patrons, a management philosophy he called 'MBWA' (Management By Walking Around). He was well-loved by his staff and colleagues, treating them like family and demonstrating gentleness and his sense of humor," reported the *Record-Eagle.*

"He knew how to work any desk," said reference librarian Sandy Robey. "He was everywhere. He knew what we needed. He would work the reference desk or the circulation desk."

Not everyone was a fan of his management style, but everyone agreed he was a true librarian at heart. "The library was his baby," said Dawn Buchanan.

"He was very caring. He cared about people and access," said Nancy McGuire.

He was also known for his collection of owl statues. Someone gave McGuire an owl statue and the number snowballed over the years. When McGuire retired in 2009, he gave all his owls away to library staff and friends. "I don't know how this started, but I never wanted to collect owls," he said.

McGuire had such an impact on the library that the library board voted to name the community room after him. Ever since 2009 it's been called the McGuire Room.

At the Woodmere library, the McGuire Community Room is named after Mike McGuire, library director from 1979 to 2009. The upstairs meeting room called the Thirlby Room honors Elsie Thirlby, a Traverse City Public Library trustee from 1918 to 1952. The Nelson Room, with its collection of Michigan and local history books, was named for Jack D. Nelson, library trustee from 1956 to 1991.

McGuire had worked at the Traverse library for nearly 35 years, and many considered him to be a local icon. He began as adult services librarian, then became assistant director, and continued as director for 31 years. His methods aggravated some, and delighted others, but there was no question that McGuire left his mark on the library. Now it was time for a new era.

Metta T. Lansdale, Jr., TADL director 2009–2014

Metta Lansdale became the next director. She had forty years of library experience as a medical librarian in Ann Arbor and as director of Chelsea District Library and Royal Oak Public Library downstate. She knew libraries, and knew what it meant to step into the shoes of a long-tenured director. It might mean there were some things to shake up. Newcomers brought new ideas.

Lansdale introduced an updated computer system, replacing a homegrown version McGuire had installed, and made major changes to revamp the circulation department and shift the library to an electronic check-out system. Lansdale also linked the Traverse district system to MelCat, a statewide catalog. Now, instead of only accessing collections within the local district, Traverse City library users could check out materials from the entire statewide library system, more than 400 libraries.

"Metta has been an outstanding director for the library," said library board member Tom Kachadurian. "She has just revolutionized this library."

Growing pains often hurt. Lansdale rearranged some staff positions and shepherded TADL through a period of change.

"Metta came in with big ideas and big changes, and there were some people who didn't like them," Kachadurian continued. "It's what happens when you have someone there for 30 years."

Lansdale led the library for five years, and stepped down for health reasons. Gail Parsons (later Juett) was tapped to be director after Lansdale. She'd already been acting as interim director for a few months. Her background was in business and finance, and she'd been working for TADL since 2008, initially as the library's business manager. She led the library through a fairly quiet period with no major changes. "It was a welcome reprieve for staff to stay 'status quo' for a few years and really integrate the changes," said administrative assistant Vicki Carpenter. Juett led the library for four years, all the time keeping a steady hand on finances, watching over building maintenance and issues (like the roof) relating to a gradually aging building. During her tenure, TADL paid off its mortgage for the Woodmere building and won voter approval for a new operating millage for ten years, ensuring stable funding until 2026. Juett retired in 2019, and TADL librarian Michele P. Howard stepped up to the director position.

Gail Parsons Juett, TADL director 2015–2019

Like many librarians and other staff (including Alice Wait, Theresa Schaub, Evelyn Brown, Marie Kulibert, and Dawn Buchanan), McGuire continued to volunteer at the library after his retirement. He came in regularly and diligently sorted library book donations until his death in 2018.

LIBRARY IN THE PANDEMIC

When Michele Howard moved to town, the Woodmere library had just opened.

"It was the first place I went," she said. She brought her oldest child to Wigglers' Story Time and settled right in. "Being a librarian, it was the first thing you do. You move in. You get a library card."

Michele Howard, TADL director 2019–

Howard worked as a librarian in Traverse City for many years before joining the TADL staff. She had an Information and Library Studies degree from the University of Michigan, first focused on law library work, then was a librarian at the NMC library. At TADL, Howard began in a part-time librarian position, then moved on to head the adult services department as adult services coordinator. Within two years, Howard became the new director.

"The library isn't just a warehouse of books, it's people and it's community," said Howard.

It's also about equal access. "It's the place where everyone knows they're welcome," said Howard. "You don't have to buy anything or believe anything to be here."

[The library is] the place where everyone knows they're welcome; you don't have to buy anything or believe anything to be here.

Then, just five months after Howard took the helm, the coronavirus pandemic hit. The library abruptly closed on March 13, 2020. No books could be checked out. No books could even be returned. It was simply too dangerous. No one knew exactly how the virus spread, and returned books could be carrying contamination. Library staff and patrons only had three hours' notice about the shutdown.

The library's closure stunned the community.

It wasn't just being cut off from books and other materials. It was being cut off from a beloved resource and a social, community hub.

Story Time for young children shifted to virtual story time. People became desperate for reading material, especially fiction. Some tried checking out digital books for the first time. Cookbooks shot up in popularity, but no one wanted travel books. Readers were also anxious to get back in the library. Patrons placed nearly 22,000 holds, waiting for the day when the library would open again.

The day before the March shut-down, people flocked to the library, trying to stock up before the lockdown. Rumors were flying. Everything was closing: schools, stores, businesses, restaurants, playgrounds, parks, and construction sites. What would happen to the library? Even before the official notice was issued, many patrons feared the worst and checked out the maximum number of items on their library cards. Altogether there were 36,075 books and other materials checked out during the spring 2020 lockdown. The main library and all its branches and member libraries stayed closed by government order for three months.

People came in and emptied the shelves. They took armfuls of books.

On June 8, 2020, TADL began to accept book returns again.

"Watching 40,000 items come back was incredible," said Howard. Returned items had to be quarantined for 3 to 4 days, and with all the quarantining, the storage rooms overflowed. Books were stacked in the staff lounge, the children's room, the Thirlby Room, and the McGuire community room. Every room was packed with boxes full of quarantined materials, and when staff ran out of cardboard boxes, they used garbage bags.

Face coverings were required after TADL libraries reopened in 2020.

Two weeks later, on June 24, 2020, TADL once again opened its doors to patrons. People lined up to get in the first day the library was open.

"People came in and *emptied* the shelves," said Howard "They took armfuls of books." That's when library staff realized just how much the library was loved.

"We're so thankful you're open," people said, again and again. "Thank you for being here."

The pandemic, with businesses and schools closed, made free Wi-Fi access in library parking lots invaluable.

Staff at the Woodmere Library and many of the other libraries in the TADL system were kept busy during the pandemic delivering books to patrons in their cars, regardless of the weather.

And some people went a step further: "We missed you more than our hairdresser!" The lockdown had also closed all barbershops and hair salons, and people were resorting to homemade haircuts and dye jobs.

Besides all the love, the pandemic also emphasized the increasing digital divide in the Traverse region. When the library closed due to statewide lockdown orders, thousands were instantly cut off from their only computer access. People needed the internet to file for unemployment. School children needed the internet to connect to remote schooling and turn in school assignments. TADL saw the need and rushed to provide access. While the library buildings remained closed, all the district libraries welcomed patrons to their parking lots.

"We put signs out," said Howard. "People would sit in the parking lot to get Wi-Fi."

Outlying libraries had their hands full. "I think our biggest 'feel good' was during the initial struggle to sign up for unemployment," said Kingsley Librarian Amy Barritt. "The system was overwhelmed, but it was even worse out in the rural parts of the county where the internet service is so intermittent or slow that patrons would be logged out of the system before they could finish filling out the forms." Kingsley library staff were on the spot to help patrons fill out unemployment forms from their cars.

The pandemic reinforced how vital the library was to the community. "I love my library," people said, and meant it. What had started out in Traverse City as a few small nineteenth century volumes on a shelf had become the lifeblood for so many people.

The coronavirus pandemic caused the library to shut down, or partially shut down, for several weeks later in 2020. During much of November and December 2020, the library was able to provide curbside-only service. The buildings closed, but staff could deliver books to patrons' vehicles. Another full shut-down, with no curbside service, occurred for two weeks from December 14 to 28, 2020. The book return slot was blocked and no materials could go in or out.

People still want books! They want to hold them and smell them and sit with a kid in their lap.

Still, people continued to be loyal to the library. New users shot up by nearly 5,000 in June 2020 when the spring lockdown lifted.

"People still want books!" Howard said. "They want to hold them and smell them and sit with a kid on their lap."

"When we were closed during COVID, I was here alone," said Vicki Shurly, Peninsula library director. "It was not a library. A library isn't just about books. It takes people and human interaction and discussion and the sharing of information. And that's what makes a library so vital."

DIGITAL INNOVATIONS

More than a million items circulate from TADL each year. Most of these are still physical books. Out of a million or more items, about 200,000 of them are electronic resources like ebooks or downloaded videos. The rest are physical items.

Librarians did not discard all their card catalogs when the book collection went online but found ways to repurpose them, such as this one holding seed packets.

Although there is an enduring love for physical books, digital resources are growing, providing patrons with an ever greater array of films, music, stories, and ideas. When Citizens for Libraries led the charge to build a new library on Woodmere, their motto was "Books N Moore." Now hashtags spring up saying #Notjustbooks. That's certainly true: TADL gives people access to a 3D printer for their projects.

These musical instruments are a great example of what TADL now lends from its Library of Things.

Digital databases have transformed modern libraries. To start, instead of searching for a book's location using the Dewey Decimal system or with paper cards in a card catalog, patrons quickly search the library's collection using an online computer system. TADL's card catalog went digital in the 1980s.

"People ask: 'Where's your card catalog?'" said Michele Howard. "Well, they're decorations now. They're very hard to get on Etsy." Old wooden card catalogs are now mainly used as tables and classy storage drawers. TADL stores its new Seed Collection of garden seeds in a former card catalog.

Access remains a challenging factor. As computers and smart phones become standard in many households, the library increasingly acts as an essential bridge to the digital world for many patrons. Thousands of county residents rely on the library for their access to the internet, ebooks, and computers.

"There's a digital divide we see all the time in libraries," said Howard. "There are patrons who come in every day who don't have credit cards, who don't have cell phones... We see it every day."

Buying a device to read ebooks can be a financial hardship. Reading digital books on a Kindle, which is owned by Amazon, requires a credit card number even if the books themselves are a free library resource.

The library offers a range of books, magazines, movies, and more through digital databases like Overdrive, Hoopla, and Kanopy. Hoopla offers an array of audio books, ebooks, comic books, TV programs, documentaries, movies, and music. Access Video provides many varieties of educational and vocational programming, including nonfiction shows like "Nova." Kanopy brings in European cinema and indie films, and Overdrive has ebooks and audio books. Each database allows patrons to check out a certain number of books or films per month.

One booming category is audio books. Listening to books is becoming increasingly popular, on car rides, while out walking, or at home. TADL checked out nearly 12,000 audio books in 2020.

The library has continued to build up its foreign language collection, and that includes access to foreign language editions of magazines. Overdrive lets patrons download a tremendous range of international magazines from Italian home design, to articles in Korean, Japanese, Russian, French, Portuguese, Canadian, and Australian publications.

Some digital databases work by streaming over the internet. Others are portable. Hoopla allows people to download items directly to their own phones or other devices. After it's downloaded, no internet connection is required.

"You can download it and literally go ice fishing," said Aaron Olson, Sight and Sound manager. "Or go to a cabin in the U.P."

There are also many specialized library databases. TADL has access to car repair databases, business databases, and demographic databases, to name a few. The library has databases to access newspaper and magazine articles. For people interested in genealogy, the Friends of the Library pays for a subscription to Ancestry.com.

In addition to all the digital offerings, there is a retro trend, too. Sight & Sound has vinyl records again, along with cassette tapes.

"Cassette tape culture is huge right now," said Olson. "Young people want an authentic experience."

THE LIBRARY OF THINGS

"We've been exploring new territory for our library," said Aaron Olson. Olson has been on the library staff since 1997, starting at the Sixth Street location when Mike McGuire was director. "We've got new items into what has been deemed The Library of Things."

The Library of Things means non-book and non-magazine, music, and movie items.

"We're getting into sewing machines, energy meters, and metal detectors," said Olson. "It all fits with giving people access to the things they need. Things they may need, but not need all the time." That includes telescopes, ukuleles, and record players. The library has a large and growing collection of musical instruments.

"I bought three ukuleles and a small parlor guitar," said Olson. "We started with that."

Musical instruments available for check-out now include: dulcimers, synthesizers, singing bowls, a Theremin, a thumb piano, xylophones, banjos, a travel guitar, and a range of other guitars and ukuleles. Electronic equipment, like digital audio recorders, microphones, and video projectors are also there. The Kingsley branch is circulating cake pans, and Peninsula Community Library offers fishing rods.

"It's not just about books anymore," said Vicki Shurly. "It's about meeting the community's needs. It's still a center for information."

All items check out for free. A few years ago the library offered use of a video camera or projector, but charged $10 to $25 for rental. TADL has now turned away from charging rental fees for circulating items.

Every non-traditional item, including puppets, board games, and musical instruments, is now under the umbrella of the Library of Things. Olson promoted the concept of the "Thing" library, and eventually the idea caught on and the Library of Things was funded.

"If a library is good at lending things, then it's good at lending things people don't want to store," said Olson.

Most library patrons are amazed by what the Library of Things can offer. "Really?" they gasp. "That is incredible. I had no idea a library could do that."

"Mike was an interesting thinker," said Olson, referring to former director Mike McGuire. "This is a natural extension of his vision."

If a library is good at lending things, then it's good at lending things people don't want to store.

Today, in the children's department, families can check out a growing range of STEM kits, fun toys, and games that teach children science, technology, engineering, and math skills. These include electrical circuit wiring and the physics of soccer and snowboarding.

One of the most popular items is a photo scanner. The library has film scanners, photo scanners, and VHS tape-to-digital video converters. Many patrons have old shoeboxes of photos or photograph albums at home, and they come to the library for digital archiving equipment. The telescopes are also extremely popular. These are offered in partnership with the Grand Traverse Astronomical Society.

"I want stuff to be *used*," said Olson.

Next, the Library of Things is moving into circulating laptop computers and Wi-Fi hot spots.

"We saw big downstate libraries doing it," said Howard. "And we just knew it would be popular from our community needs [assessment]." During the pandemic, Wi-Fi hot spots became essential for many students to attend school remotely.

Collections

In the Sixth Street days, the library was known for its extensive telephone book collection with shelves of telephone books from across the country. The emphasis has shifted. TADL has a collection of approximately 328,000 books, music, Things, and more, but it has few telephone books. It is also host to several special collections.

The Northwestern Michigan College library transferred its microfilm collection of local newspaper archives to TADL. So did the Traverse Area Historical Society. The collection includes photos and text from the former Pioneer and Historical Society. The Grand Traverse Area Genealogical Society collection, formerly housed at NMC, moved to TADL when the new Woodmere library was built. The Genealogical Society donated more than 2,000 genealogical books and other materials to the library and stores its collections in the library archives. Librarian Katheryn Carrier, affectionately known as the "genealogy genius," provides guidance.

Many local groups store their collections in the TADL archives, including the Cherry Festival, Friendly Garden Club, and the League of Women Voters. The former State Hospital has historical records at TADL, too.

Other lesser-known collections are the Al Barnes collection of photos, including 50 aerial photographs; the Camp Royale archives; the Charles Saunders jazz collection; and the Liz Bannister sheet music collection. The Bannister collection has sheet music dating from the 1890s, and the Saunders collection has thousands of jazz audio recordings.

The Nelson Room holds Michigan resources with an emphasis on local history, including yearbooks from the first Traverse City High School. The Polk directories help people researching local house histories. Homeowners often get curious about who lived in their house before, and the directory contains names and photos.

Besides these specialized collections, public browsing areas like the Sight & Sound department are still thriving.

"It was originally the passion of Mike McGuire," said Howard. "We have one of the best CD collections in the state. We got into music at the right time. Now it would be too expensive to build up. Mike used his budget wisely."

Community Spaces

From the beginning, Traverse City looked to the library for community gathering space. The Ladies' Library Association first discovered how great the need for public space was when they did a brisk business renting out Library Hall. The demand only increased.

When designing the new main library on Woodmere, Citizens for Libraries envisioned a community room with separate access, so the room could be available to county residents even after hours when the library itself was closed. That feature was installed, but not put to use. Community access still remains good since the library stays open most nights until 9 pm.

Besides adding a kitchen to the largest meeting room, the McGuire Community Room, it was important to install a good speaker system and ability to record programs. The room was already in the midst of being drywalled when Aaron Olson noticed a problem.

"You don't have any conduits for your AV," Olson pointed out.

"Get them in there," McGuire answered.

Olson marked areas on the walls needed for audio/visual access. This allowed the community room to support a sophisticated level of audio/visual equipment. It could support up to three cameras for recording. Many community groups, from public meetings of the Downtown Development Authority to forums by the League of Women Voters, use the room and record their meetings.

Community meeting rooms continue to be in high demand. Besides the large McGuire Community Room, which fits 160 at standing capacity, there are several smaller meeting rooms for groups of two to twenty. The McGuire Room hosts author talks, blood drives, ballet performances, and summer reading programs. The Grand Traverse Humanists meet there. So do veterans' groups, helping veterans draft wills, for example, on Veterans Day. The library is host to cycling clubs, French clubs, Unix coders, gamers, yoga, and rock and mineral enthusiasts.

The library is the center of your community.

"The library is the center of your community," said Howard.

Library Partnerships

The library is a natural partner when it comes to access and education. TADL has partnered with many groups over the years, from the Law Library to local schools.

Poetry is a natural fit for the library. Poets' Night Out started in 1998 with a broad partnership between Horizon Books, TADL, Friends of the Library, and Clark, Walter, Sirrine Architects. Jody Clark had the original idea, which she shared with librarian Sandy Robey. Poets' Night Out got a boost after Robey, Martha Vreeland, and poet Anne-Marie Oomen received a grant to attend a Poets' Night Out workshop in San Francisco. The local Poets' Night Out gives northern Michigan poets a platform to read and publish their work, and encourages original poetry from all ages in a ten-county area. Contest winners are published in a chapbook and read their work at the annual Poets' Night Out event.

The library supports regional book clubs by providing "Book Club Kits." The book club kits contain 4 to 8 copies of a title. This helps book club members enjoy easy access to chosen books.

SCORE is another partnership. SCORE helps small businesses through a mentorship program and often meets in the McGuire Room to offer educational programs. The library partners with area schools in a host of ways, from providing free books to families who are part of the school district free lunch and breakfast program, to being part of the Grand Traverse Battle of the Books program, a reading contest for teams of 4th and 5th graders. TADL also partners with schools in the Grand Traverse area, by providing every school child a public library account.

TADL has housed the Library for the Blind and Physically Handicapped, now called the Talking Book Library, since 1972. This branch of services is a federally mandated program, and Traverse City serves as a regional resource for residents in sixteen counties, contributing paid staff to run the program. It changed its name to the Talking Book Library in 2013, primarily due to digitization of its offerings. The Talking Book Library continues to provide audio versions of books and other texts.

The area's Law Library was also established by government statute, which requires each county to have a law library. Many times, that meant just a shelf in a judge's office, but in Grand Traverse County, the Law Library was housed for many years on the fourth floor of the historic Courthouse. The Law Library served the jail, judges, and the Bar Association, as well as the general public. During that period, TADL partnered with the court and the Bar Association to help staff the Law Library, contributing half of a part-time law librarian's salary. In 2013, the Grand Traverse County Law Library moved to the main Woodmere library when the Grand Traverse Bar Association stopped being involved. Today, TADL holds the collection, and Grand Traverse County pays for the Law Library's maintenance.

Serving the Public

The library fields all kinds of questions daily. In addition to circulating books and other materials, the reference desk is kept busy.

"What time is it?" People call the library to ask this essential question, especially if they don't have a computer and if the clock light has gone out on their stove. Many local "time and temperature" phone services have faded away, although the U.S. Naval Observatory still provides the time, if you know the number (202-762-1069).

Reference librarians field a wide range of questions, from both children and adults:

"When did puffed rice first happen?"

"I'm looking for a book and it's something like 'X' and it has a blue cover."

"My teacher wants me to read the "Wrath of Grapes."

"Do you have a photo of Jesus?"

"I need to find a biography of General Motors."

"What's the difference between coddled and poached eggs?"

Downstairs in Sight & Sound, library staff often get serenaded by patrons. "'Do you have the song…I'm not sure of the name, but it goes like this,'" explained Vicki Carpenter, who used to work that department. "Then they would sing or hum a few bars," she said.

One library user was searching for recipes for vegan cookies. After reference librarian Katheryn Carrier helped her, she brought in some of the finished cookies to share. Carrier is one of many TADL librarians who have a long-term commitment to the library.

Whatever the community education and access need, TADL tries to meet it. For years, Munson Medical Center ran the Munson Community Health Library, which included popular "medical kits." When Munson closed its public medical library in 2020, TADL began offering its own medical kits. These health kits included books, videos, and information sheets on such topics as diabetes, heart disease, mental health, autism, and Alzheimer's.

"Often people come in with a recent diagnosis," said Howard. "Sometimes people sit in our stacks and cry."

And, as always, the library looks out for individuals, including the right of patrons experiencing homelessness to use the public library. Staff receive empathy-based training designed to work with homeless patrons, but find the trainings useful for interacting with other patrons, too.

Library staff have even been involved in helping to save patrons' lives. In the past few years, quick-thinking staff used CPR to save a man who had a heart attack and a woman who had overdosed and was unresponsive.

A library has room for everyone. Howard described watching a typical library scene unfold. "There's a multimillionaire…and two tables down is a group of homeless people. How often do we ever have those two groups of people sitting together?" asked Howard, marveling that both groups know they can be there. "It's a unique space, your community library."

Over in the children's area, children play as well as read. Dogs are regular patrons, too, at least the giant, gentle dogs who act as reading therapy dogs. These dogs offer a friendly, non-judgmental ear to young readers who read aloud. And Summer Reading programs are not just for children anymore. TADL involves a growing number of adults in summer reading challenges.

The children's area opens to the main lobby, and often noise spills out, mixing with adult chatter. "I don't think you have to keep the noise of children away from the rest of the library because everyone is pretty noisy now," said Bernadette Groppuso. "It's better. It fits with what people need and want today."

Mike McGuire would agree. The day after the Woodmere library opened, McGuire was quoted in the *Traverse City Record Eagle* as saying: "I like to see a very lively library. Screaming, no, but a modest amount of noise."

Patrons who need silence can book a private study room or use the designated quiet spaces, but overall the library has a more vibrant feel. That's as it should be, said Groppuso.

"A public library isn't a research library, where you might work away in your little cubby. It's become a community center."

The main Traverse City library is the centerpiece of the whole Traverse Area District Library network, a modern community library system.

As long as they're willing to evolve, then there will always be a place for the library.

Vicki Shurly

Chapter 17

TADL into the Future

Strategic Plans for the Future

"City LIBRARY" is boldly carved in stone above the doors of the Carnegie library on Sixth Street. But, surprisingly, there's no sign at the Woodmere library.

"There's no sign out front," said Director Michele Howard. "It says on the building, but you can't see it because of the trees. People don't know what our building is. You have to *know* it's a library." That's something she'd like to change.

Strategic planning for the public library will always involve the community. Howard envisions plenty of public input on how TADL grows and changes. On her list for the main library, she'd like to improve space for the Local History Collection, the Talking Book Library, and the teen department. "They've outgrown their space," she said.

She'd also like to finally close the hole in the floor. The library could use the space, and the open air space makes the library extra noisy.

The Bookmobile will return, too. TADL received a grant from Rotary Charities in 2021 to help host a bookmobile program to bring the library to outlying neighborhoods. The modern bookmobile will bring books, movies, music, technology, and Wi-Fi hot spots to new patrons. This is one more embodiment of what Mike McGuire urged staff to envision: "a library without walls."

"It will be incredible for the community," said Howard. "To cruise around and spread love of the library." The idea of spreading the library beyond library walls is continuing to gain traction. Former TADL staff Kristin Talaga brought to life the Book Bike, which visits the Sara Hardy Farmers' Market and Friday Night Live in Traverse City, and other area events like Kingsley's Heritage Days. She also helped arrange the region's first Little Free Library, one of the earliest to be set up in Michigan. Little Free Libraries are book-sharing boxes placed in neighborhoods to encourage reading and book exchanges.

Another possibility is getting rid of the fine system for overdue books. Fines for late children's materials have already been abolished. This is a trend among libraries in general, because of concerns about access. When people rack up high fines, they normally can't pay them. Instead, they just stop coming to the library. That's not the point, said Howard.

"That's lost materials and lost patrons," she said. "They don't get back to the library."

Doing away with fines certainly worked in the past. During "Free From Overdue Fee Week," in the late 1960s, Traverse City patrons unearthed several long-overdue books. One man brought in a copy of *A Man Without a Country,* originally checked out from the Traverse City library on October 7, 1919 and returned in 1969, according to the *Lansing State Journal.* It was fifty years overdue and had accumulated $260 in fines, which were waived by Library Director Bernard Oppenneer. Removing fines completely is a far cry from the days when the Traverse City library threatened patrons with arrest for overdue library books (see page 84).

What else could be in store? As Citizens for Libraries leader Anne Magoun said, "Libraries are all about possibilities."

BUILDING BOOM FOR COMMUNITY LIBRARIES

"When we came here in 1982," said Interlochen resident and longtime library advocate John Trezise, "Carnegie was a wreck. There was no library in Interlochen, the library in Kingsley occupied a storefront...Fife Lake library was in an old one-room school, and the Peninsula library was located in the elementary school.

"Today there is a brand-new library in Interlochen, a brand-new library in Kingsley, a brand-new library in Fife Lake, a brand-new library out on the Peninsula, a branch in East Bay, and a new, modern library at Woodmere. The effort by the library community resulted in this county having a really good network of modern libraries all linked together with really good service."

Since the main Woodmere library was built, there's been a boom in building modern, exceptional libraries throughout Grand Traverse County.

Fife Lake Public Library

The first was Fife Lake. Until 2005, Fife Lake's library had continued in a one-room schoolhouse. Quaint and homey, but not adequate. They shared space with the township treasurer, and two voting booths were stored in the back.

"We need a bigger library, we need a bigger library, we need a bigger library," director Julie Gray told Mike McGuire. Her family had been involved in the Fife Lake library for decades, including her grandfather, who used to fill the library's old pot-bellied stove.

"It will take at least ten years," McGuire told her.

"We got it in eight," said Gray.

The effort started with a grant Gray wrote to the Grand Traverse Band of Ottawa and Chippewa Indians. She submitted the request, but

Fife Lake's new library building opened in 2005.

didn't hear from them. "Then I opened the mail one day and here's a check for $36,000!"

The fund drive for a new Fife Lake library building took off from there. Brothers Jeff and Jim Hayes, of Hayes Manufacturing, donated land. Local contractors pitched in. Since Fife Lake was an independent member library in the TADL system, the full cost of building a new library building was up to them. TADL donated $10,000 in shelves, but the new building—from its well to its windows—was fully a community effort.

Current Fife Lake Library Director Julie Kintner agrees, saying "Working for the Fife Lake Library has been the most fulfilling experience. Our Library is the gem of our rural community."

KINGSLEY BRANCH LIBRARY

Kingsley was next. Kingsley built a new library building in 2009, complete with a local genealogy room, clock tower, and garden. They'd managed 70 years in the 800-square-foot bank building, even using the old bank vault for processing books. The library had no room for programs, so programs had to be held off-site. The push for the new building came soon after Kingsley became a branch library in 1999. At that point, the independent Kingsley library board disbanded, and the former board transformed into a Kingsley Friends of the Library group.

Kingsley's new branch library building opened in 2009.

"Man, were they on fire! That's how the whole thing started," said Mary Fraquelli, Kingsley library director when the new building was built. "They needed to direct their energies, and did they ever!" Kingsley hosted 5K runs, penny collections, plant walks, and a BBQ on the Boardman, along with a major capital campaign. As a branch library, Kingsley was also able to receive funds directly from TADL for construction. Today the Kingsley Branch Library hosts its programs on-site, including a Monarch butterfly release program in the library garden.

Interlochen Public Library

In Interlochen, four years of fundraising led to a modern new building in 2018. Jane Hardwicke stepped up with a major gift to kick off the campaign, and her daughter, Dr. Mary Beth Hardwicke, ran the campaign and also contributed generously. Both Hardwickes have been deeply involved in the Interlochen library over the years and served as Interlochen library trustees.

The new building doubled the library's size and is located prominently on the main street in Interlochen, instead of being hidden away on a side street. Now patrons enter a friendly, modern library with an up-north cabin feeling, complete with sweeping high ceilings, exposed wood design, and cozy gas fireplaces. It includes a community room, commercial kitchen, and children's area. It's a far cry from the pole-barn days when the Interlochen library shared space with the Golden Fellowship and a day care center.

Interlochen Public Library's new building opened in 2018.

"When I first walked into the community room and saw the kitchen," said a library patron, "I got choked up." The building cost approximately $3 million.

Peninsula Community Library

Peninsula Community Library remained mostly content with its school building location, but when the school district closed the Old Mission Peninsula School in 2017, the library's existence was in jeopardy.

"You will always have a library on the Old Mission Peninsula," Peninsula Library Director Vicki Shurly reassured township residents. The library had owned a separate parcel of land for many years, and now it was time to use it. Peninsula Community Library moved out of the school building they'd shared for 63 years and built their own $2.5 million library. More than one thousand people donated for the new community library. "We asked people to dream," said Shurly. "Dream the perfect library. We did everything except the cat café."

We asked people to dream, dream the perfect library. We did everything except the cat café.

The doors opened in 2019. The new Peninsula Community Library building is highly visible, right on Center Road, and attracts new patrons, many of whom used to be reluctant to enter the school-housed

Peninsula Community Library's new building opened in 2019.

library. As security tightened, being part of a school meant public access was somewhat limited. "We had to buzz people in," explained Shurly.

East Bay Branch Library

The East Bay Branch Library remains in its historic town-hall setting, which imbues this beloved eastside branch with a sense of history and local flavor. The "east side" no longer ends at Franklin Street in Traverse City as it did in the early 1900s. Today the East Bay branch serves patrons from Acme, Williamsburg, and outlying areas.

East Bay branch library in the old township hall opened in 1991.

At East Bay, Story Time and arts programs are vibrant. Librarian Rosie May offers Ukrainian egg decorating, miniature making, and other crafts. She also leads the popular Filmstrip Festival, which shows children's filmstrips every summer at the library to join in the fun of the Traverse City Film Festival. East Bay's Filmstrip Festival debuted in 2006. May, the daughter of long-time TADL librarian Martha Vreeland, credits the branch's home in the old East Bay Town Hall building for some of its charm.

"It's a two-room library that's kind of old-timey and nostalgic," said May. "So we like to reinforce that culture of family and community with old-fashioned holiday open house parties and our annual ice cream social in the summer."

A NETWORK OF COMMUNITY LIBRARIES

Besides beautiful new facilities and modern programming, there's an easy camaraderie between TADL and its member and branch libraries. The earlier fears from the 1980s are gone, relationships are strong, and the district has found its balance.

"It became a good partnership," said Fife Lake's Julie Gray.

Each member library gets equitable funding, based on its library class size and other factors. "Right now it's really good," said Howard. "Libraries are thriving."

For Kingsley, transforming from an independent district library to a branch of TADL took some getting used to. Would the main library let them keep their library programs? Their staff? Their choice of materials? Mary Fraquelli changed from being Kingsley's independent director to being branch manager.

"Oh my gosh, it was the perfect thing to happen at the time for our community," said Fraquelli. "It really ended up being the best thing... Especially the technology support, and computers, and new computers, and *more* computers."

It was the perfect thing to happen at the time for our community.

"It was definitely advantageous to us when we became part of it," agreed Gray, from Fife Lake. "Once we became part of the district, our growth was phenomenal. Circulation went from 300 a month to 2,000 a month." That growth also helped allay fears of being shut down. "We proved we were needed and being used."

One of the ways the district helps outlying libraries is by preparing books for the shelves and increasing collections through interlibrary loan.

"You'd be surprised how many books came from Fife Lake to the other libraries," said Gray. "We were very small. We weren't able to update our inventory...A lot of books that people wanted were older books and we still had them!"

"It's a real asset," Gray added. "We support each other. We help each other."

"We have a very good relationship," agreed Peninsula Library Director Vicki Shurly. "I wouldn't trade it for anything now."

TADL Today

"It turned out very nicely," said Suzanne Antosh Connor, who moved back to Traverse City a few years ago. It's lovely," she said of the Woodmere main library. "Not historic, but beautiful. It was probably an excellent choice." Connor now serves on the city's Human Rights Commission.

"The entire system now is such an effective library system for people up here," said John Trezise. "It's an accomplishment for an awful lot of people."

I can't imagine a community without a library. It would be like Death Valley.

"I can't imagine a community without a library," said Fred Nelson. "It would be like Death Valley."

"Libraries are living entities," said Vicki Shurly. "Libraries managed to redefine themselves, to become community centers. There's hunger for community space."

Rosie May, East Bay Branch Library manager, agreed. "Come step inside and see what's happening at libraries," she said.

Many of the leaders who threw their energies into establishing and improving Traverse area library services have died, whether it was Clymene Bates and Martha E. Cram Bates of the Ladies' Library Association; Betty Parker, Ellie Long, Arline Howe, Ruth Gamble, and Pat Trezise of the League of Women Voters; or Citizens for Libraries and TADL staff and board members such as David Hacker, Dick Rosser, Mike McGuire, Bryan Crough, Don Pratt, and Frank Senger. This is their story, and the story of our changing community. It is a story of labor. And in some ways, a love story. A love story for a library.

"A library, like a hospital, is a precious community possession, vital to our daily lives," said Citizens for Libraries leader David Hacker in a speech at Woodmere's groundbreaking. "But these are only bricks and mortar. They are brought to life by a community's spirit…By saying Yes to the new library, the Grand Traverse area issued its first welcome to the Twenty-first Century and the next millennium. It is a gift to the imaginations and knowledge and learning of all."

"We'll always be here," said Shurly. "As long as they're willing to evolve, then there will always be a place for the library."

Final Note

We set out to tell the story of building the new Woodmere library. Instead, it's been a journey into the nature of the library itself.

What is a Library?

Libraries did not die out in the 1990s with the advent of the internet. They evolved and thrived. Since libraries have changed so dramatically, it seems fitting to search for a new definition.

An older definition says a library is a building filled with books, periodicals, and other resources. A new definition from the American Library Association describes the library as a collection of resources in a variety of formats, organized by experts, with the mission of educating, informing, or entertaining, and the goal of "stimulating individual learning and advancing society as a whole." That's grandiose, but appropriate.

So the library is more than books, it's a vast collection of resources. A place where fun and education overlap. A place of infinite possibility.

Yet a *thriving* library is something more. It's aptly been called the heartbeat of the community.

As we saw when the COVID-19 pandemic closed the library doors in 2020, a library is more than its resources. It's a bastion of equality. A foundation for democracy. And most simply, a place of human interaction. "We missed you more than our hairdresser!" people cried. To many, the library is more like a member of the family.

Libraries live and change as we do. That's where *you* come in.

Welcome to the library.

Director Michele Howard welcomes patrons after three-month closure.

Traverse City Head Librarians/ Library Directors

Dr. David Goodale, postmaster	1853
Various Township Clerks	1850s–1890s
Ruth Barlow	1890s
Tina Holdsworth	1890s
Lucille Dusenbery Keith	1900–1903
Helen Stout	1903–1911
Alice Wait	1911–1949
Karl O. Burg	1949–1951
Terese O'Connor Flaherty	1951–1966
Bernard Oppenneer	1966–1970
Robert "Scotty" Olney	1970–1979
Michael L. McGuire	1979–2009
Metta T. Lansdale, Jr.	2009–2014
Gail Parsons Juett	2014–2019
Michele Howard	2019–

Citizens for Libraries Executive Committee

Fred Bimber
Margaret Braden
Bryan Crough
David Hacker
Judith Halsted
Ted Kidd
Mike McGuire
Karen Nielsen
Don Pratt
Anne Rock
Dick Rosser
Frank Senger
MacKay Taylor
John Trezise
Guy Wood

Community Support

Assistance

Many thanks to the people who gave generously of their time to enrich the stories of this book by researching, proofing, and offering general guidance.

Phyllis Babel
Bruce Bennett
Leslie Bilbey
Barbara Berry
Bruce Borchardt
Nancy Bordine
Jane Boursaw
Heather Brady
Dawn Buchanan
Vicki Carpenter
Katheryn Carrier
Melissa Cartwright
Cherry Capital Foods
Jody Clark
Jordan Cloud
Eunice Crockett
Duane Dodge
Fred Dohm
Becky Ewing
Facebook Group: *I Grew Up in Traverse City*
Richard Fidler
Mike Gillis
George Gregory
Mary Grover
Judith Halsted
Joelle Hannert
Marlas Hanson
Kelly Haug
Bob Holdeman
Ann Hoopfer
Donna Hornberger
Ann Hosler
Michele Howard
Sharon Jennings
Seth Johnson
Peg Jonkhoff
Julie Kintner
Charlene Lutes
Anne Magoun
Peter Magoun
Melissa McKenna
Andrea Melvin
Alison Metiva
Joanne Michalski
Laura Mills
Mary Morgan
Shirley Murray
Betsy Myers
Fred Nelson
Karen Nielsen
Aaron Olson
Laura Quackenbush
Paul Riess
Amy Shamroe
Jackie Shinners
Vicki Shurly
Peg Poeschl Siciliano
Stephen Siciliano
Russ Soyring
Liam Strong
Ann Swaney
Gerry Swaney
Jerry Swanson
Monica Taylor
John Trezise
United Way of NW Michigan
Diane Viskochil
Martha Vreeland
Alicia Walker
Jan Warren
Doug Weaver
Kimberly Wiggins
Guy Wood

Donations

Generous community donors who appreciate libraries and history and who helped bring this project to fruition.

Friends of Traverse Area District Library
Traverse Area Historical Society
Donna Hornberger
Nancy Hoagland
Bruce Borchardt
Ann Swaney
Peter Magoun
John B Trezise
Michele Howard
Bob Holdeman
Martha Vreeland
Anonymous (2)
Amy Barritt
Ruth Bay
Friends of Peninsula Community Library
Mary and Ward Gillett
Charlene Anne Lutes
Shirley Murray
Karen Ann Nielsen
Jackie Shinners
John and Tracey Welch
Rotary Endowment/ Grand Traverse Regional Community Foundation
Arlene Dean
Jerry Beasley
Barb Berry
Vicki Carpenter
Jody Clark
Nancy W. Davy
Carol Hale
Joseph Jonika
Nancy McGuire
Mary Morgan
Fred Nelson
Lynne Rae Perkins
Carol A Sullivan
William Twietmeyer
Jane Brainard
Liz Lint
Elizabeth Strawbridge
Eunice Crockett
Margaret Monsour

Tributes

Some donors chose to honor a person or organization through a generous tribute gift.

Peg Jonkhoff in honor of Jeanne Snow

Anne Magoun in memory of Betty and Ken Parker

Mary Ann Tompkins Galic in memory of George J. Galic and Jim and Ida Tompkins

Mary M. Grover in honor of League of Women Voters–Grand Traverse Area

Michael and Marina Deering in honor of her mother, Leonor Rodriguez

Jerry and Gail Dennis in memory of Gerald Dennis, Sr.

Nancy A. Freund in honor of History of Traverse City

Susan Goering in memory of Judy Diane Opie

Judith Halsted in memory of my mother, Ruth Shriver Wynn, who quietly modeled a life enriched through reading

Horizon Books in honor of Victor Herman

Robert W. Parker in memory of Kenneth and Betty Parker

Nikki Sobkowski in honor of Vicki Shurly

Nancy and Kent Walton in honor of Ladies Library Association

Janice Warren in honor of Betty Parker

Price and Jane Watts in honor of Judith Halsted

Marly Hanson in memory of Bob Hanson

Michael and Joanie Jackson in honor of Carol Hale

Susan Lynn Odgers in memory of Mrs. Vivian Prindl

Ann Rogers in memory of Derek Bailey

Paul Swaney in honor of Ann Swaney

Tina Ulrich in memory of Elaine Beardslee

Jeffrey J. Wescott in honor of Jeffrey Wescott

Melissa Cartwright in honor of Liz Messing

Rochelle and Steve Hammontree in memory of NMC Librarian Elaine Beardslee

Sources

List of Interviews

Interviews were conducted with author Heather Shumaker

Barb Berry, phone interview July 21, 2020
Holly T. Bird, Zoom interview January 29, 2021
Dawn Buchanan, phone interview July 23, 2020
Katheryn Carrier, Zoom interview October 23, 2020
Jody Clark, phone interview June 29, 2020
Kimberly Conaghan, Zoom interview January 29, 2021
Suzanne Connor, phone interview July 22, 2020
Mary Fraquelli, phone interview February 10, 2021
Julie Gray, phone interview February 8, 2021
Bernadette Groppuso, phone interview October 22, 2020
Carol Hale, phone interview October 12, 2020
Judith Halsted, phone interview June 24, 2020
Ann Hoopfer, phone interview October 15, 2020
Michele Howard, phone interview October 14, 2020
Peg Jonkhoff, phone interview November 2, 2020
Emily Kuschell, Zoom interview January 29, 2021
Richard Kuschell, phone interview January 29, 2021
Anne Magoun, phone interview July 23, 2020
Nancy McGuire, phone interview July 9, 2020
Joe Muha, phone interview September 15, 2020
Shirley Murray, phone interview July 14, 2020
Fred Nelson, personal interview June 25, 2020
Karen Nielsen, phone interview July 2, 2020
Aaron Olson, phone interview October 9, 2020
Sandy Robey, phone interview July 30, 2020
Grace Rudd, phone interview July 17, 2020
Vicki Shurly, Zoom interview July 14, 2020
Peg Siciliano, phone interview October 23, 2020
Ann Swaney, FaceTime interview October 22, 2020

John Trezise, phone interview June 23, 2020
Diane Viskochil, phone interview July 10, 2020
Martha Vreeland, FaceTime interview July 1, 2020
John Welch, Zoom interview July 6, 2020
Guy Wood, phone interview August 18, 2020

Main Resources Consulted

Traverse City Public Library History 1905-2006, compiled by Marie Kulibert, Traverse Area District Library librarian, 2006.

Traverse City Library Binder, containing newspaper articles from 1869-2020, compiled by Anne Magoun, 2020.

Citizens for Libraries personal files, courtesy of Judith Halsted, 1988-1999.

Jones, Theodore. *Carnegie Libraries Across America: A Public Legacy*, 1997; John Wiley & Sons.

Traverse City Public Library: A Brief History, by Helen Langworthy, Traverse City Library librarian, September 1980.

"Ladies Library Association," 1878 speech by Mrs. Martha E. Cram Bates at dedication ceremony of Ladies' Library Association new building on Front Street, Traverse City. Extracted from "The Traverse Region, Historical and Descriptive….," Chicago: H.R. Page & Co. 1884; Genealogy Trails Transcription Team.

Handwritten letter to Andrew Carnegie from Leon Titus, January 3, 1902, on microfilm.

Speeches given by Elvin L. Sprague and Dr. Albert H. Holliday at the Carnegie library dedication, as reported in the *Traverse City Evening Record,* March 11, 1905.

Speech given by Esther Hatch at the dedication of the second Ladies' Library Association building on Cass Street, Traverse City, as reported by the *Traverse City Evening Record*, July 23, 1909.

History of the Traverse City Public Library, in the handwriting of Miss Alice Wait.

Carnegie Corporation of New York Records, Series II microfilm files (Reel 32), Rare Book & Manuscript Library, Columbia University, notes transcribed by Anne Magoun.

Ten-year anniversary video, courtesy of Traverse Area District Library, Sight & Sound department [Aaron Olson]. Twelve-minute video of Woodmere library building groundbreaking, Carnegie library goodbye, and opening day celebration, 1999.

Speech given by Judith Halsted, dedication of main Woodmere library, April 1999.

"Composing the Next Chapter," news magazine produced by the Traverse Area District Library, undated. Approximately January 1999.

Trezise, John. *A History of the Interlochen Public Library 1976-2000*, October 2000.

"The Traverse City Public Library," Timeline 1885–1962, courtesy of Traverse Area District Library.

"Timeline for History of the Traverse City Carnegie Library," 1902-1906, researched by Sharon Jennings, August 2020.

Timeline of articles 1869 – 1999, compiled by Anne Magoun and Ann Swaney.

Personal files on Traverse Area District Library formation, courtesy of Joe Muha, 1981-1983.

Annual reports of the Board of Library Trustees of the Traverse City Public Library 1800s-1984, and board minutes, annual reports and newsletters of the Traverse Area District Library.

FOR FURTHER READING

"Records of the Rebellion," *The Morning Record*, November 16, 1897.

"Women Want Bread, Not the Ballot," speech by Susan B. Anthony, compiled by PBS for Ken Burns *Not For Ourselves Alone*, transcript by Ida Husted Harper in *Life and Work of Susan B. Anthony*, V2, Chapter XXVII, published 1898-1908.

"Anthony, Susan B., most noted woman in U.S. will lecture at Library Hall under auspices of Y.M.C.A.," *Grand Traverse Herald*, February 27, 1879.

"Holocaust at Lake Ann," *Traverse City Morning Record*, July 4, 1897.

The Gospel of Wealth, Andrew Carnegie, June 1889.

"Under a New Charter: Ladies' Library Association Has Made Slight Change of Name," *Traverse Bay Eagle*, August 2, 1901.

"This is the Report in Full: of the Joint Carnegie Library Site Committee which the City Council Refused to Have Published," *Traverse City Evening Record*, August 19, 1902.

"Turned Down: Free Site Favored," *Traverse City Evening Record*, August 19, 1902.

"Differences of Opinion," editorial, *Traverse City Evening Record*, October 29, 1902.

"Back to the Board," *Traverse City Evening Record*, November 4, 1902.

"Settled: Carnegie Library Will Go on Cass Street," *Traverse City Evening Record*, November 6, 1902.

"A Clever Cartoon," *Traverse City Evening Record*, October 31, 1902.

"Latest Move: Another Clever Cartoon by R.W. Rastall," *Traverse City Evening Record*, November 5, 1902.

"Broke Out Again: Another Clever Cartoon by R.W. Rastall," *Traverse City Evening Record*, November 15, 1902.

"Site Still Unsettled: Carnegie Library Matter Again Fought Over. Hot Time Last Evening," *Traverse City Evening Record,* January 6, 1903.

"Message of Mayor Santo," *The Evening Record,* May 5, 1903.

"It is Up Once More: Library Site Fight On Again as Fresh as Ever," *Traverse City Evening Record,* May 12, 1903.

"Handsome $20,000 Home of the Traverse City Public Library," *The Daily Eagle,* March 11, 1905.

"Cornerstone Laid Today," *Traverse City Evening Record*, July 23, 1909.

"History of the Ladies Library Association 1869-1950," by Larry Wakefield.

"L.L.A. Building was First Theater Built," *Traverse City Evening Record,* June 7, 1909.

"Dear Observer," letter to the editor by Mabel Bates Williams, *Traverse City Record-Eagle*, May 21, 1946.

The Observer, column by Jay Smith, *Traverse City Record-Eagle,* February 28, 1961.

"Mrs. Terese Flaherty to Retire," *Traverse City Record-Eagle,* September 24, 1966.

"Library Book Fines," by Katherine J. Hall, *Traverse City Record-Eagle*, 1979.

"How Many Elections?" letter to the editor by Eilene Reamer, Lorene Sedlacek, and Dorothy Westrate, librarians, Kingsley Public Library, *Traverse City Record-Eagle,* November 3, 1983.

"District Library Millage Passes," by Loraine Anderson, *Traverse City Record-Eagle,* November 9, 1983.

"TC Library Inadequate," letter to the editor by Richard F. Rosser, *Traverse City Record-Eagle*, April 10, 1995.

"Library Improvement," letter to the editor by Judith Halsted, chair, Library Action Committee, Charlene White, president, League of Women Voters–Grand Traverse Area, *Traverse City Record-Eagle,* May 16, 1995.

"Book Lovers: Local Advocates Connect to Lead Citizens For Libraries," by Shirley Murray, *Prime Time News and Observer*, May 1996.

"Book Aficionado Leads Charge for new TC Library," by Jeff Couzens, *Grand Traverse Herald*, May 29, 1996.

"TC Library – Do the Right Thing," editorial by David Hacker, *Northern Express,* July 31, 1996.

"Hannah vs. Hull: City Fathers Quarreled Over Site for First Library," by Jeff Couzens, with resources from historian Mary Brown-McChrystal, *Grand Traverse Herald,* December 26, 1996.

"Former Library: Looking back, looking forward," by Bill O'Brien, *Traverse City Record-Eagle,* January 5, 2000.

"A Lot in Common: The League of Women Voters and Public Libraries," by Arthur Solomon Meyers. *Public Libraries,* American Library Association, Jan/Feb 2000

"Women Leaders, Trail-blazers, and Community Builders of early TC," compiled by Loraine Anderson for the Women's History Project of Northwest Michigan, October 31, 2009.

"ALA's Proudest Moments," by Wayne Wiegand. *American Libraries,* American Library Association, June 2016.

"Letter from Andrew Carnegie to the People of Traverse City, 1902," by Amy Barritt, *Grand Traverse Journal,* August 1, 2016.

"Finding the Founding Mothers," by Loraine Anderson, *Traverse City Record-Eagle,* September 17, 2017.

"Quiet Man Built Up a Strong Community," by Peg Siciliano, *Traverse City Record-Eagle,* February 23, 2018.

"Libraries Turn a Page," by Laura Michels, *Traverse City Record-Eagle,* March 7, 2021.

Photo Credits

By page number

American Library Association: 184
Boursaw, Jane: Old Mission Gazette: 210
Brady, Heather, TADL Marketing Department: 193, 214
Carnegie Corporation Records - Rare Book and Manuscript Library, Columbia University: 30
Carnegie Library of Pittsburgh: 24
Carpenter, Vicki: 152
Clark, Jody: 196
Fife Lake Area Historical Society: 74
Halsted, Judith: 118
Harper's Magazine Company: 28 (top)
Hoopfer, Ann: 180, 182
Howard, Michele: 192
Interlochen Public Library: 209
Jonkhoff, Peg: 179
Kingsley Branch Library: 208
League of Women Voters: 112
Library of Congress: 22
Magoun, Anne: x, 146, 174, 194 (bottom)
Maxson, Julie: 68
Prime Time News & Observer, May 1996: 122
Roosevelt University Archives: 64 (right)
Swancy, Ann: 69, 176, 195, 207, 211
Swanson, Jerry, GIS Coordinator, City of Traverse City, adapted by Anne Magoun and Angela Saxon: 32
Traverse Area District Library: 38, 53, 64 (left), 66 (bottom), 76, 78–80, 82, 83, 86, 89, 92, 99, 100, 102, 110, 115–117, 130, 142, 150, 151, 153, 154, 157, 160, 168, 169, 171-173, 188, 190, 191, 194 (top), 204
TADL Local History Collection: xvi, 2, 4, 7, 10, 11, 16, 17, 20, 34, 45, 47–50, 52, 54–56, 60, 66 (top), 70, 134
Traverse City Record-Eagle (including archives): 8, 28 (bottom), 40, 55 (top), 77, 84 (both), 90, 137, 148, 158, 164, 166

Index

Note numbers in **bold** *indicate a photo*